This book is dedicated to Roy and Janice Harbour

ACKNOWLEDGMENTS

A big thank you once again to Emi Smith, Jenny Davidson, and Joshua Smith for another great book—I think we make a good team, and I couldn't have done it without you! This book was a very enjoyable project due to the subject matter, and I was thrilled to have the opportunity to write it. I trust the end result reflects the attention that went into it.

Thanks to Jennifer and our children, Jeremiah, Kayleigh, Kaitlyn, and Kourtney, for bringing such joy to my life!

I am again grateful to Eden Celeste for sharing her talent to produce the cover art and the concept drawings of the hero and monster game characters. See her work at www.edenceleste.com.

Thanks again to Reiner Prokein for his sprite artwork, which made the examples in this book possible. The game artwork is all from his free resources at www.reinerstileset.de.

VISUAL C# GAME PROGRAMMING FOR TEENS

JONATHAN S. HARBOUR

Course Technology PTR

A part of Cengage Learning

COURSE TECHNOLOGY
CENGAGE Learning™

Australia • Brazil • Japan • Korea • Mexico • Singapore • Spain • United Kingdom • United States

COURSE TECHNOLOGY
CENGAGE Learning

Visual C# Game Programming for Teens
Jonathan S. Harbour

Publisher and General Manager,
Course Technology PTR: Stacy L. Hiquet

Associate Director of Marketing:
Sarah Panella

Manager of Editorial Services:
Heather Talbot

Marketing Manager: Jordan Castellani

Senior Acquisitions Editor: Emi Smith

Project Editor: Jenny Davidson

Technical Reviewer: Joshua Smith

Interior Layout Tech: MPS Limited, a Macmillan Company

Cover Designer: Mike Tanamachi

Indexer: Larry Sweazy

Proofreader: Mike Beady

For product information and technology assistance, contact us at
Cengage Learning Customer & Sales Support, 1-800-354-9706

For permission to use material from this text or product,
submit all requests online at **www.cengage.com/permissions**
Further permissions questions can be emailed to
permissionrequest@cengage.com

All trademarks are the property of their respective owners.

All images © Cengage Learning unless otherwise noted.

Library of Congress Control Number: 2011920277

ISBN-13: 978-1-4354-5848-2

ISBN-10: 1-4354-5848-6

Course Technology, a part of Cengage Learning
20 Channel Center Street
Boston, MA 02210
USA

Cengage Learning is a leading provider of customized learning solutions with office locations around the globe, including Singapore, the United Kingdom, Australia, Mexico, Brazil, and Japan. Locate your local office at: **international.cengage.com/region**

Cengage Learning products are represented in Canada by Nelson Education, Ltd.

For your lifelong learning solutions, visit **courseptr.com**

Visit our corporate website at **cengage.com**

Printed by RR Donnelley. Crawfordsville, IN. 1st Ptg. 03/2011

Printed in the United States of America
1 2 3 4 5 6 7 13 12 11

About the Author

Jonathan S. Harbour has been programming video games since the 1980s. His first game system was an Atari 2600, which he disassembled on the floor of his room as a kid. He has written on numerous subjects such as C++, C#, Basic, Java, DirectX, Allegro, Lua, DarkBasic, Pocket PC, and game consoles. He is the author of the recent books *Beginning Java SE 6 Game Programming, Third Edition*; *Visual Basic Game Programming for Teens, Third Edition*; *XNA Game Studio 4.0 for Xbox 360 Developers*; and *Multi-Threaded Game Engine Design*. He holds a master's degree in Information Systems Management. Visit his web log and game-development forum at www.jharbour.com.

Contents

INTRODUCTION

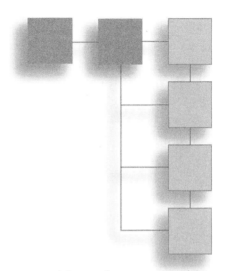

Imagine this scenario: You create a hunter character with random stats and hit points and enter the dungeon to begin exploring for treasure. You stumble upon a zombie pacing near a pile of gear and gold! You attack the zombie and it strikes back! You roll 1D20 and score a critical hit! The 20 point die plus dexterity, against the zombie's armor class, nets a guaranteed hit. Your damage roll is 1D8 plus your strength and weapon modifier, which is 1D4, more than enough to kill the monster! It falls to the ground motionless. Lying next to the unmoving zombie is leather armor that you pick up and equip, giving your hunter a huge boost in defense points. You also pick up some gold coins and gain experience points. Now you dream of finding a better bow... Off to the right, you spot a whole group of undead monsters that are surely guarding loot you could use... and you head toward them to battle!

You *will* learn to build a game with *every* feature just described! This book will teach you how to create your own fully functional role-playing game (RPG) using Visual C#. You will learn step-by-step how to construct each part of the game engine using Windows Forms and GDI+, including a tiled scroller, game editors, and scripting. If you think role-playing games are fun to play, wait until you start working on one of your own design! Constructing an RPG is more fun than playing one, because you are in complete control over the game world, and you can let your imagination loose to create adventures for others to enjoy. However, it is not easy! Just as your game character must gain experience and level up, so must you level up by reading each chapter to learn new skills!

Before you can get to the point where you are able to design an adventure and build an RPG with Visual C#, you will need to learn the basics of RPG game mechanics. My goal with this book is to teach you just what you need to know in order to make this happen. You will learn how to construct a dungeon-based RPG called the Dungeon Crawler. When you have finished this book, you will have learned several new skills including game programming and tools programming. In addition, you will have complete creative control over how the game operates, and will be able to make many games from the same code and tools.

Pacing and Experience

This book is aimed toward the serious RPG fan with discussions about to-hit and damage rolls during combat, and RPG character creation with random stats and character classes and so forth. This is not just a pure programming book, it's very much about creating an RPG, while C# programming comes second in the list of priorities. The primary purpose of this book is to help you to have fun learning about game programming. Typing in long source code listings out of a book is not fun, so I don't ask you to do that in this book. Instead, you will learn by studying the short examples in each chapter. There is no memorization required here, as I'm a firm believer that repetition and practice is the best way to learn, not theory and memorization. The Dungeon Crawler game is built from one chapter to the next, with new features and gameplay elements added in each new chapter. You will learn to create this game completely *from scratch* in a very short amount of time.

The finished game in the last chapter includes all the source code to make your own game with the features described above, including: combat with monsters; talking with NPCs; picking up treasure and gold; creating items with the custom item editor; picking up items; managing the player's inventory bag; equipping gear with buffs (stat modifiers) such as armor and weapons; creating NPCs with the character editor; rolling new player characters; saving and loading the game; and creating the dungeon with a custom level editor. Whew! That sounds like a lot of work, but we make all of this happen in the pages of this book, and you will have a playable, customizable RPG game system by the time you reach the last chapter.

Prerequisites

The goal of this book is to teach you how to create an RPG. You will most definitely benefit from a solid grasp of the C# language. If you are a C# beginner, you may struggle with the source code in this book. But, all of the projects are available in the downloadable resources, so you can still enjoy learning while running the working examples if that is your desire. Programming an RPG is a serious challenge, but if you pay attention and study the examples, you'll be able to do it! The Dungeon Crawler game is large and complex, and it's very hard to program your own RPG from scratch, but that is exactly what we do! I'll try to explain it one step at a time, but there are some programming matters that you will just need to know in advance. If you ever feel lost, then a good primer on the C# language will be helpful. All of the game editors for the RPG are also covered in the book. We cover the key code for the editors but don't list all of the source code because that would take up 500 pages!

Visual C# 2008 and the .NET Framework

This book supports Visual C# 2008 and requires the .NET Framework 2.0. Although the project files are slightly different, the code will compile without issues under Visual C# 2010 as well. If you have 2010 you will still be able to run all of the code in the book, but you will have to convert the projects to the 2010 format (an automatic process performed by Visual Studio when you open a 2008 project). I have left the projects in the 2008 format so that more readers will be able to open the projects with either version. You cannot open 2010 projects using 2008, but the opposite is true.

I recommend that you download the free version of Visual C# Express Edition. You can find it at http://www.microsoft.com/express/downloads. Since web links change frequently, I recommend you instead search Google for "Visual C# Express download." There are links to the 2008 version as well, but 2010 is now the officially supported current version so go ahead and use that version if you want. Just note that the 2008 projects will need to be converted when you open them in 2010. This should not pose a problem, it's just one additional step, and it allows us to support both versions.

There is one caveat: the LuaInterface library requires the .NET Framework 2.0, so when it comes to the script examples in Chapter 15, you may need to create a *new* Visual C# 2010 project and then import the sources to it, in order for

LuaInterface to work correctly. As an option, an advanced reader may recompile the LuaInterface library with Visual C# 2010 and then use the later .NET Framework. If you feel confused about this issue, please visit the author's web forum at www.jharbour.com/forum with any questions. This book was never intended to be complicated—we can thank Microsoft for that.

Managed DirectX?

This book does *not* use the .NET version of DirectX (called Managed DirectX). Instead, this book focuses on Windows Forms programming with the Windows GDI+ (Graphics Device Interface). Managed DirectX is no longer supported by Microsoft and does not work with modern 64-bit versions of Windows. Not to worry, though, because the demos in this book run at 100+ FPS on even an older PC using just GDI+ code.

Contacting the Author

My website is located at http://www.jharbour.com. It has information about this book that you may find useful. This site also features an online forum where you can pose questions and keep up to date with the latest discussions with other programmers about Visual C# and the Dungeon Crawler. If you have any problems working through this book, visit the site to find answers.

Book Contents

The book is divided into three major parts.

"Part I, Dungeon Prerequisites," includes five chapters that form the foundation of the role-playing game that is developed in the book. These chapters cover subjects like Windows Forms, bitmaps, sprite animation, user input, collision detection, and sound effects.

"Part II, Building the Dungeon," includes four chapters devoted to building the game engine components needed to manage and render dungeon levels. The core of this rendering system is a tiled scroller and a level editor.

"Part III, Exploring the Dungeon," includes six chapters that develop all of the gameplay components of the engine that make the Dungeon Crawler game truly playable. This part offers additional game editors and classes that make it possible to fight monsters, pick up treasure, manage the player's inventory and equipped gear, gain experience and level up, and talk with NPCs.

CONVENTIONS USED IN THIS BOOK

Source code is presented in fixed-width font for easy readability.

```
//This is what source code will look like in the text
public void Hello()
{
    Console.WriteLine("Hello World");
}
```

The following styles are used in this book to highlight portions of text that are important. You will find definition, hint, and tip boxes here and there throughout the book.

Definition

Definitions provide additional details about a key word or subject.

Hint

Hints offer guidance and suggestions on what to do or not do in a given situation.

Tip

Tips give additional information about the current subject being covered.

COMPANION WEBSITE DOWNLOADS

You may download the companion website files from www.courseptr.com/downloads. Please note that you will be redirected to our Cengage Learning site.

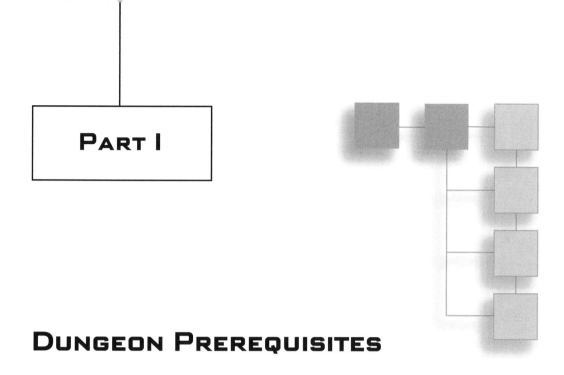

PART I

DUNGEON PREREQUISITES

Welcome to the first part of the book, covering the fundamental building blocks needed to develop the game engine that will be used for the Dungeon Crawler game.

- Chapter 1: Welcome to the Dungeon
- Chapter 2: Drawing Shapes and Bitmaps with GDI+
- Chapter 3: Sprites and Real-Time Animation
- Chapter 4: Collision Detection
- Chapter 5: Playing Sound Effects and Music

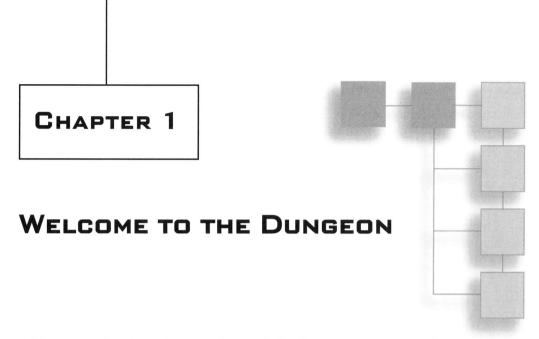

CHAPTER 1

WELCOME TO THE DUNGEON

Welcome to the first chapter of *Visual C# Game Programming for Teens*. This chapter gives you a little overview of what to expect in future chapters and helps set the pace at which we will delve into Visual C#. The goal of the book is to take you step by step through the development of a dungeon crawler–style role-playing game (RPG). First, we'll learn the core techniques in 2D game programming in order to fill our "toolbox" with tools—the classes and functions needed for most games, such as bitmaps and sprites. Next, we'll develop several game editors (including the most important one—the Level Editor), build the dungeon, and populate it with monsters and non-player characters (NPCs). In order to accomplish these goals, we have to start with the basics.

Here's what we'll cover in this chapter:

- Game programming is an art
- Get your feet wet first, ask questions later
- Let your creativity fly
- Creativity, talent, and hard work
- The sky's the limit
- Learning the tricks of the trade
- Taking a look at Dungeon Crawler

GAME PROGRAMMING IS AN ART

Visual C# is a good tool for beginners to use for writing games because the language is fairly easy to use and Forms-based graphics programming produces good, fast results, which we need for a high-speed game loop. This book treats C# like a professional game development language. What makes Visual C# so popular in application development will be useful for our needs as well—we just won't be using any data flow diagrams or flowcharts here! Although this is a "For Teens" book, that certainly doesn't mean any person of any age can't read it! The series simply reflects the reading and programming level of the average reader who is likely to read the book.

I spent quite a few years doing .NET programming with Visual C# and Visual Basic and I appreciate the .NET environment. But, I have to admit something: for every line of application code I have ever written, I was daydreaming about the source code for a game. Now, no matter what I do day by day, I *love* game programming, and let me tell you, it's *still* fun when you grow up. I've been working with C++ most of the time for the last few years, using DirectX and other SDKs, so I have a good perspective on where and how Visual C# fits into things. As a game development tool, it does a pretty good job in the hands of a decent programmer. But, as is the case with even a more powerful language like C++, in the hands of a beginner, it simply will not meet its potential. What you'll need to do over the next few chapters is learn how to get the most out of the C# language, and push it to its limits! We're not using DirectX here, but our gameplay goals are simple enough in the graphics department—we need a 2D scrolling game world with RPG fantasy characters and dungeon artwork. The "Visual" in Visual C# allows us to *also* create some game editors as well—and that's something you *can't* do easily in C++ (I've tried!). Making a 2D RPG is feasible with just about any language and platform, but we're going to explore RPG creation with C#.

Note

If you also like the Basic language and want to learn even *more* role-playing game development tricks, then check out the sister book, *Visual Basic Game Programming for Teens, 3rd Edition*! That book builds an open world with towns, trees, and beaches, and quests. The Basic language is quite different from C# but the .NET Framework and Forms code is similar. A lot of the code between these two books is very similar, so it would be a good way to learn both languages.

However, you have to keep something in mind: This is a small book, and our goal is to create a dungeon-based role-playing game (RPG) with all the trimmings within these pages. If you feel that you are completely lost within the next few chapters, my advice is to pick up a Visual C# primer to get up to speed, and then return to this book. All of the examples are intentionally kept on the simple side, but a lot of information is presented at a fast pace, so you don't want to get left behind. If you are totally new to C#, then I recommend you study all of the code carefully in each chapter, or pick up a beginner's book on C# (such as *Visual C# Programming for the Absolute Beginner*).

Getting Your Feet Wet

For every great game idea that someone has, a thousand more ideas are waiting to be thought up by a creative person. One thing I want you to do while reading this book is learn to think outside the box. I realize that is a cliché that you have heard many times, but it is an important concept because it helps you visualize the point very clearly. Most people, and many programmers for that matter, are unable to think beyond the experience of their collected memories. A very rare person is able to think about something completely foreign, the likes of which has never been thought of before. The phrase "thinking outside the box" can mean many things, depending on the context, but when I'm talking about writing a game, I mean you should think of ideas that are *above and beyond* what has already been done. The greatest game ideas have *not* all been taken already!

For every *Doom* game that takes the industry by storm, there are a dozen more trend-setting game ideas waiting to be invented. Don't be discouraged, believing that the best ideas have been discovered already! That is what many gamers believed before real-time strategy games *took over* the game industry a few years ago. (If you don't believe me, just take a look at sales for *StarCraft II*, shown in Figure 1.1.) What's the next great game genre? It hasn't been *invented* yet. That is your job!

Tip

Before you can let your creativity flow, you need a foundation in the basics of programming, so you aren't always bogged down, not knowing how to make your imagination come to life on the screen. Learn as much as you can so your ideas can be put into motion without losing your momentum while looking up basic programming issues. Get up to speed *quickly* so you can create games, and move beyond the learner stage.

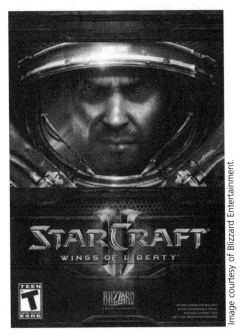

Image courtesy of Blizzard Entertainment.

Figure 1.1
StarCraft II: Wings of Liberty.

Back in 1992, I was playing Sid Meier's *Civilization* on my PC, *Super Mario World* on my Super NES, and *Dragon Crystal* on my Game Gear. Contrast those with amazing new games like *Goldeneye 007* for the Nintendo Wii! (See Figure 1.2.) The fact is, most people did *not* play games back then, unlike today, when almost everyone does! A game like *Doom* was unbelievable at the time, which is why people are still sharing fond memories about it today; that is why *Doom III* was created, and that is why David Kushner wrote the book *Masters of Doom*. *Doom* was so dramatically different from all the other games at the time that a whole new genre was created: the first-person shooter (FPS). FPS games dominate the game world today, unlike any other genre, partially because it consumed the virtual reality market that was flagging at the time.

Do you want to create a game like *Doom* using Visual C#? That goal *is* possible, but it would be a challenge. The Visual C# compiler creates intermediate

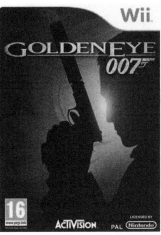

Figure 1.2
Goldeneye 007 for Nintendo 64 and Wii (cover art).

language (IL) code that looks the same regardless of whether you're using Basic or C#, and then that IL code is compiled to an object file and linked into an executable file. That compiled Visual C# game code *could* deliver a gaming experience like *Doom*. There are quite a few third-party libraries available for C#—and even more for C++. For example, most C++ games use helper libraries like Perlin (a texture generator), ZLIB (for reading Zip files), LIBOGG (for audio playback), and some of these are available for C#, but not all. So, even though we could technically build a game like *Doom* in C#, we would have to re-invent a lot of things on our own, or link up those C++ libraries through a complex interop library with .NET wrappers for each of the C++ functions we need. It's just a lot of work! Why stop there? How about *Quake*? The first two *Quake* games were not extremely advanced beyond *Doom*. Oh, sure, they used matrix trans-formations and lighting and 3D models, but it would be no problem for your modern video card to handle brute force rendering *without* any optimization. But, again, it comes down to the language. So, we're not going to build a *Doom*-style game in C#, but we *are* going to create an incredibly fun role-playing game!

What if we wanted to make a game like *World of Warcraft*? You *could* create a smaller, less ambitious version of *WoW* using C# and Managed DirectX (which is now obsolete—replaced by XNA Game Studio), but we can't do that kind of 3D rendering with Forms-based graphics. The most challenging aspect of the game is the server, and in the case of *WoW*, there is not a single server, or even a bunch of servers; there are *racks* and *racks* with hundreds of servers at several geographical locations around the *world*. So, while it is technically feasible to play *WoW* with your friend from Australia (by signing on to the same region), the odds are that bandwidth would be a challenge. The limitation has to do with latency, or lag, due to the number of jumps required to send a packet of data around the world. In a game like *WoW*, you need a fast Internet connection with very few latency problems in order for the gaming experience to be realistic.

I'm sure you've experienced the rare and humorous "slideshow effect" in some games where the server becomes overburdened and cannot keep up, so players do not receive server updates for several seconds until the server can catch up. This primarily happens when a number of players are connecting with high latency, causing the connections to lag. In sufficient numbers, this causes the game to stutter or go into "slideshow mode." (The phrase comes from the frequent exclamation by gamers to the effect of, "I'm enjoying the slideshow today!" which was more common in the heyday of modems, before broadband.) Although Blizzard makes millions of dollars in player fees every month, the company *spends* millions on Internet bandwidth to make the game even possible.

On Programming Languages

So, what kind of hardware do you need to play a game built using Forms-based Visual C#? Basically, we're talking about the same kind of gaming hardware needed to play just about any game currently on store shelves, but we can get by with lower-end PCs since we will not be invoking any 3D rendering devices. Consider the typical NHRA dragster. It can make usually only a few passes down the quarter mile before the engine needs to be rebuilt. It can do it in about *four seconds*, but only once. On the other hand, your average family sedan or minivan will take about 20 seconds to reach the 1,320-foot mark, and a sports car will do it in about 12 seconds. But what about ease of use, multipurpose functionality, fuel mileage, and so on? You can't exactly strap a child's car seat to a dragster to go to a doctor's appointment. Although you could potentially get there a lot faster, the darned car can barely turn left or right, let alone navigate in traffic. How about we use a more realistic race car as an example: a *NASCAR race car*. Here, we have a little more versatility, and the *power potential* is still stratospheric. But there are no headlights, taillights, or any modern conveniences such as air conditioning or *mufflers*. Do you know how loud a car sounds without mufflers? You don't even need a racing engine to deafen yourself. At any rate, a typical *NASCAR* vehicle is insanely fast, but very inflexible and error-prone, unable to withstand the abuses of stop-and-go city traffic.

The same might be said of C++; it is incredibly fast and powerful, but very fragile. I write a lot of C++ code. I have about 15 years of experience with the language. And even after all that, I still get stuck for hours at a time trying to figure out a syntax error in my C++ programs. This happens all the time! It's part of the understanding one must have with this language. But if you show it the proper respect, understand its power, and try not to get frustrated, then little by little you make progress, wrapping the lowest-level features of a game in a layer of protective classes, then another layer, and so on until you have a well-behaved program that is error free. Windows itself—yes, the operating system— was written in C++. When you work with the DirectX SDK using C++, you literally are working with the internals of the Windows OS, and can tinker with the Windows.h source code file.

Here's one that will blow your mind: Visual C# was created with the C++ language! (Technically, we're talking about Visual Studio.) Weird, isn't it? I'm talking about the compiler, the editor, and so on. I've written about another game programming tool for beginners called DarkBASIC Professional, developed by The Game Creators (www.thegamecreators.com), and this tool (along with its DirectX game engine) was also created in C++. Even the latest version of Visual C++ was created with the *previous* version of Visual C++. That can kind of mess with your head if you think about it.

Building a modern first-person shooter (FPS) game requires a lot more than just rendering polygons. You have to write the code to load a BSP level, the code to load hierarchical meshes, the shader code to render meshes with lighting and special effects, the code to load and play sound effects and music, and that's just the technical side. You also have to consider the game's *design*, because a game that just looks cool is not all that great without a good story, and that's where the designer comes in. *Quake II* didn't have much of a design behind it, and actually it seems to me that id Software sort of tacked on the story after the game was nearly finished. But we're talking about a world famous game studio here, not "*<insert your name> Studios.*"

Let Your Creativity Fly

The important thing to realize, though, is that thinking outside the box and coming up with something unprecedented is just the first step toward creating a great game. But, before you can be creative, you must have an understanding of the technology first! You must have the technical know-how to pull it off. In the field of video games, that means you must be a skilled programmer. If you are just getting started, then this book is perfect because Visual C# allows you to practice some of your game ideas without getting too bogged down with a difficult programming language (such as C++). These languages have a tendency to suck away all of your time and leave your mind numb and unable to think creatively. Writing solid code has a tendency to do that to a person, which is why it is a huge help when you start with a not-too-difficult language, such as C#.

Tip

You don't need to be a C++ programmer to write a killer game! All it takes is good artwork, a good story, and well-written code. You don't need to write *fancy* code with complex algorithms; you simply must follow through and *complete the game.* That is really what it's all about—and *that* is what game industry professionals are looking for in a candidate.

ON CREATIVITY, TALENT, AND HARD WORK

I have seen some high-quality games created with DarkBASIC. After you have finished with this book, I encourage you to consider *DarkBASIC Pro Game Programming, Second Edition* (Course Technology, 2006). Once you have mastered the C# language and written a few games with it, maybe then you will have some experience with which to support a study of C++. I've ported some games from Visual C# to C++/DirectX, and then to DarkBASIC, and then Java. In fact, the tile scroller engine developed in this book was featured in that DarkBASIC book; see Chapter 15, "2D Game Worlds: Level Editing and Tile-Based Scrolling." And for the C++ code, see Chapter 10, "Scrolling the Background" in *Beginning Game Programming, Third Edition*. Another obvious choice for further study will be XNA Game Studio, which allows you to write games for Xbox 360 using the C# language we're using here! Source code is *very similar* among languages when you understand the *concepts* behind it. The tiled layer scrolling you'll learn about in this book formed the foundation of several games created in other languages, and now we will port it again from the Managed DirectX version from the previous edition to Windows Forms and GDI+ in this new edition. Remember, it's all about *concepts*!

What you want to strive for as a budding game programmer is an understanding of these *concepts*, and the best way to do that is to write games using your favorite language. Believe it or not, I got started in programming with Microsoft Basic, which came with most of the old computers at the dawn of the PC industry (on such systems as Apple II, Commodore PET, and IBM PC). If you're at all interested in learning traditional BASIC, check out QB64 at www.qb64.net—it can compile and run all of the old BASIC code dating back to the 1960s (with line numbers) as well as more modern QuickBasic and QBasic code from the 1990s. QB64 has graphics capabilities via OpenGL!

I have to say that technical programming language skills are about equal in importance to your creativity. I've known some very talented programmers who don't have an ounce of creativity in their bones, so they are not able to do anything unique and interesting without someone else giving them the ideas first. It's okay to be a person like that—really, really good at programming but not very creative—because you can always borrow ideas from other games and things like movies, and leave the ideas to a game designer or another person who needs your technical skills. It doesn't matter if you have the technical or creative bent, because you really need to learn everything you can. Think about your favorite subjects in school, or favorite movies, and always ask yourself this question: could I make a game out of *that*?

The Sky's the Limit

Did you know that you can write your own games for the Xbox 360? Microsoft provides XNA Game Studio 4.0 for free, and it uses Visual C# 2010 Express as the compiler. For an annual membership fee, you can develop a game right on your retail Xbox 360 and upload your XNA games to a special "developer's" section on Xbox Live Arcade and sell your game using Microsoft Points (the licensing is similar to web gaming sites). Best of all, you can debug your code right on the retail Xbox 360.

You don't need to limit your creative juices to just what you *think* is possible. In fact, don't limit yourself at all, and don't assume that you *can't* do anything, even if you have tried and failed. If you can imagine something, no matter how out of this world it might seem, then it's possible to build it. That is what human imagination is all about. What Jules Verne imagined back in the late 1890s— ideas that were so crazy that everyone laughed at them—suddenly became a reality fewer than 70 years later. Imagine that—people riding around in horse carriages, on dirt or cobblestone roads, and some crazy writer suggests that people will walk on the moon. What a lunatic, right? If you lived in 1890, you probably would have thought he was crazy! It's easy for us to make fun of people when we later know better (something called *hindsight*), just as it is easy to criticize a small flaw in a complex automobile or computer. (It's *easy* to critique; it's *hard* to create. Why do you think there are so many blogs on the net today? Uncreative people tend to criticize what they are not able to create on their own.)

Jules Verne described the rocket ship that would blast off the Earth with an explosion of mighty power that would lift the huge rocket off the ground and propel men into space so they could land on the moon. Doesn't that sound familiar? If you have ever watched a video of the Apollo 11 mission, it is uncanny how Jules Verne described the launch 70 years before that time. Even today, boosters are launched into orbit using the same basic technology, although the rockets are a lot more powerful and more efficient than they were during the Apollo program (so much so that private companies are springing up with plans to usher in space tourism in the near future). What am I getting at here? Just this: don't *assume* that a wild idea is impossible before trying. I'm sure you've heard the story about how many failed light bulbs Thomas Edison built before finally getting one to work. I've found that one of the best ways to make a great game is to base it on one of my own favorite subjects—something with which I am intimately familiar! That makes it easy to build the game because no design doc is really needed.

Learn the Tricks of the Trade

The most technically skilled programmers are often those who copy the most creatively talented people in the world. From that perspective, people are still copying the work of John Carmack (of id Software), who continues to crank out unbelievable game engines. The vast majority of game developers are trying to keep up or succumb to Carmack's genius and end up paying to use his latest game engine. Carmack is one of the few who possesses both unmatched technical skill and incredible creative talent. Although he was born with the talent, he learned the technical skill purely from hard work, putting in an unbelievable number of hours at his keyboard, experimenting, tweaking, and trying new things, day after day, month after month, year after year... and he is still going at it.

If your whole purpose is just to have some fun while learning how to write your own game, and you have no real desire to become a master of it, that is perfectly okay! I am one of those people. I love writing games for the enjoyment of myself and others, and I don't really care whether my latest game is any good (because I'm not trying to sell them, in most cases). If you are approaching game development from the standpoint of a hobby, the whole point is to have fun. If you want to get serious, attend a game-development college, and then get a job as a professional game developer, you'll probably take the subject a little more seriously. There are benefits to just treating this subject as a hobby: no deadlines or pressure, and the freedom to do whatever you want. Have you always wanted to create your very own role-playing game (or another type of game), and you've decided to learn how to do it on your own? That's great! In fact, that is largely the direction this book takes. If your goal is to do this for a living, then I wish you the very best; this book may be your first stepping stone on the path toward that dream.

When I suggest you think outside the box, therefore, I'm advising that you try not to succumb to the "been there, done that" mentality of creating yet another mod (using a game engine like *Battlefield*), or another *Tetris* clone, or another version of *Breakout*. These terrific learning experiences are very common because these latter two types of games are easy to make and demonstrate important concepts in game programming. A game engine mod, on the other hand, is an entirely different issue; most mods require little or no programming. They are merely conversions with new 3D models and game levels to match a new theme (as is the case with *Desert Combat* [a *Battlefield 1942* mod] and *Counter-Strike* [a *Half-Life* mod]). Try to come up with some completely original game ideas and develop them; no matter how simple a game concept is, if it's a brand-new idea, then it will probably be interesting! Of course, the fun factor is entirely up to you, the game's designer and programmer.

TAKING A LOOK AT DUNGEON CRAWLER

This book builds just one game to teach the subject of game programming and to give an overall picture of how the topics in each chapter are put to use in a real game. The alternatives are to forego a sample game altogether or to just use small example games or graphics demos to explain how a new subject can be put to use. Small demos and mini games provide good examples of individual subjects, but an entire game will give you a better grasp of the "big picture." This game we're going to build is based on a scrolling game world and animated sprites with pre-existing royalty-free artwork, courtesy of Reiner Prokein (www. reinerstileset.de). Figure 1.3 shows the game as it will look when you are finished with it in this book's last chapter.

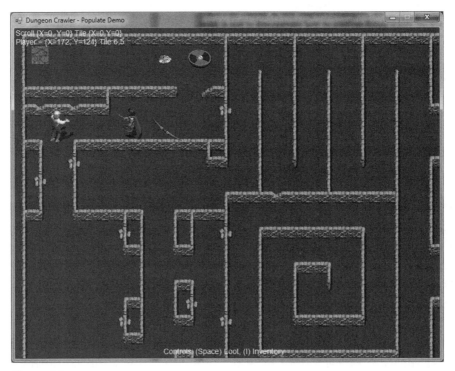

Figure 1.3
Dungeon Crawler is a game you create from scratch in this book.

Building a Role-Playing Game

I chose to create a complete RPG for this book because no other subject digs deeper into the depths of game programming than a real RPG with all of the functionality you expect from this genre. Since I come from the old school of gaming, I am still fond of classics such as *Ultima VII: The Black Gate*. There's an open source engine called *Exult Ultima7 Engine* (shown in Figure 1.4) that uses the original *Ultima VII* artwork and data files and recreates the gameplay, with complete game editors included. Download and play it from http://exult. sourceforge.net.

My second choice was a game based on *Star Trek*, but there are the obvious copyright problems when using a TV show as the basis for a game. If you really love some subject such as *Star Trek*, then I encourage you to go ahead and write a game about that subject and then give it away to your friends. The learning

Figure 1.4
Exult Ultima7 Engine. (Linux version shown here.)

experience is enhanced when you are working on a game about a subject that you really enjoy and that has a lot of texture, with a huge background story surrounding it. The RPG we will build as an overall learning experience is called Dungeon Crawler and takes place in medieval Ireland, complete with ancient Celtic history and myth as background material for our game. We'll be building this game while learning important new skills in each new chapter.

The Dungeon

The story in our Dungeon Crawler game does not include just fantasy creatures as you might find in some RPGs (vampires, skeletons, werewolves, giant snakes, giant spiders, dragons, and the like)—there will be some creatures like this to make the gameplay as fun and engaging as possible. There may also be some human characters to fight against as well as interact with as NPCs—namely, vendors in the "spawn town" where you can go to sell loot and buy new gear. Figure 1.5 shows some of the monster sprites we have available for the game, courtesy of Reiner Prokein. While fantasy characters are a lot of fun to kill in most RPGs, and Dungeon Crawler has a lot of creatures to fight, this game also features some human characters that your player will encounter.

N o t e

The images shown here for the Dungeon Crawler game were created by Reiner "Tiles" Prokein, who makes them freely available with no strings attached. You may browse Reiner's sprites and tiles at www.reinerstileset.de.

Describing the Player's Character

The most robust RPGs usually allow the player to create a custom character to play, although in recent years this has taken a backseat to hack-and-slash games like *Baldur's Gate* (which is okay because it introduces another type of gamer to

Figure 1.5
Assortment of monster sprites available for our game.

Courtesy of BioWare.

Figure 1.6
Baldur's Gate.

the great fun had with an RPG and gives the type of person who would not normally play an RPG a glimpse into a bigger world). (See Figure 1.6.) *Baldur's Gate* most certainly does let you create a character, but it's less robust than a traditional RPG system, because it is intended to be more of a "hack & slash" type of game.

Blizzard's *Diablo* series may also (arguably) fall into the category of "hack & slash" game like the *Baldur's Gate* series. See Figure 1.7.

These provide a glimpse of the *type* of game that you have an opportunity to create in this book! Of course, you can tweak and modify the game to suit your own imagination, and you will have the technical know-how after reading this book to do just that. We'll be going over the game engine for Dungeon Crawler step by step, and will develop the game in each new chapter, but the complete game with quests and goals is up to you!

I am taking this game in a slightly different direction and following a real-world scenario, as you might find in the *Ultima* and *Legend of Zelda* series. There are a lot of human characters in Dungeon Crawler (as you learn in the next few

Courtesy of Blizzard Entertainment.

Figure 1.7
Diablo III.

chapters), and the player can choose from several character classes. Good *non-player characters (NPCs)* also help the player to successfully complete the game's primary quest chain and sub-quests. In our game, we will allow the player to create a custom character based on several character classes, as shown in Figure 1.8. Some possible classes include:

Warrior	Strong melee fighter with powerful weapons and plate armor
Paladin	Balanced melee fighter who wears plate armor and heals himself
Hunter	Dexterous ranged fighter who wears leather armor
Mage	Powerful magic user who wears cloth and wields a staff

Tip

You will be able to define your own character classes using the character editor in Chapter 10, "Creating Characters and Monsters."

Figure 1.8
Some of the character class sprites available for our game.

Adventure Game or Dungeon Crawler?

Two types of classic RPGs exist in my opinion: adventure games and dungeon crawlers. The typical dungeon crawler is made up of a spawn or home town where you can equip your character (purchase weapons, armor, and so on) using the treasure you find in the dungeon, which is usually made up of many levels and driving deep into the Earth, and is often portrayed as a gold mine that became infested with evil creatures. The standard of the genre is widely considered to be the classic game *Rogue*, shown in Figure 1.9. While you are killing bad guys (represented as little ASCII characters like #, %, and &), your experience is going up and you are finding gold. As your experience goes up, your skills go up as well, and this is reflected by your character's level. A level-20 warrior, for instance, can dispatch level-5 skeleton archers with the back of his hand, so to speak, while a level-18 fire dragon poses a serious threat! This type of game is typically very simple in concept, lacking any serious storyline or plot— hence the term *dungeon crawler* or *dungeon hack*. *Diablo* and *Dungeon Siege* epitomize this type of game.

The other type of RPG, the adventure game, usually takes place on the surface rather than in a dungeon or underground mine and often involves a deeper storyline with quests to challenge the player. This game allows the player's character to gain experience, weapons, and special items, such as armor, amulets, magic rings, and so on. Although the main quest of an adventure RPG might be very difficult, sub-quests allow the player's character to reach a level sufficient to beat the game's main quest. Sub-quests offer plenty of opportunity for a creative game designer to insert fascinating stories and interactions with NPCs. *Ultima VII* is a good example of this type of game. (This type of RPG is the focus of *Visual Basic Game Programming for Teens, 3rd Edition*.)

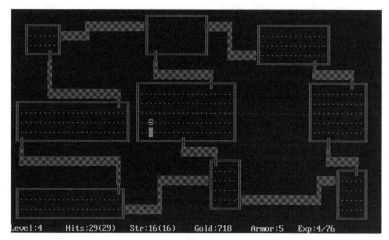

Figure 1.9
Rogue defined the RPG genre in the ancient days of computer gaming.

We will be building a dungeon level editor just for this game, entirely from scratch, beginning in Chapter 6, "Creating the Dungeon Editor." Additional game editors will be featured in later chapters: a character editor in Chapter 10, and an item editor in Chapter 13.

LEVEL UP!

This chapter introduced you to the main concepts you'll be learning about in upcoming chapters from a high-level point of view. In later chapters, you will learn how to take the first step toward writing games with Visual C# by creating your first Visual C# project and delving into Forms-based GDI+ graphics programming. This chapter was short on details but long on ideas, presenting a glimpse of the Dungeon Crawler game, an RPG that you create while following along with this book. The remaining chapters in Part I will teach you how to use the Graphics namespace of the .NET Framework to draw bitmaps and animate sprites with an introduction to GDI+ graphics programming, and the foundational code that will be needed for the game.

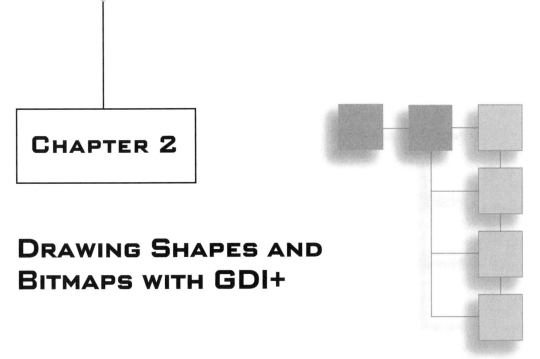

CHAPTER 2

DRAWING SHAPES AND BITMAPS WITH GDI+

We are now on the verge of getting started on the Dungeon Crawler game, which is the focus of most of this book! The first chapter should have brought you up to speed on the goals for the game, while this chapter will explain how we can merge graphics with forms and controls. We will begin studying the graphics capabilities of the .NET Framework that will make it possible to build a complex game. You will learn how to detach controls from the "Form Designer" and just create them at runtime. Although future chapters will continue to need forms and controls, the graphics code will not be dependent on controls such as PictureBox. The .NET Framework has abstracted classes around the Windows Graphics Device Interface (GDI) so that we can create drawing surfaces and render shapes onto them using classes such as Graphics and Bitmap in conjunction with a PictureBox control. We will just create what is needed at runtime.

Here's what is covered in this chapter:

- Drawing lines
- Drawing rectangles
- Drawing text
- Loading a bitmap
- Drawing a bitmap
- Rotating and flipping a bitmap

- Accessing bitmap pixels
- Creating a reusable framework

DRAWING LINES

Lines and other vector shapes may not be very exciting but we are going to use line drawing as a starting point for learning about graphics programming with the .NET Framework and GDI+. The graphics code we'll cover produces the result shown in Figure 2.1.

PictureBox Is Our Friend

For our purposes in this chapter, we will just look at the features specific to 2D graphics programming using the Image property of a PictureBox control. The PictureBox can be added to a form manually, but it's easier to use a global PictureBox control and just create it at runtime in the Form1_Load function. In fact, we will just configure the form in code as well so that no manual property

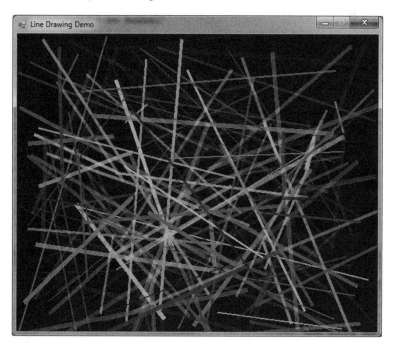

Figure 2.1
Drawing lines with managed GDI+ objects.

editing is needed. Any property you see in the Properties window of the Form Designer can be modified in code—and it's easier to do that in code. So, in the globals section of `public partial class Form1`, let's add some variables, including a `PictureBox` control:

```
PictureBox pb;
Timer timer;
Random rand;
```

In `Form1_Load`, we will create this new `PictureBox` and add it to the form. The `Parent` property is used to attach the control to `Form1` (referred to with the `this` keyword—which refers to the current `Form`). `DockStyle.Fill` causes the `PictureBox` to fill the entire form, so that we can set the size of the form and the `PictureBox` will resize with it.

```
pb = new PictureBox();
pb.Parent = this;
pb.Dock = DockStyle.Fill;
pb.BackColor = Color.Black;
```

While we're working in `Form1_Load`, let's just go ahead and set the form's settings. Again, this is being done in code while it could also be done using the Properties window in the Form Designer.

```
//set up the form
this.Text = "Line Drawing Demo";
this.FormBorderStyle = System.Windows.Forms.FormBorderStyle.FixedSingle;
this.MaximizeBox = false;
this.Size = new Size(600, 500);
//create random generator
rand = new Random();
```

Surfaces and Devices

Back in the globals sections at the top of the code, we need two new objects: a `Bitmap` and a `Graphics` object.

```
Bitmap surface;
Graphics device;
```

The `Bitmap` represents a drawing surface and is really just a pointer to the data in memory. After drawing something using the `Graphics` object (onto a

PictureBox.Image), we then set the Bitmap variable (which is a pointer) equal to the PictureBox.Image, and that Bitmap can then be treated as an independent surface—which can be copied elsewhere, saved to a file, and other things. The Bitmap should be created with the same dimensions as the PictureBox control. This code goes in Form1_Load:

```
//create graphics device
surface = new Bitmap(this.Size.Width, this.Size.Height);
pb.Image = surface;
device = Graphics.FromImage(surface);
```

There are quite a few versions of the Graphics.DrawLine() function with various parameter variations that use Points, float- and int-based X,Y coordinates, and drawing modes. The version I use will use a Pen defined with the desired color and line width. The drawLine() function creates a pen with a random color and random line size, and two random points for the line ends that fit inside the dimensions of the form. After calling DrawLine(), then the PictureBox.Image is refreshed.

```
public void drawLine()
{
    //make a random color
    int A = rand.Next(0, 255);
    int R = rand.Next(0, 255);
    int G = rand.Next(0, 255);
    int B = rand.Next(0, 255);
    Color color = Color.FromArgb(A, R, G, B);
    //make pen out of color
    int width = rand.Next(2, 8);
    Pen pen = new Pen(color, width);
    //random line ends
    int x1 = rand.Next(1, this.Size.Width);
    int y1 = rand.Next(1, this.Size.Height);
    int x2 = rand.Next(1, this.Size.Width);
    int y2 = rand.Next(1, this.Size.Height);
    //draw the line
    device.DrawLine(pen, x1, y1, x2, y2);
    //refresh the drawing surface
    pb.Image = surface;
}
```

4D Programming with a Timer

We can even create a `Timer` in code without using the Form Designer. There is just one extra step to take and then the new `Timer` will work like usual—when setting its properties, we have to create an event handler.

```
Timer timer;
```

The `Timer` object is created in `Form1_Load`:

```
//set up the timer
timer = new Timer();
timer.Interval = 20;
timer.Enabled = true;
timer.Tick += new System.EventHandler(TimerTick);
```

When a new event handler is created, then it becomes "visible" to the event handler system in Visual C#, and can be used as an event trigger even when we write the function ourselves (rather than having Visual C# generate it for us). In this example, I want the `drawLine()` function to run every 20 milliseconds, which is 50 frames per second (50 Hz).

```
public void TimerTick(object source, EventArgs e)
{
    drawLine();
}
```

One final point: we should free memory after we finish with objects created in our programs. Visual C# (or, more specifically, the runtime) will free objects automatically in most cases, but it's a good programming habit to free memory that you use. This is best done in the `Form1_FormClosed` event. At a certain point, it becomes too difficult to manage *everything* in code; some events like this one are best left up to the event handler in the Form Properties. To bring up the Events, open the `Form1.cs` in design view, then in the Properties window click the Events button (which looks like a lightning bolt). You will see all of the events, as shown in Figure 2.2. I wouldn't say that freeing memory is *crucial*, but it's a good idea.

```
private void Form1_FormClosed(object sender, FormClosedEventArgs e)
{
    device.Dispose();
    surface.Dispose();
    timer.Dispose();
}
```

Figure 2.2
The list of Form events.

DRAWING RECTANGLES

Once we have the framework in place to draw lines, there are many other vector shapes that can be drawn with only a few minor changes in the code. One such shape is a rectangle, which we will look at next. Figure 2.3 shows the result.

For reference, we'll go over the entire code listing (which is still quite short). First up are the global variables, Form1_Load, which initializes the program, and Form1_FormClosed, which frees memory.

```
using System;
using System.Drawing;
using System.Windows;
using System.Windows.Forms;
public partial class Form1 : Form
{
    PictureBox pb;
    Timer timer;
    Bitmap surface;
```

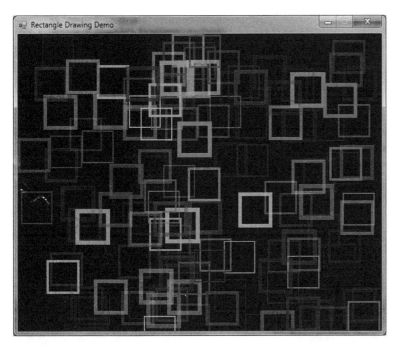

Figure 2.3
Drawing rectangles with GDI+.

```
Graphics device;
Random rand;

public Form1()
{
    InitializeComponent();
}

private void Form1_Load(object sender, EventArgs e)
{
    //set up the form
    this.Text = "Rectangle Drawing Demo";
    this.FormBorderStyle = System.Windows.Forms.FormBorderStyle.
        FixedSingle;
    this.MaximizeBox = false;
    this.Size = new Size(600, 500);
    //create a new picturebox
    pb = new PictureBox();
```

```
        pb.Parent = this;
        pb.Dock = DockStyle.Fill;
        pb.BackColor = Color.Black;
        //create graphics device
        surface = new Bitmap(this.Size.Width, this.Size.Height);
        pb.Image = surface;
        device = Graphics.FromImage(surface);
        //create random generator
        rand = new Random();
        //set up the timer
        timer = new Timer();
        timer.Interval = 20;
        timer.Enabled = true;
        timer.Tick += new EventHandler(timer_Tick);
    }

    private void Form1_FormClosed(object sender, FormClosedEventArgs e)
    {
        device.Dispose();
        surface.Dispose();
        timer.Dispose();
    }
```

Lastly, we have the `timer_Tick` event and the `drawRect()` function, which does the actual rasterizing of rectangle shapes. Again, there are several versions of the `Graphics.DrawRectangle()` function, and I have just chosen the easiest one, but there are others that let you use a `Point` for the coordinates instead of individual X and Y values.

```
    private void drawRect()
    {
        //make a random color
        int A = rand.Next(0, 255);
        int R = rand.Next(0, 255);
        int G = rand.Next(0, 255);
        int B = rand.Next(0, 255);
        Color color = Color.FromArgb(A, R, G, B);

        //make pen out of color
        int width = rand.Next(2, 8);
        Pen pen = new Pen(color, width);
```

```
        //random line ends
        int x = rand.Next(1, this.Size.Width - 50);
        int y = rand.Next(1, this.Size.Height - 50);
        Rectangle rect = new Rectangle(x, y, 50, 50);

        //draw the rectangle
        device.DrawRectangle(pen, rect);

        //refresh the drawing surface
        pb.Image = surface;
    }

    private void timer_Tick(object source, EventArgs e)
    {
        drawRect();
    }
}
```

DRAWING TEXT

We will need to draw text onto the game screen using any desired font, and the Graphics class gives us this ability too, via the DrawString() function. There are several versions of the function with various sets of parameters, but we will be using the simplest version that just needs a String (for the words we want to print out), a custom Font object, the color, and the coordinates. Figure 2.4 shows the result of this example program.

```
using System;
using System.Drawing;
using System.Windows.Forms;
public partial class Form1 : Form
{
    string[] text = {
        "AVATAR!",
        "Know that Brittania has entered into a new age of",
        "enlightenment! Know that the time has finally come",
        "for the one true Lord of Brittania to take his place",
        "at the head of his people. Under my guidance, Brit-",
        "tania will flourish. And all of the people shall",
        "rejoice and pay homage to their new... guardian!",
        "Know that you, too, shall kneel before me, Avatar.",
```

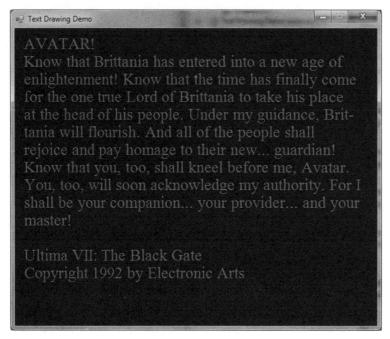

Figure 2.4
Printing text using a custom font and color.

```
            "You, too, will soon acknowledge my authority. For I",
            "shall be your companion... your provider... and your",
            "master!", "",
            "Ultima VII: The Black Gate",
            "Copyright 1992 by Electronic Arts"
    };

    PictureBox pb;
    Bitmap surface;
    Graphics device;
    Random rand;

    public Form1()
    {
        InitializeComponent();
    }

    private void Form1_Load(object sender, EventArgs e)
```

```csharp
{
    //initialize
    this.Text = "Text Drawing Demo";
    this.FormBorderStyle = System.Windows.Forms.FormBorderStyle.
        FixedSingle;
    this.MaximizeBox = false;
    this.Size = new Size(600, 500);
    rand = new Random();

    //create a new picturebox
    pb = new PictureBox();
    pb.Parent = this;
    pb.Dock = DockStyle.Fill;
    pb.BackColor = Color.Black;

    //create graphics device
    surface = new Bitmap(this.Size.Width, this.Size.Height);
    pb.Image = surface;
    device = Graphics.FromImage(surface);

    //make a new font
    Font font = new Font("Times New Roman", 26, FontStyle.Regular,
        GraphicsUnit.Pixel);

    //draw the text
    for (int n = 0; n < text.Length; n++)
    {
        device.DrawString(text[n], font, Brushes.Red, 10, 10 + n*28);
    }

    //refresh the drawing surface
    pb.Image = surface;
}

private void Form1_FormClosed(object sender, FormClosedEventArgs e)
{
    device.Dispose();
    surface.Dispose();
}
}
```

There are other shapes in addition to lines, rectangles, and text that the `Graphics` class can draw. Now that you have a foundation, see if you can modify the program to use any of the following functions:

- `DrawArc`
- `DrawBezier`
- `DrawCurve`
- `DrawEllipse`
- `DrawPie`
- `DrawPolygon`

Trick

> To simplify the code in this C# project, I have removed the default namespace that Visual C# automatically added to the new project. In a larger project with many source code files and libraries, we would want to use a namespace, but for simple examples like this it is okay to skip the namespace.

DISSECTING BITMAPS

Learning to draw a bitmap is the first step toward creating a 2D game like our impending Dungeon Crawler game. When we have the ability to draw just one bitmap, then we can extend that to animation by drawing one frame after another in a timed sequence—and presto, sprite animation becomes a reality! We will focus on sprite animation in Chapter 3, and work on the basics of bitmap drawing now as a prerequisite.

Drawing on the code we learned about earlier in the chapter, a `Bitmap` object, a `PictureBox`, and a `Graphics` object work in tandem to represent a rendering device capable of drawing vector shapes as well as bitmaps. Once again for reference, we have to declare the two variables:

```
Bitmap surface;
Graphics device;
```

and then, assuming we have a `PictureBox` control called `pictureBox1`, create the objects. The `PictureBox` control can be created at runtime or we can just add it to the form manually.

```
surface = new Bitmap(this.Size.Width, this.Size.Height);
pictureBox1.Image = surface;
device = Graphics.FromImage(surface);
```

So, we already knew this startup code, but—just to lay the groundwork—this is what is needed up front as a rendering device to draw a *bitmap*.

Loading a Bitmap File

We can load a bitmap in C# by using the `Bitmap` class. But there is no `Bitmap.Load()` function (unfortunately!) so we have to use the constructor instead by passing the bitmap filename when the object is created.

```
Bitmap bmp;
bmp = new Bitmap("image.bmp");
```

Definition

A *constructor* is a class function (also called a method) that runs when an object is first created. This is where class variables (also called properties) are initialized. A *destructor* is a class function that runs when the object is being destroyed: via `object.Dispose()` or `object = null`.

Although both approaches work, and we can even pass a string rather than hard coding the filename, there is the very serious problem of error handling: if the file does not exist, an exception error will crash the program. Missing files are fairly common (usually due to their being in the wrong folder), and we want to display a friendly error message rather than watch the program crash. The solution is to wrap the bitmap loading code in a `try...catch` block. Here is an example:

```
try
{
    bmp = new Bitmap(filename);
}
catch (Exception ex) { }
```

This code will *not crash* if the file is missing or if some other error occurs while reading the file. So, let's put it into a reusable function that returns a `Bitmap` if the file exists or `Nothing` (null) if it fails. One caveat: be sure to free memory used by the bitmap when the program ends.

```
public Bitmap LoadBitmap(string filename)
{
```

```
Bitmap bmp = null;
try
{
    bmp = new Bitmap(filename);
}
catch (Exception) { }
return bmp;
}
```

If the file does not exist, then LoadBitmap() will return Nothing as the object pointer rather than crashing with an exception error. This is a very handy little function! And it demonstrates the power of code reuse and customization—whatever features we need that are not already in an SDK or library we can just write ourselves. One might even go so far as to write their own new Bitmap wrapper class (called something like CBitmap?) with a Load() function. You could easily do this yourself with just the small amount of code we have used so far. I'm just going to skip this step, though, and add bitmap loading in the Sprite class when we get to it in Chapter 3.

Hint

To ensure that created objects are properly disposed of when the program ends, I recommend putting the Form1_FormClosed() function at the top of the source code, just below the variable declarations, where it will be quick and easy to write the code needed to free an object. Always write creation/deletion code together in pairs to avoid memory leaks!

Drawing a Bitmap

There are several versions of the Graphics.DrawImage() function; the alternate versions are called *overloaded functions* in "OOP speak." The simplest version of the function calls for just a Bitmap or Image parameter and then the X and Y position. For example, this line

```
device.DrawImage(bmp, 0, 0);
```

will draw the bitmap bmp at pixel coordinates 0,0. Figure 2.5 shows an example.

We can optionally use a Point with the X and Y coordinates combined into one object, or use floating-point Single variables. There are also *scaling* features that make it possible to resize the image. By passing additional width and height

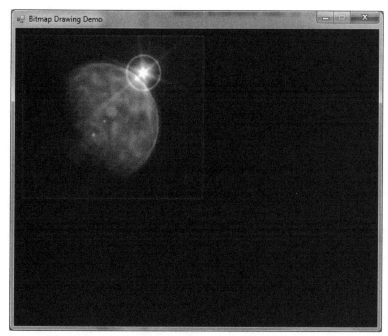

Figure 2.5
Drawing an image loaded from a bitmap file.

parameters, we can define a new target size for the image. Figure 2.6 shows another example with the addition of this line, which draws another copy of the bitmap scaled down to a smaller size.

```
device.DrawImage(planet, 400, 10, 64, 64);
```

Rotating and Flipping a Bitmap

The Bitmap class has some helper functions for manipulating the image and even its individual pixels. The Bitmap.RotateFlip() function will rotate a bitmap in 90-degree increments (90, 180, and 270 degrees), as well as flip the bitmap vertically, horizontally, or both. Here is an example that rotates the bitmap 90 degrees:

```
planet.RotateFlip(RotateFlipType.Rotate90FlipNone);
```

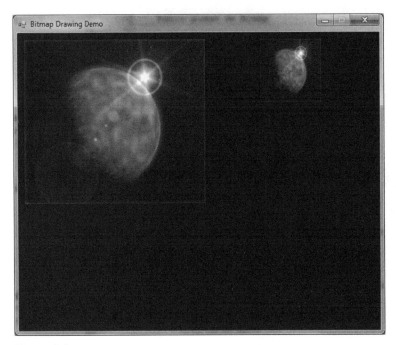

Figure 2.6
Drawing a scaled bitmap.

The RotateFlipType options are as follows:

- Rotate180FlipNone
- Rotate180FlipX
- Rotate180FlipXY
- Rotate180FlipY
- Rotate270FlipNone
- Rotate270FlipX
- Rotate270FlipXY
- Rotate270FlipY
- Rotate90FlipNone
- Rotate90FlipX
- Rotate90FlipXY
- Rotate90FlipY

Figure 2.7
Rotating and flipping a bitmap.

- RotateNoneFlipX
- RotateNoneFlipXY
- RotateNoneFlipY

The Bitmap Drawing demo has several buttons on the form to let you explore rotating and flipping a bitmap in various ways, as you can see in Figure 2.7. In addition to calling RotateFlip(), we still need to draw the image again and refresh the PictureBox like usual:

```
image.RotateFlip(RotateFlipType.Rotate180FlipNone);
device.DrawImage(planet, 0, 0);
pictureBox1.Image = surface;
```

Accessing Bitmap Pixels

We can also examine and modify the pixel buffer of a bitmap directly using functions in the Bitmap class. The Bitmap.GetPixel() function retrieves the pixel of a bitmap at given X,Y coordinates, returning it as a Color variable. Likewise,

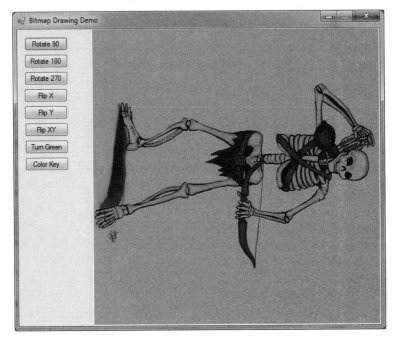

Figure 2.8
Modifying the color value of pixels in a bitmap.

the `Bitmap.SetPixel()` will change the color of a pixel at the given coordinates. The following example reads every pixel in the planet bitmap and changes it to green by setting the red and blue components of the color to zero, which leaves just the green color remaining. Figure 2.8 shows the Bitmap Drawing demo with the pixels modified—not very interesting but it does a good job of showing what you can do with this capability.

```
for (int x = 0; x < image.Width - 1; x++)
{
    for (int y = 0; y < image.Height - 1; y++)
    {
        Color pixelColor = image.GetPixel(x, y);
        Color newColor = Color.FromArgb(0, pixelColor.G, 0);
        image.SetPixel(x, y, newColor);
    }
}
```

Here is the source code for the Bitmap Drawing demo. There are controls on the form, so you must open the project in order to run it; the source code here does not build the user interface like some of our simpler examples have done.

```csharp
using System;
using System.Drawing;
using System.Windows.Forms;
public partial class Form1 : Form
{
    Bitmap surface;
    Graphics device;
    Bitmap image;

    public Form1()
    {
        InitializeComponent();
    }

    private void Form1_Load(object sender, EventArgs e)
    {
        //set up the form
        this.Text = "Bitmap Drawing Demo";
        this.FormBorderStyle = System.Windows.Forms.FormBorderStyle.
            FixedSingle;
        this.MaximizeBox = false;
        //create graphics device
        surface = new Bitmap(this.Size.Width, this.Size.Height);
        pictureBox1.Image = surface;

        device = Graphics.FromImage(surface);
        //load the bitmap
        image = LoadBitmap("skellyarcher.png");
        //draw the bitmap
        device.DrawImage(image, 0, 0);
    }

    public Bitmap LoadBitmap(string filename)
    {
        Bitmap bmp = null;
        try
        {
            bmp = new Bitmap(filename);
```

```
    }
    catch (Exception ex) { }
    return bmp;
}

private void Form1_FormClosed(object sender, FormClosedEventArgs e)
{
    device.Dispose();
    surface.Dispose();
    image.Dispose();
}

private void button9_Click(object sender, EventArgs e)
{
    image.RotateFlip(RotateFlipType.Rotate90FlipNone);
    device.DrawImage(image, 0, 0);
    pictureBox1.Image = surface;
}

private void button10_Click(object sender, EventArgs e)
{
    image.RotateFlip(RotateFlipType.Rotate180FlipNone);
    device.DrawImage(image, 0, 0);
    pictureBox1.Image = surface;
}

private void button11_Click(object sender, EventArgs e)
{
    image.RotateFlip(RotateFlipType.Rotate270FlipNone);
    device.DrawImage(image, 0, 0);
    pictureBox1.Image = surface;
}

private void button12_Click(object sender, EventArgs e)
{
    image.RotateFlip(RotateFlipType.RotateNoneFlipX);
    device.DrawImage(image, 0, 0);
    pictureBox1.Image = surface;
}
```

```csharp
private void button13_Click(object sender, EventArgs e)
{
    image.RotateFlip(RotateFlipType.RotateNoneFlipY);
    device.DrawImage(image, 0, 0);
    pictureBox1.Image = surface;
}

private void button14_Click(object sender, EventArgs e)
{
    image.RotateFlip(RotateFlipType.RotateNoneFlipXY);
    device.DrawImage(image, 0, 0);
    pictureBox1.Image = surface;
}

private void button15_Click(object sender, EventArgs e)
{
    Color white = Color.FromArgb(255, 255, 255);
    Color black = Color.FromArgb(0, 0, 0);
    for (int x = 0; x < image.Width - 1; x++)
    {
        for (int y = 0; y < image.Height - 1; y++)
        {
            if (image.GetPixel(x,y) == white)
                image.SetPixel(x, y, black);
        }
    }
    device.DrawImage(image, 0, 0);
    pictureBox1.Image = surface;
}

private void button16_Click(object sender, EventArgs e)
{
    for (int x = 0; x < image.Width - 1; x++)
    {
        for (int y = 0; y < image.Height - 1; y++)
        {
            Color pixelColor = image.GetPixel(x, y);
            Color newColor = Color.FromArgb(0, pixelColor.G, 0);
            image.SetPixel(x, y, newColor);
        }
```

```
        }
        device.DrawImage(image, 0, 0);
        pictureBox1.Image = surface;
    }
}
```

CREATING A REUSABLE FRAMEWORK

We have enough code now at this point to begin constructing a game framework for our future C# projects. The purpose of a framework is to take care of repeating code. Any variables and functions that are needed regularly can be moved into a Game class as properties and methods where they will be both convenient and easily accessible. First, we'll create a new source code file called Game.cs, which will contain the source code for the Game class. Then, we'll copy this Game.cs file into the folder of any new project we create and add it to that project. The goal is to simplify the whole process of creating a new game project and make most of our C# game code reusable. Let's get started:

```
using System;
using System.Drawing;
using System.Diagnostics;
using System.Windows;
using System.Windows.Forms;

public class Game
{
    private Graphics p_device;
    private Bitmap p_surface;
    private PictureBox p_pb;
    private Form p_frm;
```

You might recognize the first three of these class properties from previous examples. They have a p_ in front of their names so it's easy to tell at a glance that they are *private* variables in the class (as opposed to, say, parameters in a function). The fourth property, p_frm, is a reference to the main Form of a project, which will be set when the object is created. Yes, our Game class will even customize its form so we don't have to do anything more than supply the form to the class.

Hint

A *class* is a blueprint written in source code for how an *object* should behave at runtime. Just as an object does not exist at compile time (i.e., when we're editing source code and building the project), a class does not exist during runtime. An object is created out of the class blueprint.

Game Class Constructor

The *constructor* is the first method that runs when a class is *instantiated* into an object. We can add parameters to the constructor in order to send information to the object at runtime—important things like the Form, or maybe a filename, or whatever you want.

Definition

Instantiation is the process of creating an object out of the blueprint specified in a class. When this happens, an object is *created* and the *constructor method* runs. Likewise, when the object is destroyed, the *destructor method* runs. These methods are defined in the class.

Here is the constructor for the Game class. This is just an early version, as more code will be added over time. As you can see, this is not new code, it's just the code we've seen before to create the Graphics and Bitmap objects needed for rendering onto a PictureBox. Which, by the way, is created at runtime by this function and set to fill the entire form (Dock = DockStyle.Fill). To clarify what these objects are used for, the Graphics variable is called p_device—while not technically correct, it conveys the purpose adequately. To help illustrate when the constructor runs, a temporary message box pops up which you are welcome to remove after you get what it's doing.

```
public Game(Form1 form, int width, int height)
{
    Trace.WriteLine("Game class constructor");
    //set form properties
    p_frm = form;
    p_frm.FormBorderStyle = FormBorderStyle.FixedSingle;
    p_frm.MaximizeBox = false;
    p_frm.Size = new Size(width, height);

    //create a picturebox
    p_pb = new PictureBox();
```

```
    p_pb.Parent = p_frm;
    p_pb.Dock = DockStyle.Fill;
    p_pb.BackColor = Color.Black;

    //create graphics device
    p_surface = new Bitmap(p_frm.Size.Width, p_frm.Size.Height);
    p_pb.Image = p_surface;
    p_device = Graphics.FromImage(p_surface);
}
```

Game Class Destructor

The *destructor* method is called automatically when the object is about to be deleted from memory (i.e., destroyed). In C#, or, more specifically, in .NET, the name of the destructor is Finalize(), but we create a sub-class destructor using the tilde character (~) followed by the class name. So, if our class name is Game, then the destructor method will be ~Game(). In this method, we again send a message sent to the output console using System.Diagnostics.Trace.WriteLine(). Feel free to use Trace any time you need to see debugging information, as it will be sent to the output window. Note that p_frm is not disposed—leave that alone as it is just a reference to the actual form.

```
~Game()
{
    Trace.WriteLine("Game class destructor");
    p_device.Dispose();
    p_surface.Dispose();
    p_pb.Dispose();
}
```

Bitmap Loading

Our first reusable method for the Game class is LoadBitmap:

```
public Bitmap LoadBitmap(string filename)
{
    Bitmap bmp = null;
    try
    {
        bmp = new Bitmap(filename);
    }
    catch (Exception ex) { }
```

```
    return bmp;
}
```

Game Updates

We probably will not need an `Update()` function at this early stage but it's here as an option should you wish to use it to update the `PictureBox` any time drawing occurs on the "device." In due time, this function will be expanded to do quite a bit more than its meager one line of code currently shows. Also shown here is a `Property` called `Device`. A `Property` allows us to write code that looks like just a simple class property is being used (like `p_device`), when in fact a *function call* occurs.

```
    public Graphics Device
    {
        get { return p_device; }
    }

    public void Update()
    {
        //refresh the drawing surface
        p_pb.Image = p_surface;
    }
}
```

So, for example, if we want to get the value returned by the `Device` property, we can do that like so:

```
Graphics G = game.Device;
```

Note that I did not include parentheses at the end of `Device`. That's because it is not treated as a method, even though we are able to do something with the data before returning it. The key to a property is its `get` and `set` members. Since I did not want anyone to modify the `p_device` variable from outside the class, I have made the property read-only by using a `get` without a corresponding `set` member. If I did want to make `p_device` writable, I would use a `set` member.

Properties are really helpful because they allow us to protect data in the class! You can prevent changes to a variable by making sure the change value is in a valid range before allowing the change—so in that sense, a property is like a "variable with benefits."

Framework Demo

The code in this Framework demo program produces pretty much the same output as what we've seen earlier in the chapter (drawing a purple planet). The difference is, thanks to the new Game class, the source code is *much*, much shorter! Take a look.

```
using System;
using System.Drawing;
using System.Windows.Forms;

public partial class Form1 : Form
{
    public Game game;
    public Bitmap planet;

    public Form1()
    {
        InitializeComponent();
    }

    private void Form1_Load(object sender, EventArgs e)
    {
        //set up the form
        this.Text = "Framework Demo";

        //create game object
        game = new Game(this, 600, 500);

        //load bitmap
        planet = game.LoadBitmap("planet.bmp");
        if (planet == null)
        {
            MessageBox.Show("Error loading planet.bmp");
            Environment.Exit(0);
        }

        //draw the bitmap
        game.Device.DrawImage(planet, 10, 10);
        game.Device.DrawImage(planet, 400, 10, 100, 100);
        game.Update();
```

```
    }

    private void Form1_FormClosed(object sender, FormClosedEventArgs e)
    {
        //delete game object
        game = null;
    }
}
```

Eliminating any reusable source code by moving it into a support file is like reducing a mathematical formula, rendering the new formula more *powerful* than it was before. Any code that does *not* have to be written increases your productivity as a programmer. So, look for every opportunity to cleanly and effectively recycle code, but don't reduce just for the sake of code reuse—make sure you keep variables and functions together that belong together and don't mish-mash them all together.

LEVEL UP!

This chapter gave us the ability to create a rendering system in code and bypass the Form Designer by creating controls at runtime instead of design time. Using this technique, we created a `PictureBox` for use in rendering. We also learned how to work with bitmaps and manipulate them in interesting ways that will be very useful in a game. We have now learned enough about 2D graphics programming to begin working with sprites in the next chapter!

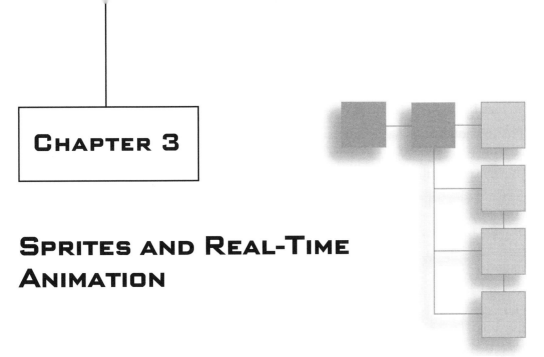

CHAPTER 3

SPRITES AND REAL-TIME ANIMATION

This chapter will show how to create a sprite using the code developed in the previous chapter for working with bitmaps. We have a lot of ground to cover here, and we'll be going through it thoroughly because this is the foundation of the Dungeon Crawler game. You will finish this chapter with a solid grasp of sprite programming knowledge, with the ability to load a sprite sheet and draw a sprite with timed animation. Because we want a sprite to draw transparently over any background image in a game, we'll also learn how to work with an alpha channel in a bitmap image to render an image with transparency. This chapter moves along at a pretty good clip, so you don't want to skip ahead or you might miss some important detail.

Here's what we'll cover in this chapter:

- What is a sprite?
- Sprite animation theory
- Creating a Sprite class
- Improving the Game class
- Adding a real-time game loop
- Gameplay functions

WHAT IS A SPRITE?

The first question that often arises when the discussion of sprites comes up is, "What is a sprite?" To answer this question simply, a *sprite* is a small, transparent, animated game object that usually moves on the screen and interacts with other sprites. You might have trees or rocks or buildings in your game that don't move at all, but because those objects are loaded from a bitmap file when the game starts running, and drawn in the game separately from the background, it is reasonable to call them sprites. There are two basic types of sprites. One type of sprite is the "normal" sprite that I just described, which I refer to as a *dynamic sprite*. This type of sprite is often called an *actor* in game design theory. The other type of sprite might be called a *static sprite*; it is the sort that doesn't move or animate. A static sprite is used for scenery or objects that the player uses (such as items that might be picked up in the game world). This type of sprite is often called a *prop*.

Definition

A *sprite* is a small, transparent, animated game object that usually moves on the screen and interacts with other sprites. There are two types of sprites: actors and props.

I'm going to treat any game entity that is loaded and drawn separately from the background as a sprite. So, I might have a whole house, which normally would be considered part of the background, as a sprite. I use that concept in the sample program later in this chapter.

Figure 3.1 shows an example sprite of a dragon. The sprite is really just the detailed pixels that you see at the center of the image, showing the dragon flying. The sprite itself only takes up about half of the actual size of the image because the computer only sees sprites in the shape of a rectangle. It is physically impossible to even store a sprite without the rectangular boundary because bitmap images are themselves rectangular. The real problem with a sprite is what to do about all the transparent pixels that should *not* be shown when the image is displayed on the screen (or rather, on the back buffer surface).

The amateur game programmer will try to draw a sprite using two loops that go through each pixel of the sprite's bitmap image, drawing only the solid pixels. Here is some *pseudo-code* for how one might do this:

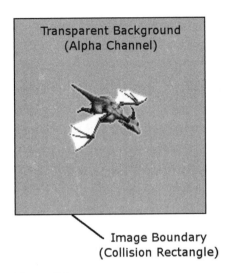

Figure 3.1
The sprite boundary is a rectangle that encloses the sprite with transparent pixels.

```
For Y = 1 To Sprite_Height
  For X = 1 to Sprite_Width
    If Pixel At X,Y Is Solid Then
      Draw Pixel At X,Y
    End
  Next X
Next Y
```

This *pseudo-code algorithm* (so named because it would not compile) goes through each pixel of the sprite image, checking for solid pixels, which are then drawn while transparent pixels are ignored. This draws a transparent sprite, but it runs so slowly that the game probably won't be playable (even on a top-of-the-line PC).

And yet, this is the *only* way to draw a transparent sprite! By one method or another, some process must check the pixels that are solid and render them. The key here is understanding how drawing works, because this very critical and time-consuming algorithm is quite old and has been built into the silicon of video cards for many years now. The process of copying a transparent image from one surface to another has been provided by video cards for decades now, dating back to the old Windows 3.1 and "video accelerator" cards. The process is

Figure 3.2
The sprite on the right is drawn without the transparent pixels.

called *bit block transfer* or just *blit* for short. Because this important process is handled by an extremely optimized and custom video chip, you don't need to worry about writing your own *blitter* for a game any longer. (Even older systems like the Nintendo Game Boy Advance have a hardware blitter.)

The video card uses *alpha blending* to draw textures with a translucent effect (which means you can see through them like a window) or with full transparency. Fifty-percent translucency means that half of the light rays are blocked and you can only see about half of the image. Zero-percent translucency is called *opaque*, which is completely solid. The opposite is 100-percent translucency, or fully transparent, which lets *all* light pass through. Figure 3.2 illustrates the difference between an opaque and transparent sprite image.

When an image needs to be drawn with transparency, we call the transparent color a *color key*, and the process of alpha blending causes that particular pixel color to be completely blended with the background. At the same time, no other pixels in the texture are affected by alpha blending, and the result is a transparent sprite. Color key transparency is not often used today because it's a pain. A better way to handle transparency is with an alpha channel and a file format that supports it such as tga or png. (Note: bmp files do not support an alpha channel.)

How Visual C# Handles Pathnames

A path is a complete description of a directory location. Consider a file with an absolute path, as in the following example:

C:\Program Files\Microsoft Visual Studio 8\Common7\IDE\devenv.exe

The filename is located at the end, "devenv.exe," while the path to this filename is everything else in front of the filename. The complete "path" to a file can be described in this absolute format.

The problem is, Visual C# compiles programs into a subdirectory under your project directory called *bin*. Inside bin, depending on whether you're building the Debug or Release version of your program, there will be a folder called bin\Debug or bin\Release. You need to put all of your game's asset files (bitmaps, waves, etc.) inside this folder in order for it to run. You would not want to store your game's files inside the main folder of the project because when it runs (inside bin\Debug, for instance) it will not know where the files are located, and the program will crash.

You can hard-code the path into your game (like C:\Game), but this is a bad idea because then anyone who tries to play your game will have to create the exact same directory that you did when you created the game. Instead, put your artwork and other game resources inside bin\Debug while working on your game. When your game is finished and ready for release, then copy all of the files together into a new folder with the executable.

ANIMATING A SPRITE

After you have written a few games, you'll most likely find that many of the sprites in your games have similar behaviors, to the point of predictability. For instance, if you have sprites that just move around within the boundaries of the screen and wrap from one edge to the other, you can create a subroutine to produce this sprite behavior on call. Simply use that subroutine when you update the sprite's position. If you find that a lot of your sprites are doing other predictable movements, it is really helpful to create many different behavioral subroutines to control their actions.

This is just one simple example of a very primitive behavior (staying within the boundary of the screen), but you can create very complex behaviors by writing subroutines that cause sprites to react to other sprites or to the player, for instance, in different ways. You might have some behavior subroutines that cause a sprite to chase the player, or run away from the player, or attack the player. The possibilities are truly limited only by your imagination, and, generally, the most enjoyable games use movement patterns that the player can learn while playing. The Sprite demo program in this chapter demonstrates sprite movement as well as animation, so you may refer to that program for an example of how the sprite movement code is used.

Sprite Animation Theory

Sprite animation goes back about three decades, when the first video game systems were being built for arcades. The earliest arcade games include classics such as *Asteroids* that used vector-based graphics rather than bitmap-based graphics. A *vector-based* graphics system uses lines connecting two points as the basis for all of the graphics on the screen. Although a rotating vector-based spaceship might not be considered a sprite by today's standards, it is basically the same thing. Any game object on the screen that uses more than one small image to represent itself might be considered a *sprite*. However, to be an *animated sprite*, the image must simulate a sequence of images that are cycled while the sprite is being displayed.

Animation is a fascinating subject because it brings life to a game and makes objects seem more realistic. An important concept to grasp at this point is that *every* frame of an animation sequence must be treated as a distinct image that is stored in a bitmap file; as an alternative, some animation might be created on the fly if a technique such as rotation or alpha cycling is used. (For instance, causing a sprite to fade in and out could be done at runtime.) In the past, professional game developers did not often use rotation of a sprite at runtime due to quality concerns, but we can do that today with pretty good results.

Animation is done with the use of a *sprite sheet*. A sprite sheet is a bitmap containing columns and rows of tiles, with each tile containing one frame of animation. It is not uncommon for a sprite with eight directions of movement to have 64 or more frames of animation just for one activity (such as walking, attacking, or dying).

Figure 3.3 shows a dragon sprite with 64 frames of animation. The dragon can move in any of eight directions of travel, and each direction has eight frames of animation. We'll learn to load this sprite sheet and then draw it transparently on the screen with animation later in this chapter. The source artwork (from Reiner Prokein) comes in individual bitmap files—so that a 64-frame dragon sprite starts out with 64 individual bitmap files.

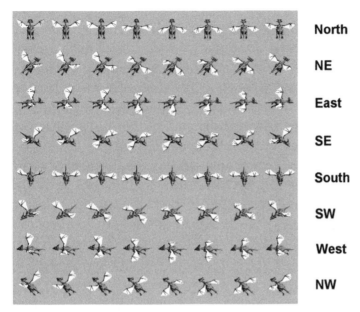

North

NE

East

SE

South

SW

West

NW

Figure 3.3
A dragon sprite sheet with an 8 × 8 layout of animation frames.

Tip

This dragon sprite was provided courtesy of Reiner "Tiles" Prokein at www.reinerstileset.de. Most of the other sprite artwork in this book is also from Reiner's sprite collection, which includes a royalty-free license.

The trick to animating a sprite is keeping track of the current frame of animation along with the total animation frames in the animation sequence. This dragon sprite is stored in a single, large bitmap image and was actually stored in 64 individual bitmaps before I converted it to a single bitmap using Pro Motion.

Trick

Cosmigo's Pro Motion is an excellent sprite animation editor available for download at www.cosmigo.com/promotion. All of the sprite sheets featured in this book were converted using this great, useful tool.

After you have exported an animation sequence as a sprite sheet image, the trick is to get a handle on animating the sprite in source code. Storing all the frames of animation inside a single bitmap file makes it easier to use the animation in your program. However, it doesn't necessarily make it easier to set up; you have to deal with the animation looping around at a specific point, rather than looping through all 64 frames. Now we'll start to see where all of those odd properties and subroutines in the Sprite class will be used. I have animated the dragon sprite by passing a range to the Animate function that represents one of the four directions (up, down, left, right), which is determined by the user's keyboard input. Although the sprite sheet has frames for all eight directions, including diagonals, the example program in this chapter sticks to the four main directions to keep the code simpler.

To get the current frame, we need to find out where that frame is located inside the sprite sheet in the least amount of code possible. To get the Y position of a frame, you take the current frame and divide by the columns to get the appropriate row (and then multiply that by the frame height, or height of each tile).

To get the X position of the frame, perform that same division as before, but get the remainder (modulus result) from the division rather than the quotient, and then multiply by the sprite's width. At this point, the rest of the rectangle is set up using the sprite's width and height. The destination rectangle is configured to the sprite's current position, and then a call to the existing Draw subroutine takes care of business. Figure 3.4 shows the numbered columns and rows of a sprite sheet. Note that the numbering starts at 0 instead of 1. That is a little harder to follow when reading the code, but using a base of 0 makes the calculations *much* simpler. See if you can choose a frame number and calculate where it is located on the sprite sheet on your own!

Creating a Sprite Class

We could get by with a couple of reusable functions and a Bitmap. But, that would involve a lot of duplicated code that could very easily be put into a class. So, that is what we will do. There aren't very many classes in this book, in the interest of making source code easier to understand, but in some cases it's more difficult to *not* use a class—as is the case with sprite programming. The first

COLUMNS

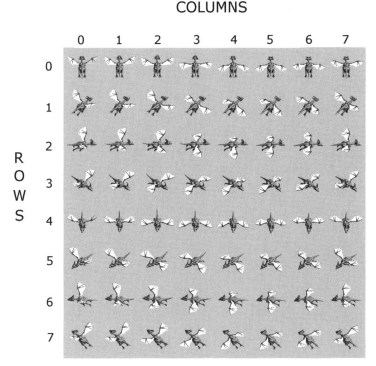

Figure 3.4
The numbered columns and rows of the dragon sprite sheet.

thing you will notice is the use of a new namespace called RPG. This helps to organize things in our project now that we have some classes as well as the Form code. You can call the namespace what you wish, as long as every source code file uses the same namespace name (in order for them to "see" each other). "RPG" is sort of the name of the *engine* for Dungeon Crawler—it has no real meaning beyond organizing the code.

I have some goals for our new Sprite class. First, it will be self-contained, with the exception that it needs the rendering device in our Game class (Game.Device) for drawing. We can pass a reference to the game object to a sprite's constructor at runtime and that should take care of it.

Second, the class should handle both drawing *and* animation with enough variation to support any needs we'll have in Dungeon Crawler, with numerous properties to keep the code clean and tidy. This is a pretty good start, but we will make small changes to Sprite over time to meet any new needs as the game begins to take shape.

```
using System;
using System.Drawing;
namespace RPG
{
    public class Sprite
    {
        public enum AnimateDir
        {
            NONE = 0,
            FORWARD = 1,
            BACKWARD = -1
        }
        public enum AnimateWrap
        {
            WRAP = 0,
            BOUNCE = 1
        }
        private Game p_game;
        private PointF p_position;
        private PointF p_velocity;
        private Size p_size;
        private Bitmap p_bitmap;
        private bool p_alive;
        private int p_columns;
        private int p_totalFrames;
        private int p_currentFrame;
        private AnimateDir p_animationDir;
        private AnimateWrap p_animationWrap;
        private int p_lastTime;
        private int p_animationRate;
```

The Sprite constructor method is next. The variables and references are initialized at this point. It's good programming practice to set the initial values for the properties on our own.

```
        public Sprite(ref Game game)
        {
            p_game = game;
            p_position = new PointF(0, 0);
```

```
            p_velocity = new PointF(0, 0);
            p_size = new Size(0, 0);
            p_bitmap = null;
            p_alive = true;
            p_columns = 1;
            p_totalFrames = 1;
            p_currentFrame = 0;
            p_animationDir = AnimateDir.FORWARD;
            p_animationWrap = AnimateWrap.WRAP;
            p_lastTime = 0;
            p_animationRate = 30;
        }
```

The Sprite class includes numerous properties to give access to its private variables. In most cases this is a direct get/set association with no real benefit to hiding the variables internally, but in some cases (such as AnimationRate) the values are manipulated within the property's set.

```
        public bool Alive
        {
            get { return p_alive; }
            set { p_alive = value; }
        }

        public Bitmap Image
        {
            get { return p_bitmap; }
            set { p_bitmap = value; }
        }

        public PointF Position
        {
            get { return p_position; }
            set { p_position = value; }
        }

        public PointF Velocity
        {
            get { return p_velocity; }
            set { p_velocity = value; }
        }
```

```csharp
public float X
{
    get { return p_position.X; }
    set { p_position.X = value; }
}

public float Y
{
    get { return p_position.Y; }
    set { p_position.Y = value; }
}

public Size Size
{
    get { return p_size; }
    set { p_size = value; }
}

public int Width
{
    get { return p_size.Width; }
    set { p_size.Width = value; }
}

public int Height
{
    get { return p_size.Height; }
    set { p_size.Height = value; }
}

public int Columns
{
    get { return p_columns; }
    set { p_columns = value; }
}

public int TotalFrames
{
    get { return p_totalFrames; }
    set { p_totalFrames = value; }
}
```

```
        }

        public int CurrentFrame
        {
            get { return p_currentFrame; }
            set { p_currentFrame = value; }
        }

        public AnimateDir AnimateDirection
        {
            get { return p_animationDir; }
            set { p_animationDir = value; }
        }

        public AnimateWrap AnimateWrapMode
        {
            get { return p_animationWrap; }
            set { p_animationWrap = value; }
        }

        public int AnimationRate
        {
            get { return 1000 / p_animationRate; }
            set
            {
                if (value == 0) value = 1;
                p_animationRate = 1000 / value;
            }
        }
```

Sprite animation is handled by the single Animate() method, which should be called from the gameplay functions Game_Update() or Game_Draw(). Animation timing is handled automatically in this function using a millisecond timer, so it can be called from the extremely fast-running Game_Update() without concern for animation speed being in sync with the drawing of the sprite. Without this built-in timing, the Animate() function would have to be called from Game_Draw(), which is timed at 60 Hz (or frames per second). Code such as this Animate() function really should be run from the fastest part of the game loop whenever possible, and only real drawing should take place in Game_Draw() due to timing considerations. If you were to put all of the gameplay code in Game_Draw() and hardly anything in Game_Update(), which is the fast-running function, then the game would slow down quite a bit. We will also need the default Animate() function which defaults to animating the *whole* range of animation automatically.

```
public void Animate()
{
    Animate(0, p_totalFrames - 1);
}


public void Animate(int startFrame, int endFrame)
{
    //do we even need to animate?
    if (p_totalFrames <= 0) return;

    //check animation timing
    int time = Environment.TickCount;
    if (time > p_lastTime + p_animationRate)
    {
        p_lastTime = time;

        //go to next frame
        p_currentFrame += (int)p_animationDir;
        switch (p_animationWrap)
        {
            case AnimateWrap.WRAP:
                if (p_currentFrame < startFrame)
                    p_currentFrame = endFrame;
                else if (p_currentFrame > endFrame)
                    p_currentFrame = startFrame;
                break;

            case AnimateWrap.BOUNCE:
                if (p_currentFrame < startFrame)
                {
                    p_currentFrame = startFrame;
                    p_animationDir = AnimateDir.FORWARD;
                }
                else if (p_currentFrame > endFrame)
                {
                    p_currentFrame = endFrame;
                    p_animationDir = AnimateDir.BACKWARD;
```

```
            }
          break;
      }
    }
  }
```

The single `Draw()` method can handle all of our sprite drawing needs, including animation! However, there is an optimization that can be made for sprites that do not animate (i.e., "props"): the modulus and division calculations being done in this function make sprite sheet animation possible, but this code can slow down a game if quite a few sprites are being drawn without any animation. The `Game.DrawBitmap()` function can be used in those cases, because it does not take up any processor cycles to calculate animation frames.

```
public void Draw()
{
    Rectangle frame = new Rectangle();
    frame.X = (p_currentFrame % p_columns) * p_size.Width;
    frame.Y = (p_currentFrame / p_columns) * p_size.Height;
    frame.Width = p_size.Width;
    frame.Height = p_size.Height;
    p_game.Device.DrawImage(p_bitmap, Bounds, frame,
        GraphicsUnit.Pixel);
}
```

Oddly enough, even though we have not discussed the subject yet, this class already has collision detection included. We have a chapter dedicated to the subject: the very next chapter. So, let's just briefly take a look at this as-yet-unused code with plans to dig into it soon. There is one very useful property here called `Bounds`, which returns a `Rectangle` representing the bounding box of the sprite at its current position on the screen. This is used both for drawing *and* collision testing. When drawing in the `Draw()` method, `Bounds` provides the destination rectangle which defines where the sprite will be drawn on the screen, and with scaling of the image if you want. The `IsColliding()` method below *also* uses `Bounds`. One very handy function in the `Rectangle` class is `IntersectsWith()`. This function will return true if a passed rectangle is intersecting with it. In other words, if two sprites are touching, then we will know by using this function that is built in to the `Rectangle` class. We don't have to even write our own collision code!

Nevertheless, we'll explore advanced collision techniques in the next chapter (including distance or circular collision).

```
public Rectangle Bounds
{
    get {
        Rectangle rect = new Rectangle(
            (int)p_position.X, (int)p_position.Y,
            p_size.Width, p_size.Height);
        return rect;
    }
}

public bool IsColliding(ref Sprite other)
{
    //test for bounding rectangle collision
    bool collision = Bounds.IntersectsWith(other.Bounds);
    return collision;
}
    }
}
```

Sprite Drawing Demo

The Sprite demo program shows how to use the new Sprite class, the improved Game class (coming up), and the new Form/Module code presented in this chapter to draw an animated sprite. The result is shown in Figure 3.5. The dragon sprite is actually comprised of animation frames that are each 128 × 128 pixels in size, but I have enlarged the sprite sheet so the dragon is twice as large as normal. This isn't a great idea for a game, because we can resize the sprite at runtime (with the Bitmap.DrawBitmap() method), but it was a simple solution to make it appear bigger for the sake of illustration.

Improving the Game Class

It is completely possible to make a game within the source code file of the Form, without any support or helper code or external libraries. But, there will come a point where the complexity of the source code (in a single file) will exceed our ability to manage it effectively, and progress on the game will grind to a halt with new and frustrating bugs cropping up every time one is apparently fixed.

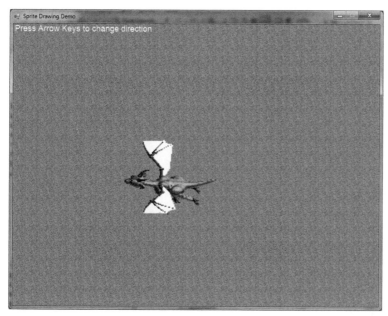

Figure 3.5
The user controls an animated dragon sprite in the Sprite demo program.

We have already seen an early first attempt at a Game class in the previous chapter. Now that we have added a new Sprite class to our toolbox, we will revise Game to give it new features too. In the next section we will build a real-time game loop with new gameplay method calls that will enable us to write code that runs extremely fast, and that is detached from the Forms architecture. The new and improved Game class still has the primary responsibility of creating the rendering device (i.e., the PictureBox/Graphics/Bitmap concoction), but added to that is support for printing text in various fonts and loading and drawing bitmaps. At one point I had considered putting the game loop in the Game class, but it proved to be too complex and we're going for simple, fast, and practical, keeping the source code flexible and easy to understand so changes can be made if needed. This is my best guess at this early stage, and I'm sure changes will be made later.

```
using System;
using System.Drawing;
using System.Diagnostics;
using System.Windows;
```

```csharp
using System.Windows.Forms;

namespace RPG
{
    public class Game
    {
        private Graphics p_device;
        private Bitmap p_surface;
        private PictureBox p_pb;
        private Form p_frm;
        private Font p_font;
        private bool p_gameOver;

        public Game(ref Form form, int width, int height)
        {
            Trace.WriteLine("Game class constructor");

            //set form properties
            p_frm = form;
            p_frm.FormBorderStyle = FormBorderStyle.FixedSingle;
            p_frm.MaximizeBox = false;
            //adjust size for window border
            p_frm.Size = new Size(width + 6, height + 28);

            //create a picturebox
            p_pb = new PictureBox();
            p_pb.Parent = p_frm;
            //p_pb.Dock = DockStyle.Fill;
            p_pb.Location = new Point(0, 0);
            p_pb.Size = new Size(width, height);
            p_pb.BackColor = Color.Black;

            //create graphics device
            p_surface = new Bitmap(p_frm.Size.Width, p_frm.Size.Height);
            p_pb.Image = p_surface;
            p_device = Graphics.FromImage(p_surface);

            //set the default font
            SetFont("Arial", 18, FontStyle.Regular);
        }
```

```
~Game()
{
    Trace.WriteLine("Game class destructor");
    p_device.Dispose();
    p_surface.Dispose();
    p_pb.Dispose();
    p_font.Dispose();
}

public Graphics Device
{
    get { return p_device; }
}

public void Update()
{
    //refresh the drawing surface
    p_pb.Image = p_surface;
}
```

We studied rudimentary text printing in the previous chapter, which showed how to use `Graphics.DrawString()` to print text using any TrueType font installed on the system. Now, it's possible to use just `Font` and `Graphics.DrawString()` for our text output needs, but I propose a simpler, more convenient approach. Instead of recreating the font object in each game, let's add some text printing code to the `Game` class. This will handle *most* text output needs, while giving us the freedom to still create a custom font in the game if we want. Below is the new printing support in the `Game` class. You can change the default font using the `SetFont()` function and then use `Print()` to print text anywhere on the screen. A word of warning, though: changing the font several times per frame will slow down a game, so if you need more than one font, I recommend creating another one in your gameplay code and leaving the built-in one at a fixed type and size.

```
/*
 * font support with several Print variations
 */
public void SetFont(string name, int size, FontStyle style)
{
```

```
        p_font = new Font(name, size, style, GraphicsUnit.Pixel);
    }

    public void Print(int x, int y, string text, Brush color)
    {
        Device.DrawString(text, p_font, color, (float)x, (float)y);
    }

    public void Print(Point pos, string text, Brush color)
    {
        Print(pos.X, pos.Y, text, color);
    }

    public void Print(int x, int y, string text)
    {
        Print(x, y, text, Brushes.White);
    }

    public void Print(Point pos, string text)
    {
        Print(pos.X, pos.Y, text);
    }
```

Next is the new Bitmap support code in our Game class. We will still need the old LoadBitmap() method, but will add several versions of the DrawBitmap() method. When a method name is repeated with different sets of parameters, we call that an *overload*—one of the fundamentals of object-oriented programming, or OOP. While still in the source code for the Game class, here is the final portion of code for the new and improved Game class:

```
    /*
     * Bitmap support functions
     */
    public Bitmap LoadBitmap(string filename)
    {
        Bitmap bmp = null;
        try
        {
            bmp = new Bitmap(filename);
        }
        catch (Exception ex) { }
```

```
            return bmp;
        }

        public void DrawBitmap(ref Bitmap bmp, float x, float y)
        {
            p_device.DrawImageUnscaled(bmp, (int)x, (int)y);
        }

        public void DrawBitmap(ref Bitmap bmp, float x, float y, int width,
            int height)
        {
            p_device.DrawImageUnscaled(bmp, (int)x, (int)y, width, height);
        }

        public void DrawBitmap(ref Bitmap bmp, Point pos)
        {
            p_device.DrawImageUnscaled(bmp, pos);
        }

        public void DrawBitmap(ref Bitmap bmp, Point pos, Size size)
        {
            p_device.DrawImageUnscaled(bmp, pos.X, pos.Y, size.Width,
                size.Height);
        }
    }
}
```

Form1 Source Code

The Form source code will be on the short side because its job is now only to pass control to the Main() method and pass along events to the gameplay methods. This code is found in the Form1.cs file in the project. Note that each event calls only one method, and we haven't seen them before. The main gameplay code will also be located in the Form1.cs file.

```
using System;
using System.Drawing;
using System.Windows.Forms;
using RPG;

namespace Sprite_Demo
```

```
{
    public partial class Form1 : Form
    {
        private bool p_gameOver = false;
        private int p_startTime = 0;
        private int p_currentTime = 0;
        public Game game;
        public Bitmap dragonImage;
        public Sprite dragonSprite;
        public Bitmap grass;
        public int frameCount = 0;
        public int frameTimer = 0;
        public float frameRate = 0;
        public PointF velocity;
        public int direction = 2;

        public Form1()
        {
            InitializeComponent();
        }

        private void Form1_Load(object sender, EventArgs e)
        {
            Main();
        }

        private void Form1_KeyDown(object sender, KeyEventArgs e)
        {
            Game_KeyPressed(e.KeyCode);
        }

        private void Form1_FormClosed(object sender, FormClosedEventArgs e)
        {
            Shutdown();
        }
```

Adding a Real-Time Game Loop

As you'll recall, in past chapters we used a Timer control to make things happen. In those cases, the Timer was sort of the *engine* for the program, causing something to happen automatically. Otherwise, the only thing we can do in our code is respond to events from the controls on a Form. The Timer control works pretty well for this, but we need to dig a bit deeper to get more performance out of our code, and to do that we have to use our own timed loop. The function below is called Main(), which makes it somewhat resemble the main() function of a C++ program, or the WinMain() function of a Windows program. Before the While loop gets started, we create the game object and call Game_Init(), which is sort of the gameplay loading function where you can load game assets before the timed loop begins. After the loop exits, then the gameplay function Game_End() is called, followed by End.

```
public void Main()
{
    Form form = (Form)this;
    game = new Game(ref form, 800, 600);

    //load and initialize game assets
    Game_Init();

    while (!p_gameOver)
    {
        //update timer
        p_currentTime = Environment.TickCount;

        //let gameplay code update
        Game_Update(p_currentTime - p_startTime);

        //refresh at 60 FPS
        if (p_currentTime > p_startTime + 16)
        {
            //update timing
            p_startTime = p_currentTime;

            //let gameplay code draw
            Game_Draw();

            //give the form some cycles
            Application.DoEvents();

            //let the game object update
            game.Update();
```

```
        }

        frameCount += 1;
        if (p_currentTime > frameTimer + 1000)
        {
            frameTimer = p_currentTime;
            frameRate = frameCount;
            frameCount = 0;
        }
    }

    //free memory and shut down
    Game_End();
    Application.Exit();
}
```

Calling the Shutdown() function from anywhere in the program causes it to end. No other code is needed besides setting p_gameOver to true, because that variable controls the real-time game loop, and when that ends, then two things will happen: 1) Game_End() is called, allowing the gameplay code to clean up; 2) Application.Exit() is called, which closes the program.

```
public void Shutdown()
{
    p_gameOver = true;
}
```

Gameplay Functions

We're continuing to work on the Form1.cs source code file, now moving into the gameplay methods. I call them by that name because the Main() method and everything else might be thought of as the game *engine* code, and now we're dealing with just gameplay code (that is, code that directly interacts with the player). While the engine code seldom changes, the gameplay code changes frequently and certainly will be different from one game to the next. There is no rule that we must use these particular method names—you are welcome to change them if you wish.

1. The first method to run is Game_Init(), and this is where you can load game assets.

2. The Game_Update() method is called repeatedly in the untimed portion of the game loop, so it will be running code as fast as the processor can handle it.

3. The Game_Draw() method is called from the *timed* portion of the game loop, running at 60 FPS.

4. The Game_End() method is called after the game loop exits, allowing for cleanup code such as removing gameplay assets from memory.

5. The Game_KeyPressed() method is called from Form1_KeyDown(), and receives the code of any key being pressed. This is a bit of a workaround, when we could have just responded to the key press directly in Form1_KeyDown(), but we want the gameplay code to be separated. Eventually we'll have mouse input as well.

```
public bool Game_Init()
{
    this.Text = "Sprite Drawing Demo";
    grass = game.LoadBitmap("grass.bmp");
    dragonImage = game.LoadBitmap("dragon.png");
    dragonSprite = new Sprite(ref game);
    dragonSprite.Image = dragonImage;
    dragonSprite.Width = 256;
    dragonSprite.Height = 256;
    dragonSprite.Columns = 8;
    dragonSprite.TotalFrames = 64;
    dragonSprite.AnimationRate = 20;
    dragonSprite.X = 250;
    dragonSprite.Y = 150;
    return true;
}

//not currently needed
public void Game_Update(int time) { }

public void Game_Draw()
{
    //draw background
    game.DrawBitmap(ref grass, 0, 0, 800, 600);
```

```
        //move the dragon sprite
        switch (direction)
        {
            case 0: velocity = new Point(0, -1); break;
            case 2: velocity = new Point(1, 0); break;
            case 4: velocity = new Point(0, 1); break;
            case 6: velocity = new Point(-1, 0); break;
        }
        dragonSprite.X += velocity.X;
        dragonSprite.Y += velocity.Y;

        //animate and draw dragon sprite
        dragonSprite.Animate(direction * 8 + 1, direction * 8 + 7);
        dragonSprite.Draw();

        game.Print(0, 0, "Press Arrow Keys to change direction");
    }

    public void Game_End()
    {
        dragonImage = null;
        dragonSprite = null;
        grass = null;
    }

    public void Game_KeyPressed(System.Windows.Forms.Keys key)
    {
        switch (key)
        {
            case Keys.Escape: Shutdown(); break;
            case Keys.Up: direction = 0; break;
            case Keys.Right: direction = 2; break;
            case Keys.Down: direction = 4; break;
            case Keys.Left: direction = 6; break;
        }
    }

    }
}
```

LEVEL UP!

The most remarkable accomplishment in this chapter is the creation of a robust Sprite class. Any time we need to give our sprites some new feature or behavior, it will be possible with this class. But no less significant is the start of a reusable game engine in C#! From the new real-time game loop to the new sprite animation code to the new gameplay functions, it's been quite a romp in just a few pages! But we've set a foundation now for the Dungeon Crawler game, and in a very short time we will begin discussing the design of the game and begin working on the editors. But first, there are a couple more essential topics that must be covered—collision detection and audio.

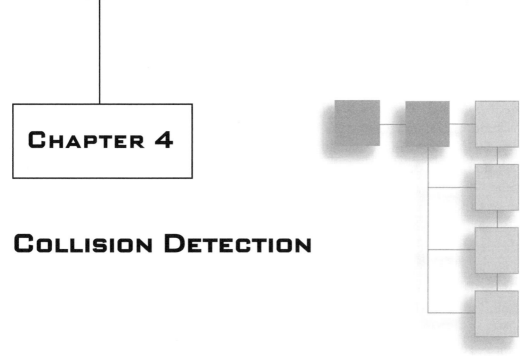

CHAPTER 4

COLLISION DETECTION

Thanks to the code developed over the last two chapters, we can draw and animate sprites on the screen. In this chapter, we will make them more lifelike by giving them the ability to bump into each other. This is done using a technique called *collision detection*. A collision occurs when two sprites touch or overlap each other. To demonstrate this new concept, we will create a simple project called Archery Game. Collision is a higher-level technique than previous topics you have learned so far, which have focused more on just getting something up on the screen. This is a very direct way to test for collisions. Another technique, which is ultimately used in Dungeon Crawler, is to calculate the distance between two sprites. Let's start with the simpler of the two in this chapter, and the distance approach down the road in the gameplay chapters.

Here's what we'll cover in this chapter:

- Reacting to solid objects
- Rectangle intersection
- Collision test
- Archery Game (Collision demo)

REACTING TO SOLID OBJECTS

Collision detection is an important technique that you should learn. It is a requirement for every game ever made. I can't think of any game that does not need collision detection, because it is such an essential aspect of gameplay. Without collisions, there is no action, goal, or purpose in a game. There is no way to interact with the game without collisions taking place. In other words, collision detection makes the sprites in a game come to life and makes the game believable. Not every situation in which collision detection occurs necessarily means that something is hit or destroyed. We can also use collision testing to prevent the player from going into certain areas (such as a lake or mountain area that is impassible).

Rectangle Intersection

Collision detection is pretty easy to do using the System.Drawing.Rectangle class. First, you will create a rectangle based on the position and size of one object, such as a sprite. Then you will need to create a similar rectangle for a second object. Once you have two rectangles, which represent the position and size of two objects, then you can test to see whether the rectangles are intersecting. We can do this with a function in the Rectangle class called IntersectsWith(). Figure 4.1 is an illustration showing the bounding rectangles

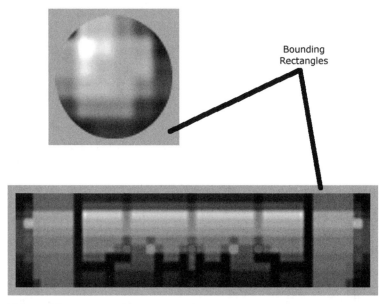

Figure 4.1
The dimensions of a sprite define its bounding rectangle.

of two sprites from the example program. In most cases, the image itself is used as the bounding rectangle, which includes the transparent pixels that usually surround an image.

Collision Test

In the previous chapter, where we learned about sprite programming with the Sprite class, we added a method called IsColliding—but didn't use it right away, as it was created in advance for our needs in *this* chapter! Here is the IsColliding() function:

```
public bool IsColliding(ref Sprite other)
{
    //test for bounding rectangle collision
    bool collision = Bounds.IntersectsWith(other.Bounds);
    return collision;
}
```

Hint

You will get better results in your game if you make sure there is very little empty space around the edges of your sprite images, since the image is used as the bounding rectangle!

Let's dissect this method to determine what it does. First, notice that IsColliding returns a bool value (true or false). Notice also that there's only one Sprite passed by reference (ref). Thus, the entire sprite object in memory (with all of its properties and methods) is not copied as a parameter, only a reference to the sprite is passed. This method is small thanks in part to the Sprite.Bounds property, which returns a Rectangle representing a sprite's position and size as it appears on the screen. Thus, two rectangles are essentially created based on the position and size of each sprite, and then IntersectsWith() is used to see whether they are overlapping each other. Figure 4.2 shows an illustration of a collision taking place between two sprites.

Definition

"Collision" is a misnomer since nothing actually collides in a game unless we write code to make it happen. Sprites do not automatically bump into each other. That's yet another thing we have to deal with as game programmers!

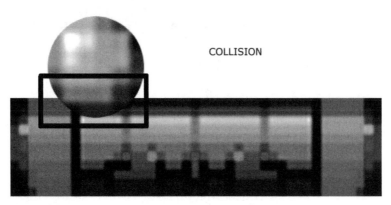

Figure 4.2
The two bounding rectangles have intersected.

Often, the code to perform a collision test is trivial compared to the code we need to write to *respond* to the collision event!

Archery Game (Collision Demo)

To demonstrate sprite collision testing with our new code, I've put together a quick demo based on the overall theme of the book, shown in Figure 4.3. Let me show you how to create this project. We'll reuse classes written previously to simplify the game and cut down on the amount of code that would otherwise be required. This new game is done entirely in graphics mode with real collision detection.

Sprite Class

Copy the Sprite.cs file from the Sprite demo project in the previous chapter over to the new one so we don't have to re-list the source code over again in this chapter! No changes have been made to the Sprite class since the previous chapter.

Game Class

We don't need to list the source code for Game.cs here again because it hasn't changed since the previous chapter either—just copy the file from your last project into the new one for this chapter.

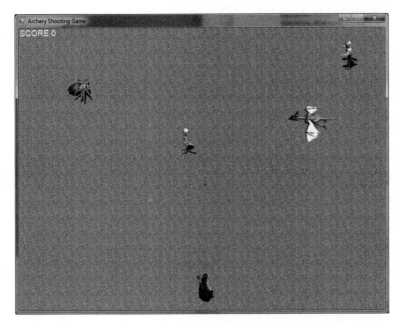

Figure 4.3
The Collision demo program demonstrates bounding rectangle collision testing.

Form1 Class

Both the game loop and gameplay code are found in the Form source code file
Form1.cs. When you create the new project, Form1 will be added automatically,
so you can open the source code for it and enter this code. Add Game.cs and
Sprite.cs to the project, grab the bitmap files, and watch it run. The collision-
specific code is highlighted in bold.

```
using System;
using System.Drawing;
using System.Windows.Forms;
using RPG;

namespace Collision_Demo
{
    public partial class Form1 : Form
    {
        Game game;
        bool p_gameOver = false;
        int p_startTime = 0;
```

```csharp
int p_currentTime = 0;
int frameCount = 0;
int frameTimer = 0;
float frameRate = 0;
int score = 0;
Sprite dragon;
Sprite zombie;
Sprite spider;
Sprite skeleton;
Bitmap grass;
Sprite archer;
Sprite arrow;

public Form1()
{
    InitializeComponent();
}

private void Form1_Load(object sender, EventArgs e)
{
    Main();
}

private void Form1_KeyDown(object sender, KeyEventArgs e)
{
    Game_KeyPressed(e.KeyCode);
}

private void Form1_FormClosed(object sender, FormClosedEventArgs e)
{
    Shutdown();
}

public bool Game_Init()
{
    this.Text = "Archery Shooting Game";

    //load the grassy background
    grass = game.LoadBitmap("grass.bmp");
```

```
//load the archer
archer = new Sprite(ref game);
archer.Image = game.LoadBitmap("archer_attack.png");
archer.Size = new Size(96, 96);
archer.Columns = 10;
archer.TotalFrames = 80;
archer.AnimationRate = 20;
archer.Position = new PointF(360, 500);
archer.AnimateDirection = Sprite.AnimateDir.NONE;

//load the arrow
arrow = new Sprite(ref game);
arrow.Image = game.LoadBitmap("arrow.png");
arrow.Size = new Size(32, 32);
arrow.TotalFrames = 1;
arrow.Velocity = new PointF(0, -12.0f);
arrow.Alive = false;

//load the zombie
zombie = new Sprite(ref game);
zombie.Image = game.LoadBitmap("zombie walk.png");
zombie.Size = new Size(96, 96);
zombie.Columns = 8;
zombie.TotalFrames = 64;
zombie.Position = new PointF(100, 10);
zombie.Velocity = new PointF(-2.0f, 0);
zombie.AnimationRate = 10;

//load the spider
spider = new Sprite(ref game);
spider.Image = game.LoadBitmap("redspiderwalking.png");
spider.Size = new Size(96, 96);
spider.Columns = 8;
spider.TotalFrames = 64;
spider.Position = new PointF(500, 80);
spider.Velocity = new PointF(3.0f, 0);
spider.AnimationRate = 20;

//load the dragon
dragon = new Sprite(ref game);
```

```
dragon.Image = game.LoadBitmap("dragonflying.png");
dragon.Size = new Size(128, 128);
dragon.Columns = 8;
dragon.TotalFrames = 64;
dragon.AnimationRate = 20;
dragon.Position = new PointF(300, 130);
dragon.Velocity = new PointF(-4.0f, 0);

//load the skeleton
skeleton = new Sprite(ref game);
skeleton.Image = game.LoadBitmap("skeleton_walk.png");
skeleton.Size = new Size(96, 96);
skeleton.Columns = 9;
skeleton.TotalFrames = 72;
skeleton.Position = new PointF(400, 190);
skeleton.Velocity = new PointF(5.0f, 0);
skeleton.AnimationRate = 30;

    return true;
}

public void Game_Update(int time)
{
    if (arrow.Alive)
    {
        //see if arrow hit spider
        if (arrow.IsColliding(ref spider))
        {
            arrow.Alive = false;
            score++;
            spider.X = 800;
        }

        //see if arrow hit dragon
        if (arrow.IsColliding(ref dragon))
        {
            arrow.Alive = false;
            score++;
            dragon.X = 800;
        }
```

```
        //see if arrow hit zombie
        if (arrow.IsColliding(ref zombie))
        {
            arrow.Alive = false;
            score++;
            zombie.X = 800;
        }

        //see if arrow hit skeleton
        if (arrow.IsColliding(ref skeleton))
        {
            arrow.Alive = false;
            score++;
            skeleton.X = 800;
        }
    }
}

public void Game_Draw()
{
    int row = 0;

    //draw background
    game.DrawBitmap(ref grass, 0, 0, 800, 600);

    //draw the arrow
    if (arrow.Alive)
    {
        arrow.Y += arrow.Velocity.Y;
        if (arrow.Y < -32)
            arrow.Alive = false;
        arrow.Draw();
    }

    //draw the archer
    archer.Animate(10, 19);
    if (archer.CurrentFrame == 19)
    {
        archer.AnimateDirection = Sprite.AnimateDir.NONE;
```

```
            archer.CurrentFrame = 10;
            arrow.Alive = true;
            arrow.Position = new PointF(
                archer.X + 32, archer.Y);
        }
        archer.Draw();

        //draw the zombie
        zombie.X += zombie.Velocity.X;
        if (zombie.X < -96) zombie.X = 800;
        row = 6;
        zombie.Animate(row * 8 + 1, row * 8 + 7);
        zombie.Draw();

        //draw the spider
        spider.X += spider.Velocity.X;
        if (spider.X > 800) spider.X = -96;
        row = 2;
        spider.Animate(row * 8 + 1, row * 8 + 7);
        spider.Draw();

        //draw the skeleton
        skeleton.X += skeleton.Velocity.X;
        if (skeleton.X > 800) skeleton.X = -96;
        row = 2;
        skeleton.Animate(row * 9 + 1, row * 9 + 8);
        skeleton.Draw();

        //draw the dragon
        dragon.X += dragon.Velocity.X;
        if (dragon.X < -128) dragon.X = 800;
        row = 6;
        dragon.Animate(row * 8 + 1, row * 8 + 7);
        dragon.Draw();

        game.Print(0, 0, "SCORE " + score.ToString());
    }

    public void Game_End()
    {
```

```
        dragon.Image.Dispose();
        dragon = null;
        archer.Image.Dispose();
        archer = null;
        spider.Image.Dispose();
        spider = null;
        zombie.Image.Dispose();
        zombie = null;
        grass = null;
    }

    public void Game_KeyPressed(System.Windows.Forms.Keys key)
    {
        switch (key)
        {
            case Keys.Escape: Shutdown(); break;
            case Keys.Space:
                if (!arrow.Alive)
                {
                    archer.AnimateDirection = Sprite.AnimateDir.FORWARD;
                    archer.CurrentFrame = 10;
                }
                break;
            case Keys.Right: break;
            case Keys.Down:  break;
            case Keys.Left:  break;
        }
    }

    public void Shutdown()
    {
        p_gameOver = true;
    }

    /*
     * real time game loop
     */
    public void Main()
    {
        Form form = (Form)this;
```

```
            game = new Game(ref form, 800, 600);
            Game_Init();
            while (!p_gameOver)
            {
                p_currentTime = Environment.TickCount;
                Game_Update(p_currentTime - p_startTime);
                if (p_currentTime > p_startTime + 16)
                {
                    p_startTime = p_currentTime;
                    Game_Draw();
                    Application.DoEvents();
                    game.Update();
                }
                frameCount += 1;
                if (p_currentTime > frameTimer + 1000)
                {
                    frameTimer = p_currentTime;
                    frameRate = frameCount;
                    frameCount = 0;
                }
            }
            //free memory and shut down
            Game_End();
            Application.Exit();
        }
    }
}
```

LEVEL UP!

That's about all there is to sprite collision detection at this point. You learned about the basic collision between two sprites—or more accurately, between two rectangles—using the `Rectangle.IntersectsWith()` method, encapsulated in the `Sprite` class within the method called `IsColliding()`, which simplifies the collision code that you would otherwise have to write yourself. We will be using another form of collision detection later on when we are working with the dungeon levels, made up of a tile map, in which certain areas in the world will be impassible based on the tile values.

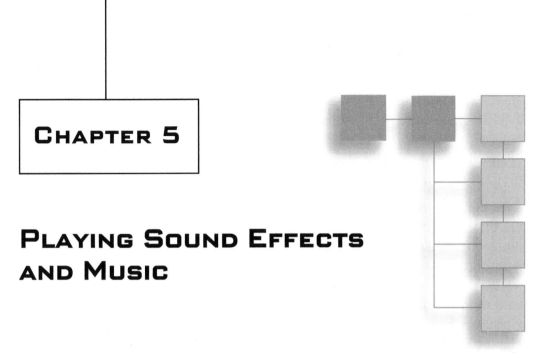

CHAPTER 5

PLAYING SOUND EFFECTS AND MUSIC

In years past, programming sound and music for games was an enormous task. Custom sound code was usually too difficult to write due to the conflicting standards among the various sound cards in the industry. Today, that is no longer a problem. Now a single, dominant hardware maker sets the PC audio standard and a single, dominant sound library sets the software standard. While some may argue the point, I believe that Creative Labs had the sound card market wrapped up with their Sound Blaster line of products, but today most motherboards include very capable audio hardware. This chapter is a quick jaunt through the basic audio features of Visual C#, with an example program to show how to play sound effects and music files in Visual C#, including the versatile MP3 format.

Here's what we'll cover in this chapter:

- Playing wave files
- Playing wave resources
- Referencing the Media Player
- Playing MP3 and MIDI files

PROGRAMMING AUDIO

Audio is always a fun subject to explore because sound effects and music can influence our emotions so dramatically. Could you imagine playing a game like

Halo: Reach without audio? It would be a different experience entirely! What is a game without sound? Little more than a graphics demo, all but unplayable in my opinion (unless you're playing late at night and don't want anyone to know!). Sound is absolutely essential for the success of any game, in both the professional and indie market.

Even the simplest game needs some form of background music, or it is difficult for the player to remain interested. Remember this important rule of game development: Any game without sound and music is just a technology demo. It is absolutely essential that you spend some of your development time on a game working on the music and sound effects. In fact, it is probably a good idea to do so during development. As the game takes shape, so should the sounds and music. Background music should reflect what is going on in the game and can even be used to invoke the emotions of the player. Consider a scene in which a beloved game character dies. Upbeat music would spoil the mood, whereas dark and menacing background music would engender feelings of remorse and sorrow (and perhaps even anger).

Keep this in mind when working on sections of a game and try to have a different background sequence for different circumstances. Victory should be rewarded with upbeat music, while menacing or dangerous situations should be accompanied by low-beat, low-tempo songs that reinforce the natural emotions that arise in such a circumstance. Later in this chapter, under the heading, "Using Windows Media Player," I'll show you how to use Windows Media Player to play an MP3 file in your game projects.

Ambient sound is a term that I borrowed from *ambient light*, which you might already understand. Just look at a light bulb in a light fixture on the ceiling. The light emitted by the bulb pretty much fills the room (unless you are in a very large room). When light permeates a room, it is said to be *ambient*; that is, the light does not seem to have a source. Contrast this idea with directional light and you get the idea behind ambient sound. *Ambient sound* refers to sound that appears to have no direction or source. Ambient sound is emitted by speakers uniformly, without any positional effects. This is the most common type of sound generated by most games (at least most older games—the tendency with modern games is to use positional sound).

Loading and Playing Audio Files

We can load and play a wave file using the class called `System.Media.SoundPlayer`. This class has limited features but gets the job done for simple sound effects needs. First, we create an object:

```
System.Media.SoundPlayer audio;
```

By adding `System.Media` to the `using` list, we can refer to just `SoundPlayer`:

```
audio = new SoundPlayer();
```

There are two overloads of the `SoundPlayer()` constructor, one to specify the audio file and another to specify a `System.IO.Stream` for loading the file. So, one way to load an audio clip is to pass the filename to the constructor:

```
audio = new SoundPlayer("sound.wav");
```

An option is to just use the default constructor and instead load the audio file manually. The `SoundPlayer.SoundLocation` property is used to specify the filename. Once set, we can use `SoundPlayer.Load()` to load the file.

```
audio.SoundLocation = "sound.wav";
audio.Load();
```

In either case, trapping errors is a good idea since a bad filename will generate an exception. We can write a `LoadSoundFile()` function to trap errors and return a `SoundPlayer` object if loading succeeds.

Hint

If you have a very large wave file that may take a few seconds to load, use the `SoundPlayer.LoadAsync()` and `SoundPlayer.IsLoadCompleted()` methods to find out when loading has finished.

```
public SoundPlayer LoadSoundFile(string filename)
{
    SoundPlayer sound = null;
    try
    {
        sound = new SoundPlayer();
        sound.SoundLocation = filename;
        sound.Load();
    }
    catch (Exception ex)
```

```
{
    MessageBox.Show(ex.Message, "Error loading sound");
}
return sound;
}
```

Using Audio Resources

We can play an audio file that has been added to the project as a resource by using `Properties.Resources` to get the audio file resource as a `SoundPlayer` object. We can use `SoundPlayer` to play waves loaded from a file or a resource, so there's some flexibility there. One great advantage to using a resource file is that your game's asset files are compiled into the executable and are no longer exposed so that the user can access them. Let me show you how to add a resource file to the project.

First, open the Project menu and choose Add New Item. Choose the list of General items, and then Resources File, as shown in Figure 5.1.

Next, double-click the `Resource1.resx` file to open the project's resources. Open the drop-down list of resource types and choose Audio, as shown in Figure 5.2.

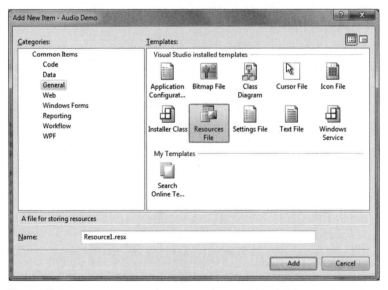

Figure 5.1
Adding a resource file to the project.

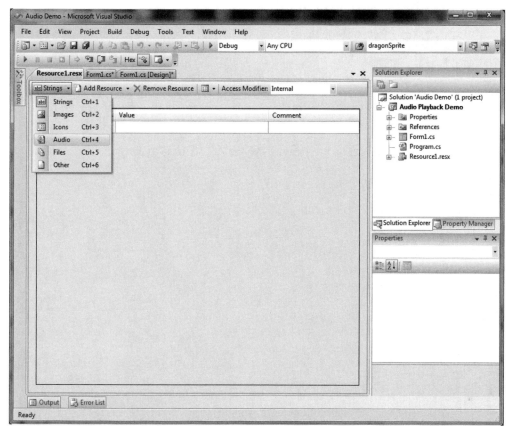

Figure 5.2
Selecting the Audio resources list.

Next, you can use the Add Resource drop-down list and choose a wave file to load, or you can just drag a wave file from Windows Explorer into the resource file asset pane, as shown in Figure 5.3.

To play an audio file from a resource, we can use `Properties.Resources` to access the resource object directly in our code.

```
SoundPlayer audio = new SoundPlayer();
audio.Stream = Properties.Resources.foom;
```

Tip

If you are using Visual C# 2010, you will not be able to load an audio clip as a resource like this section suggested. Instead, just use the default resource or load an audio clip from a file instead.

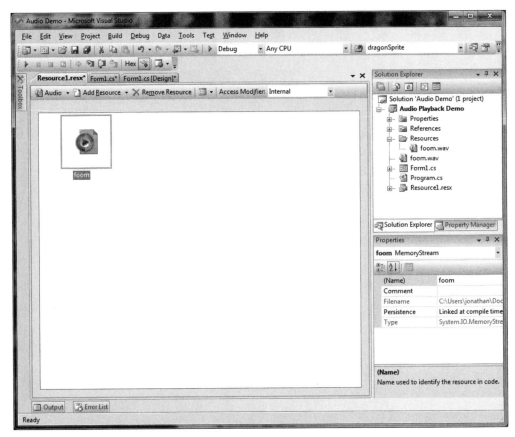

Figure 5.3
The foom.wav file has been added to the project as a resource.

Built-In System Sounds

The System.Media namespace contains a class called SystemSounds. By using this class, we gain access to the built-in system sounds that can be played directly without any preparation. Here is a list of the system sounds available:

- SystemSounds.Asterisk
- SystemSounds.Beep
- SystemSounds.Exclamation
- SystemSounds.Hand
- SystemSounds.Question

These system sound objects can be played directly in code using the `Play()` method with no other loading or preparation needed.

The Audio Playback Demo Program

The Audio Playback demo program demonstrates how to load audio files into memory and play them using `System.Media.SoundPlayer`, as well as how to play the built-in system sounds. To demonstrate how sounds are automatically mixed, the program actually loads up another sound file as well. There are several buttons on the form; each plays one of the sound clips. There is not much to this program other than the simple form. There are ten buttons to the form, simply called `button1`, `button2`, etc., as shown in Figure 5.4.

```
using System;
using System.Media;
using System.Reflection;
using System.IO;
using System.Windows.Forms;

namespace Audio_Playback_Demo
{
    public partial class Form1 : Form
    {
        System.Media.SoundPlayer[] audio;

        public SoundPlayer LoadSoundFile(string filename)
        {
```

Figure 5.4
The Audio demo program demonstrates how to play audio files.

```
        SoundPlayer sound = null;
        try
        {
            sound = new SoundPlayer();
            sound.SoundLocation = filename;
            sound.Load();
        }
        catch (Exception ex)
        {
            MessageBox.Show(ex.Message, "Error loading sound");
        }
        return sound;
    }

    public Form1()
    {
        InitializeComponent();
    }

    private void Form1_Load(object sender, EventArgs e)
    {
        audio = new SoundPlayer[5];

        //load audio using constructor
        audio[0] = new SoundPlayer("launch1.wav");

        //load audio using Load method
        audio[1] = new SoundPlayer();
        audio[1].SoundLocation = "launch2.wav";
        audio[1].Load();

        //load audio from wave file
        audio[2] = LoadSoundFile("missed1.wav");
        audio[3] = LoadSoundFile("laser.wav");

        //load audio from resource
        audio[4] = new SoundPlayer();
        audio[4].Stream = Properties.Resources.foom;
    }
```

```
private void button_Click(object sender, EventArgs e)
{
    Button button = (Button)sender;
    if (button.Text == "Asterisk")
    {
        SystemSounds.Asterisk.Play();
    }
    else if (button.Text == "Beep")
    {
        SystemSounds.Beep.Play();
    }
    else if (button.Text == "Exclamation")
    {
        SystemSounds.Exclamation.Play();
    }
    else if (button.Text == "Hand")
    {
        SystemSounds.Hand.Play();
    }
    else if (button.Text == "Question")
    {
        SystemSounds.Question.Play();
    }
    else if (button.Text == "Launch1")
    {
        audio[0].Play();
    }
    else if (button.Text == "Launch2")
    {
        audio[1].Play();
    }
    else if (button.Text == "Missed1")
    {
        audio[2].Play();
    }
    else if (button.Text == "Laser")
    {
        audio[3].Play();
    }
```

```
            else if (button.Text == "Foom")
            {
                audio[4].Play();
            }
        }
    }
}
```

USING WINDOWS MEDIA PLAYER

What if you want to use a more advanced audio file, such as an MP3, for your game's music? Although we don't have a library available for this, there is an alternative that works quite well that I'll introduce to you: the Windows Media Player control. You may be wondering: why would I want to use a Media Player control when we can already play audio files? Here's the reason: for simple music playback, System.Media.SoundPlayer is preferred. But there is a draw-back—limited options. Sure, you can play back an audio file, but that's about all you can do. Beyond that, the features are pretty slim. The Media Player control, on the other hand, is full of features, as the Music Playback demo program demonstrates.

So how does this work? Visual C# has the ability to embed an object on a form, and this capability is called OLE (*Object Linking and Embedding*). You can, for instance, embed an Excel spreadsheet on a form, and it will be fully functional! There are some obvious licensing issues when you embed a whole application onto a form, and usually applications that do this sort of thing just assume that the software (such as Excel) has already been preinstalled on the end user's PC. (The Excel control simply won't work unless Excel is already installed.) But there are some Windows applications that are so common that we can pretty much count on them being available. One example is Windows Media Player, which is automatically installed on Windows systems today. Even if someone is still using an older version of Windows, odds are they have Windows Media Player installed because it is free.

Referencing the Media Player

I've included a project with this chapter called Music Playback demo, which shows how to use WMPLib and a class called WindowsMediaPlayerClass. This is not a normal .NET component, and not part of the .NET Framework, so we have to

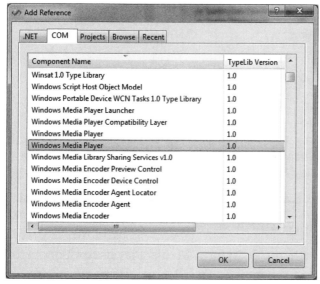

Figure 5.5
Adding a reference to the Windows Media Player control.

add it from the list of COM/ActiveX components (see the COM tab in the Add Reference dialog box). We need to add a reference to a COM component in order to use the Windows Media Player component. See Figure 5.5.

Definition

COM stands for Component Object Model, a technology created by Microsoft to make it easier to share useful software libraries.

Tip

If you see two items called "Windows Media Player" as shown in Figure 5.5, choose the one associated with wmp.dll (not msdxm.tlb).

When the Windows Media Player component is visible to the project, then an object can be created at runtime and used to play music. The COM library component is called WMPLib and can be added to the project with a using statement:

```
using WMPLib;
```

A media player object can then be created with the `WindowsMediaPlayerClass` class:

```
WindowsMediaPlayerClass player =
    new WindowsMediaPlayerClass();
```

Tip

Visual C# 2010 users will need to note another change to the architecture here. After adding WMPLib to the project (via wmp.dll), you *must* change the object's "Embed Interop Type" property to *False*. It defaults to *True*, but that causes a compile error. Thanks to Joshua Smith for solving this extremely difficult problem!

Playing MP3 and MIDI Files

You can play any media file with the Windows Media Player component by setting its URL property equal to a filename (or a URL to a file on a website, for instance). This is deceptively simple, because there is really no "play" function at all. Once you set the URL property to a filename, playback will automatically start. Likewise, if you want to stop playback, set the URL to an empty string (""). The control can support the same media file formats supported by the full-blown media player application, including MP3! Interestingly enough, you can specify a URL to an audio file on a remote website:

```
player.URL = "song.mp3";
```

To stop playback, just set the URL to an empty string:

```
player.URL = "";
```

I have included a generic MIDI file with the example but you may replace it with any MP3 file from your music collection!

Level Up!

This chapter was a quick overview of Visual C# audio support, giving you just enough information to add sound effects and music to your own games. By loading multiple sound files into memory and playing them at certain points in your game, you greatly enhance the gameplay experience. In a sense, you are the conductor of this orchestra by directing what happens in the source code. You also learned how to use the Windows Media Player component for advanced audio file support to make it possible to add music to a game. Just keep in mind that you cannot distribute copyrighted music.

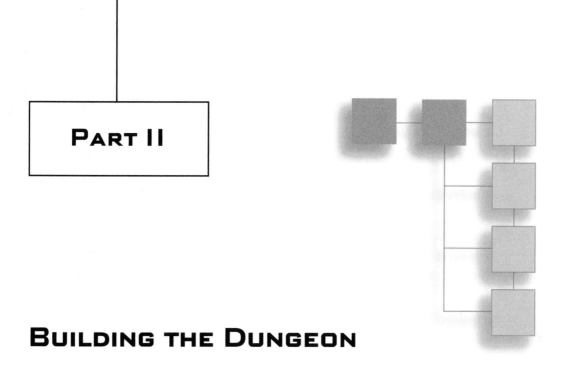

PART II

BUILDING THE DUNGEON

Welcome to the second part of the book, which focuses on designing and building a dungeon for the player to explore. Now that we have a good foundation laid in the previous five chapters of Part I, we can spend time on somewhat higher-level code involving larger subjects than just bitmaps, sprites, and sound files. Moving into the design and development stage of the Dungeon Crawler game will be much more engaging as we begin to see the game take shape!

- Chapter 6: Creating the Dungeon Editor
- Chapter 7: Rendering a Dungeon Level
- Chapter 8: Adding Objects to the Dungeon
- Chapter 9: Going Deeper into the Dungeon with Portals

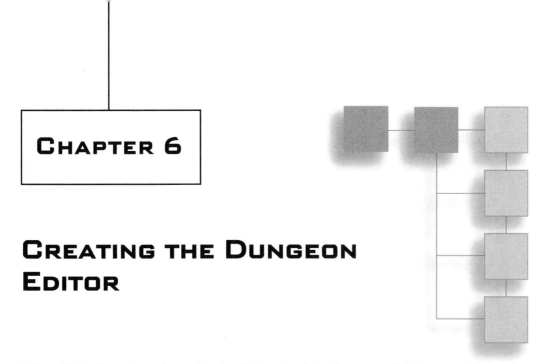

CHAPTER 6

CREATING THE DUNGEON EDITOR

We will be learning about level editing in this chapter, which is a subset of a larger field called tools programming. A simple review of the employment statistics reveals this truth: tools programmers are among the highest paid people in the game industry, commanding salaries far greater than that of game designers, gameplay programmers, and even engine programmers. So, what does a tools programmer do? This is a high-demand skill set simply because it is not taught in schools, and few programmers have found a need to develop this particular type of skill in their daily activities. A "tool" in this context is any program or script that is needed during the game development process. Examples include Max and Maya scripts, file format converters, workflow pipeline programs, automated build scripts, and yes, even level editors.

We are going to focus on the level editing aspect of tools programming in this chapter. You will learn how to build a simple tilemap level editor. The level or "game world" defines the rules of the game and presents the player with all of the obstacles that must be overcome to complete the game. Although the world is the most important aspect of a game, it is not always given the proper attention when a game is being designed. This chapter provides an introduction to world building, or more specifically, map editing. You learn to create the game world for Dungeon Crawler, as well as levels for your own games, using a custom level editor. We will explore the features of this level editor to gain some insights and inspiration for creating our game levels.

Here's what we'll cover in this chapter:

- Designing our own level editor
- Building the editor
- Creating a new tilemap level
- Loading and saving level files

LEVEL EDITOR DESIGN

A tilemap is a two-dimensional array of tiles with a set width and height that resembles a tiled floor. Perhaps you have a tiled floor or know someone who has a house with tile? The concept behind a tiled floor is similar to a tilemap used for a video game. But, unlike a real tiled floor, in a video game we use many different tiles to make up the "ground" for a game. To create a tilemap for a game, you need a map editor, which is the purpose of this chapter.

We're going to build a custom level editor for the Dungeon Crawler game so that we have full control over the tile format. One of the most popular tilemap editors used by professionals and hobbyists alike over the years has been an editor called Mappy (http://www.tilemap.co.uk). Mappy works well, especially for handheld game systems like Nintendo GBA and DS—see Figure 6.1. But, despite the usefulness of Mappy, it will never meet the needs of a custom game project quite like a custom editor. We need a level editor to save tilemap data in such a way that it can be loaded into the game without too much effort. Mappy supports several of its own file formats that we *could* load into our game, but a custom level editor also sets boundaries for a game level that cannot be done with Mappy (such as the maximum size of the level).

So, let me explain the editor a bit. This is a new editor, created just for this game, not some recycled level editor from another project. (Similar gameplay is found in the sister book covering Visual Basic.) Since we're building the editor from scratch in Visual C#, we also have the ability to make changes to the editor over time to meet future needs—another thing that cannot be said of Mappy. Nothing in this creative industry is ever finished, but we can make a solid effort to make the editor as useful as possible with the understanding that it can be modified if new features are needed. It is shown in Figure 6.2.

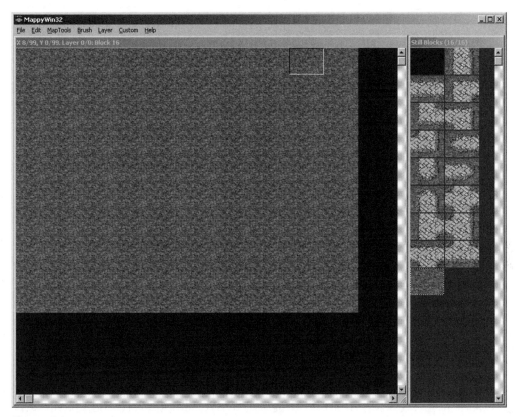

Figure 6.1
Mappy is a "proven" tilemap editor used over the years on many commercial games.

Tile Properties

The key to a level editor is making it possible to *edit* the tiles that make up a game level. The tiles themselves are represented by a single field—the tile identifier or tile ID. When you "draw" tiles onto the tilemap with the mouse, what you're doing is setting the tile ID value to the number of the tile that has been selected in the *tile palette*. Referring back to Figure 6.2 again, note that the tile palette is on the left side in a scrolling area. That is just the beginning! After that, we can add as many additional fields to the editor as we want, it's just a matter of designing the graphical user interface (GUI) to support the tile data. In the level editor, I've used the lower-left corner of the GUI for tile data, as you can see in Figure 6.2. The level editor uses XML—Extensible Markup Language—to store tilemap levels. So, our game will also need to be able to

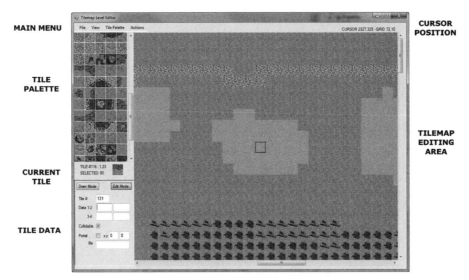

Figure 6.2
The level editor is a game development tool custom made for this game.

read the .xml files. To make the editor seem a little more, well, *professional*, the tilemap files have an extension of .level—but they just contain XML data.

So, how does the editor store data for each tile? We could use the Mappy approach by giving each tile several generic data fields that can be used in any game. An editor with just two or three fields per tile would be sufficient to make almost any kind of game. But why limit ourselves? We want to make some tiles solid so the player can't walk through them, so we need a Collision field. We will want to allow the player to teleport to new areas of the map or to completely different levels so we also need a Portal field. These can be defined in the editor directly without the need to convert generic fields into our desired tile properties.

For things such as item drops—where we want to assign a sprite to show up in the game world at a certain location automatically by the game engine—we can use one of the four Data fields. The .xml file format can handle as many fields as we want to use, so there's no need to limit the design of the level editor due to file concerns. Even 100 properties for each tile would not cause the game to slow down any. But, the fact is, we don't need that many fields. The four generic data fields store strings so you can put any data you want there—whole numbers, decimal numbers, text descriptions, etc. You could use one as a searchable item name field and then add an item to the game world at that tile location, or even something as exotic as a script function name. Here are the data fields for each tile:

- Tile palette number
- Collidable (flag)
- Data 1
- Data 2
- Data 3
- Data 4
- Portal (flag)
- Portal X
- Portal Y
- Portal file

This may not seem like very many tile properties to be used for a large and complex RPG, but believe it or not, this is more than enough! In fact, we could get by with just the four data fields alone but the others make editing and programming more convenient.

Using the Level Editor

Before getting into the development of the editor, we'll first learn how to *use it*. The following will explain the GUI and menus of the level editor with included figures for reference.

Creating a New Tilemap Level

One of the most obvious requirements of any editor is the ability to start over with a fresh, new canvas (or file). Within the File menu, shown in Figure 6.3, is the option New Tilemap. When you select this, the tilemap and all data will be wiped clean from the editor so that you can start working on a new tilemap from scratch.

Loading and Saving

Under the File menu (shown in Figure 6.3) is the Load Tilemap menu item, used to load an existing tilemap editor file. The Save Tilemap item will save any

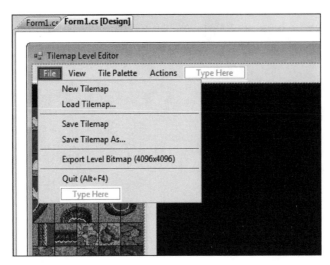

Figure 6.3
The File menu.

current tilemap file being edited (without user prompt). The Save Tilemap As option will prompt for a filename, and is especially useful if you want to make a quick backup of a level before making changes to the main level file you are working on. Designing a very large level can take many *hours*, so it would be tragic to lose all of that hard work—save often!

The tilemap level files are saved in .xml format. XML is similar to HTML (the language used for websites), in that it is a text format that you can open and read with a simple text editor. The following listing shows the first and last tiles in the tilemap.xml file saved by the level editor. Every tile is contained in a tag called "tiles," with an opening tag, <tiles>, and closing tag, </tiles>.

```
<?xml version="1.0" standalone="yes"?>
<DocumentElement>
  <tiles>
    <tile>0</tile>
    <value>145</value>
    <data1 />
    <data2 />
    <data3 />
    <data4 />
    <collidable>true</collidable>
    <portal>false</portal>
```

```
        <portalx>0</portalx>
        <portaly>0</portaly>
        <portalfile />
    </tiles>
    .
    .
    .

    <tiles>
        <tile>16383</tile>
        <value>158</value>
        <data1 />
        <data2 />
        <data3 />
        <data4 />
        <collidable>false</collidable>
        <portal>false</portal>
        <portalx>0</portalx>
        <portaly>0</portaly>
        <portalfile />
    </tiles>
</DocumentElement>
```

Exporting the Level as a Bitmap

Also under the File menu is an option called Export Level Bitmap. This menu item will cause the entire tilemap to be saved as a single huge bitmap! This is a pretty interesting option that lets you see the whole game level as one huge image—suitable for framing, perhaps? I'm not sure if it's very useful in a game since it's so large, but there are some interesting uses for it (such as being used in a game manual or tutorial). The dimensions of the complete tilemap are 4096x4096 pixels, which is 65 MB of memory in an uncompressed bitmap! See Figure 6.4.

Tile Property Viewing Options

The View menu, shown in Figure 6.5, can be used to toggle several options that affect what is shown in the editor window.

Figure 6.6 shows the default display in the editor window, in which both the Collidable and Data1 field values are shown directly in the editor window. This is purely for the sake of convenience, and you may even want to modify the

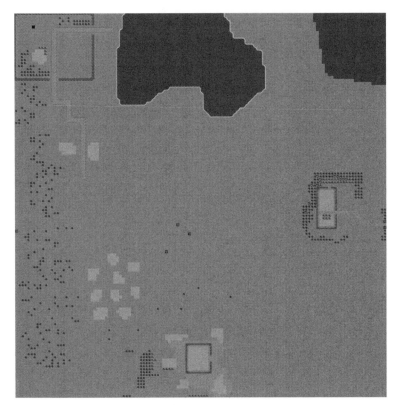

Figure 6.4
The complete tilemap is exported to a bitmap file.

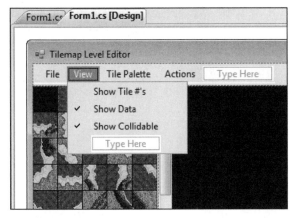

Figure 6.5
The View menu.

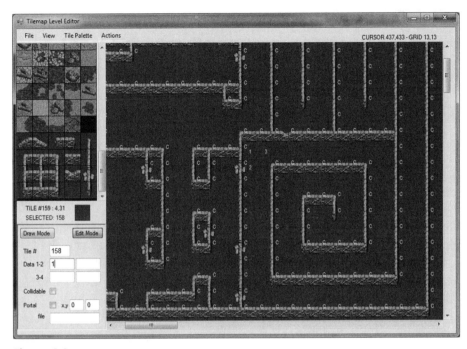

Figure 6.6
Some key tile properties are shown in the editor window by default.

editor to show *more* fields than this. Just remember that the data fields can contain text of any length so that could potentially mess up the editor display. In the example shown in Figure 6.6, I have just entered a value of "1" into the Data1 field. Note that the wall tiles all have their Collidable property set, evidenced by the "C" displayed in the editor window—perhaps the most important data to show for each tile, as far as gameplay is concerned.

Turning on the Show Tile #'s option has the effect of displaying the tile ID over every tile in the editor window—see Figure 6.7. This option is disabled by default because it makes for a messy display and it slows down the editor quite a bit. The option is there if you need it—sometimes seeing the tile numbers is helpful when editing a large and complex tilemap.

Saving the Editor Palette

The Tile Palette menu is shown in Figure 6.8. The first option in this menu, Export Palette Texture, will save the tile palette as a 512x512 bitmap file, suitable for use in a game engine that requires texture files of a uniform size. There is no

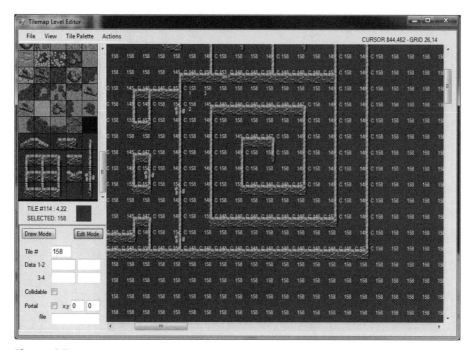

Figure 6.7
Enabling the Show Tile #'s toggle causes the tile ID to be shown over every tile.

filename prompt; it just saves the palette to the file `tilemap.bmp`, which is shown in Figure 6.9. This is usually the type of bitmap you would want to use in a game, where the tiles are arranged in the same order that they appear in the editor but with dimensions that are more friendly to game engines and graphics SDKs (some of which, like Direct3D, have a hard time using odd-shaped bitmaps, depending on the video card installed in the PC).

The second option, Export Palette Bitmap, performs a similar service to the first option, but is used more for customizing the level editor than for exporting the palette for use in a game. The result is an image that looks exactly like the palette in the editor, which is what you see in the scrolling panel. If you want to add or change the tiles used in the editor, then you can modify this bitmap and import it back into the `PictureBox` control used by the editor for the palette (its name is `picPalette`). To replace the image, open the Properties window for the `picPalette` control and select a new image using the `Image` property, as shown in Figure 6.11.

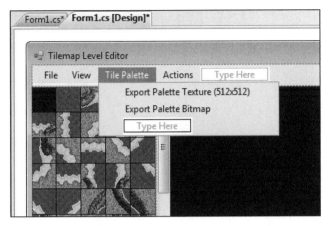

Figure 6.8
The Tile Palette menu.

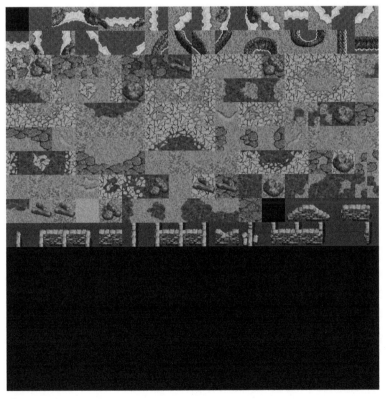

Figure 6.9
The tile palette is saved as a 512×512 texture.

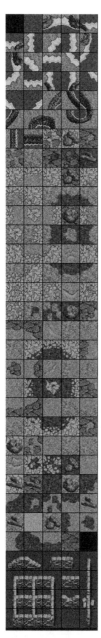

Figure 6.10
The tile palette is saved in the format used by the editor.

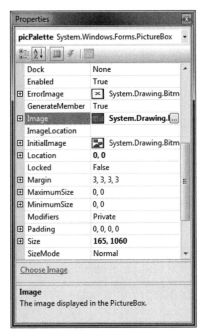

Figure 6.11
Replacing the tile palette image inside the level editor project.

Filling Empty Tiles

The Actions menu, shown in Figure 6.12, includes four options (currently) to make editing a bit easier. These are just the most useful script-like features I needed while using the editor myself. If you can think of any additional processes that would speed up level editing or make the life of a level designer easier, then I encourage you to go ahead and add them to this menu! See the source code behind the existing Action items for example code on how to manipulate the tilemap.

The first Action item, Fill Empty Tiles, will use the *currently selected tile* (so make sure you select a tile first) to fill all empty spaces in the level. So, any tile that is empty or black will be filled with the selected tile, while all tiles currently in use will be skipped! This is a very useful action. A variation that I would like to add is the ability to *replace* any tile with another, but the logic is a little bit more complex because we would have to select the tile in the editor to be replaced, then select the new one, before launching the Action item—but it could be done! Below is an example of the code:

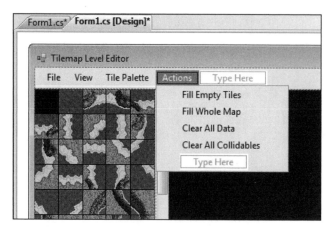

Figure 6.12
The Actions menu.

```
for (int index = 0; index < mapSize * mapSize; index++)
{
    if (tilemap[index].tilenum == 0)
        tilemap[index].tilenum = selectedPaletteTile;
}
redrawTilemap();
```

Let's see it in action. In Figure 6.13 is a sample tilemap with some tiles of the level deleted. (By the way, you can delete tiles by right-clicking them in the editor window.) Using the Actions menu, select Fill Empty Tiles. A prompt will come up in case you accidentally choose the wrong menu item. Be sure to have the desired tile selected in the palette before continuing because there's no "Undo" feature. Figure 6.14 shows the result, with all empty tiles filled in using the selected "grass" tile. All empty tiles in the entire tilemap have been similarly replaced, not just those in view.

Filling the Whole Map

The next option in the Actions menu is Fill Whole Map. As the title says, this option fills the entire map with the currently selected tile, regardless of what's already in the tilemap. Since this action replaces the entire tilemap, filling it in with a single tile, use with caution! The most common use for this is when getting started on a new tilemap, filling it in with the most commonly used "ground" tile.

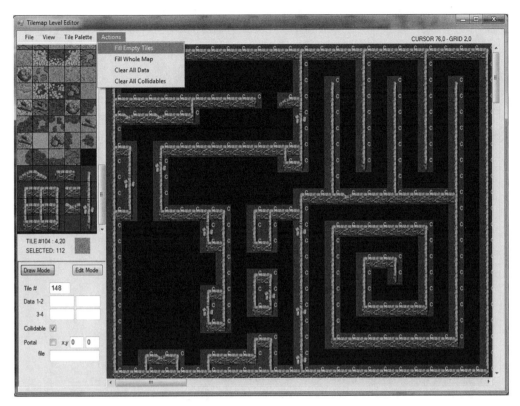

Figure 6.13
Testing the Fill Empty Tiles action item.

Clearing Data Fields

The next two options in the Actions menu, Clear All Data and Clear All Collidables, operate on the data fields of the tiles in the level. As their titles suggest, these options clear the data fields or the collidable field of every tile. What's missing here are similar actions to clear the portal fields independently from the others. There's definitely a lot of great things we could do with this menu to improve the level editor from a designer's point of view!

BUILDING THE EDITOR

The GUI for the level editor is a bit complicated. For one thing, it was created using splitter panels (System.Windows.Forms.SplitContainer), regular panels (System.Windows.Forms.Panel) as well as a PictureBox here and there, a menu (System.Windows.Forms.MenuStrip), and numerous scrollbars. Suffice it to say, it

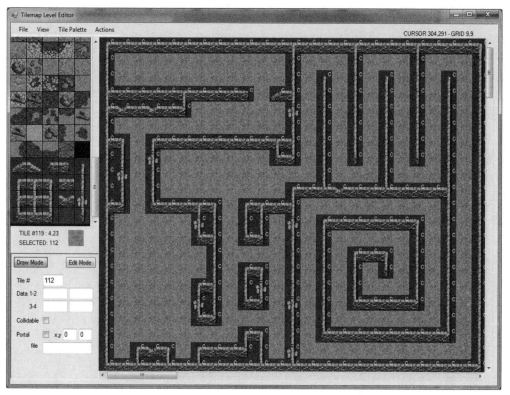

Figure 6.14
All empty tiles have been filled with the grass tile.

would take a lot of explanation to create the GUI from scratch here in this chapter. So, I'm going to recommend you open the project that is included in this chapter's resource files to see the Form. We'll go over the source code for the editor so you can see how it all works—the source is like the glue that makes the Form controls work together.

Importance of the Tile Palette

Let's consider the tile palette, which is arguably the most important part of the editor (refer back to Figure 6.10 to see the tiles). The tile palette is fixed for now with the tiles we need for the game at this point, but since the palette is a PictureBox with an associated Graphics and Bitmap object, we *can* modify it as needed—adding tiles, removing tiles, and so on. The tiles are fixed at 32x32 pixels—it's a good size for editing, especially when you're dealing with huge game levels. There's no reason why we can't use a different tile size, since the source code can work with 32x32 or 64x64 or any other reasonable dimension as a variable just as well as a hard-coded pair of numbers. Since the 3D-looking wall tiles (which we might call "2.5D" tiles) are much smaller than the character artwork, we may very well have to use a larger tile size *in the game* than is used in the editor. (The next chapter covers characters.)

I'll just presume you have the project open, and we'll go over the source code while explaining how the editor works. Figure 6.15 shows the editor in the form designer of Visual Studio.

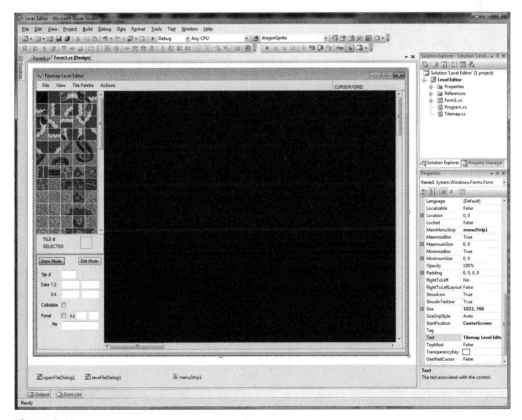

Figure 6.15
Editor GUI in the Form Designer of Visual Studio.

On the left is the tile palette. This is the collection of source tiles used to create a game level, and each tile is 32x32 pixels in size. There is also a one-pixel border separating each tile in the palette. If you create your own palette or add to this one, be sure to maintain that one-pixel border between each tile because the editor (and the game!) counts on that space being there to work correctly. If you want to replace the palette image, just open up the `PictureBox` control's properties and choose a new image using its `Image` property. The height may be shorter or taller, but it's very important that you maintain the same *width* as the one currently in the editor! The current one has five tiles across. Just be sure any replacement palette image you want to use has the same five tiles in width and the replacement palette image should work fine!

Tip

If you replace the tile palette, be sure to change the `picPalette.Height` property to match the actual height of the new palette image.

Quick Jaunt through the Sources

Like I mentioned before, we aren't going to look at *every line* of source code for the level editor, just the most interesting and relevant parts. There's a ton of code needed to make the `Form` controls work, and we just don't need to go over all of that rather mundane code. So, let's get started. First, these are the .NET Framework namespaces needed:

```
using System;
using System.Xml;
using System.IO;
using System.Collections.Generic;
using System.ComponentModel;
using System.Data;
using System.Drawing;
using System.Linq;
using System.Text;
using System.Windows.Forms;
using System.Runtime.InteropServices;
```

The last one, `InteropServices`, is an odd one! Turns out, we need this to enable mouse wheel support in the editor. Although we can't scroll left or right, we *can* scroll up and down in both the tile palette and the editor window by linking the mouse wheel to the vertical scroll bars—and that requires the `InteropServices` namespace.

Next, we have two structures. First, `tilemapStruct` contains the tile fields. Then, `selectionStruct` is a helper structure for working with the tile palette.

```
public struct tilemapStruct
{
    public int tilenum;
    public string data1;
    public string data2;
    public string data3;
    public string data4;
    public bool collidable;
    public bool portal;
    public int portalx;
    public int portaly;
    public string portalfile;
}

public struct selectionStruct
{
    public int index;
    public int oldIndex;
    public int x, y;
}
```

Next up, we have the `Form1` class definition, global variables, and startup and shutdown events. The `IMessageFilter` base class makes the mouse wheel work with the scrollbar controls.

```
public partial class Form1 : Form, IMessageFilter
{
    const int paletteColumns = 5;
    const int mapSize = 128;
    Bitmap drawArea;
    int mousex, mousey;
    Graphics gfx;
    int gridx, gridy;
    Bitmap selectedBitmap;
    Graphics gfxSelected;
    Font fontArial;
```

```csharp
    string g_filename = "";
    tilemapStruct[] tilemap;
    int paletteIndex = 0;
    int selectedPaletteTile = 0;
    selectionStruct selectedTile;

    private void Form1_FormClosed(object sender, FormClosedEventArgs e)
    {
        gfx.Dispose();
        drawArea.Dispose();
        gfxSelected.Dispose();
        selectedBitmap.Dispose();
    }

    public Form1()
    {
        InitializeComponent();
        Application.AddMessageFilter(this);

        //create tilemap
        tilemap = new tilemapStruct[mapSize*mapSize];

        //set up level drawing surface
        drawArea = new Bitmap(pictureBox1.Size.Width, pictureBox1.Size.
            Height);
        pictureBox1.Image = drawArea;
        gfx = Graphics.FromImage(drawArea);

        //selected image
        selectedBitmap = new Bitmap(picSelected.Size.Width, picSelected.
            Size.Height);
        picSelected.Image = selectedBitmap;
        gfxSelected = Graphics.FromImage(selectedBitmap);

        //create font
        fontArial = new Font("Arial Narrow", 8);
    }
```

Now for some truly ugly looking code—tapping into the core Windows messaging system to add mouse wheel support to the vertical scrollbars.

```
//adds mouse wheel support to scrollable controls
[DllImport("user32.dll")]
private static extern IntPtr WindowFromPoint(Point pt);
[DllImport("user32.dll")]
private static extern IntPtr SendMessage(IntPtr hWnd, int msg,
    IntPtr wp, IntPtr lp);
public bool PreFilterMessage(ref Message m)
{
    if (m.Msg == 0x20a)
    {
        Point pos = new Point(m.LParam.ToInt32() & 0xffff,
            m.LParam.ToInt32() >> 16);
        IntPtr hWnd = WindowFromPoint(pos);
        if (hWnd != IntPtr.Zero && hWnd != m.HWnd &&
            Control.FromHandle(hWnd) != null)
        {
            SendMessage(hWnd, m.Msg, m.WParam, m.LParam);
            return true;
        }
    }
    return false;
}
```

Now, *here* is a really important function! At its core, this is basically *sprite animation* code that we're borrowing to make the tile palette work as a single large image. When you select a tile, the program figures out which tile you clicked on based on the dimensions of the palette image and known factors like the fact that there are five tiles across and that each tile is 32x32 pixels in size. This code is primarily of concern if we ever wanted to change the tile size to anything other than this size.

```
public void setSelectedTile()
{
    int sx = (selectedPaletteTile % paletteColumns) * 33;
    int sy = (selectedPaletteTile / paletteColumns) * 33;
    Rectangle src = new Rectangle(sx, sy, 32, 32);
    Rectangle dst = new Rectangle(0, 0, 32, 32);
    gfxSelected.DrawImage(picPalette.Image, dst, src,
        GraphicsUnit.Pixel);
    picSelected.Image = selectedBitmap;
}
```

Next up, we have the core *drawing functions* used by the editor. A primary function, drawTileNumber(), is used by the others and is therefore highly reusable. This function also handles the special data information (Collidable, Data1, and the Tile # values), so if you wanted to add more information to the editor window, this is where you can make those changes (or additions).

```
public void drawTileNumber(int x, int y, int tile)
{
    //save tilemap data
    tilemap[y * mapSize + x].tilenum = tile;

    //draw tile
    int sx = (tile % paletteColumns) * 33;
    int sy = (tile / paletteColumns) * 33;
    int dx = x * 32;
    int dy = y * 32;
    Rectangle src = new Rectangle(sx, sy, 32, 32);
    Rectangle dst = new Rectangle(dx, dy, 32, 32);
    gfx.DrawImage(picPalette.Image, dst, src, GraphicsUnit.Pixel);

    //print tilenum
    if (menuViewShowTileNum.Checked)
    {
        if (tile > 0)
            gfx.DrawString(tile.ToString(), fontArial, Brushes.White,
                x * 32, y * 32);
    }

    //print data value
    if (showDataToolStripMenuItem.Checked)
    {
        string data = tilemap[y * mapSize + x].data1;
        gfx.DrawString(data, fontArial, Brushes.White, x * 32,
            y * 32 + 10);
    }

    //print collidable state
    if (showCollidableToolStripMenuItem.Checked)
    {
        bool collidable = tilemap[y * mapSize + x].collidable;
```

```
        if (collidable)
            gfx.DrawString("C", fontArial, Brushes.White, x * 32 + 22,
                y * 32);
    }

    //save changes
    pictureBox1.Image = drawArea;
}

public void redrawTilemap()
{
    for (int index = 0; index < mapSize * mapSize; index++)
    {
        int value = tilemap[index].tilenum;
        int x = index % mapSize;
        int y = index / mapSize;
        drawTileNumber(x, y, value);
    }
}

public void drawSelectedTile()
{
    drawTileNumber(gridx, gridy, selectedPaletteTile);
}

public void hideSelectionBox()
{
    //erase old selection box
    int oldx = selectedTile.oldIndex % mapSize;
    int oldy = selectedTile.oldIndex / mapSize;
    drawTileNumber(oldx, oldy, tilemap[selectedTile.oldIndex].tilenum);

}
```

The next two functions affect the editor window, drawing the selection box (when in Edit mode) and filling the tile data fields when a tile is selected in the editor.

```
public void drawSelectionBox(int gridx, int gridy)
{
    hideSelectionBox();
```

```csharp
        //remember current tile
        selectedTile.oldIndex = selectedTile.index;

        //draw selection box around tile
        int dx = gridx * 32;
        int dy = gridy * 32;
        Pen pen = new Pen(Color.DarkMagenta, 2);
        Rectangle rect = new Rectangle(dx + 1, dy + 1, 30, 30);
        gfx.DrawRectangle(pen, rect);

        //save changes
        pictureBox1.Image = drawArea;
    }

    private void clickDrawArea(MouseEventArgs e)
    {
        switch (e.Button)
        {
            case MouseButtons.Left:
                if (radioDrawMode.Checked)
                {
                    drawSelectedTile();
                }
                else
                {
                    //show selected tile # for editing
                    selectedTile.x = gridx;
                    selectedTile.y = gridy;
                    selectedTile.index = gridy * mapSize + gridx;
                    txtTileNum.Text = tilemap[selectedTile.index].tilenum.
                        ToString();
                    txtData1.Text = tilemap[selectedTile.index].data1;
                    txtData2.Text = tilemap[selectedTile.index].data2;
                    txtData3.Text = tilemap[selectedTile.index].data3;
                    txtData4.Text = tilemap[selectedTile.index].data4;
                    chkCollidable.Checked = tilemap[selectedTile.index].
                        collidable;
                    chkPortal.Checked = tilemap[selectedTile.index].portal;
                    txtPortalX.Text = tilemap[selectedTile.index].portalx.
                        ToString();
```

```
            txtPortalY.Text = tilemap[selectedTile.index].portaly.
                ToString();
            txtPortalFile.Text = tilemap[selectedTile.index].
                portalfile;

            //draw selection box
            drawSelectionBox(gridx, gridy);
        }
        break;

    case MouseButtons.Right:
        if (radioDrawMode.Checked)
            drawTileNumber(gridx, gridy, 0); //erase
        break;
    }
}
```

The last section of code (dealing with tile editing) that I'll share with you finishes off our coverage of the basic editor logic code. The editor window is handled by a `PictureBox` control called `pictureBox1`. When you move the mouse over the control, the `MouseMove` event fires and the `pictureBox1_MouseMove()` event method handles it. When we move the mouse over the tilemap, we do want the editor to display stuff about each tile as the mouse moves over it. Likewise, clicking on a tile in the editor causes either the currently selected palette tile to be drawn at that location, or if in Edit mode, causes that tile in the editor window to be highlighted so the data fields of the tile can be edited. Note that this code does not have much error handling, so save your levels often!

```
private void pictureBox1_MouseClick(object sender, MouseEventArgs e)
{
    clickDrawArea(e);
}
private void pictureBox1_MouseMove(object sender, MouseEventArgs e)
{
    gridx = e.X / 32;
    gridy = e.Y / 32;
    mousex = e.X;
    mousey = e.Y;
    lblMouseInfo.Text = "CURSOR " + e.X.ToString() + "," +
        e.Y.ToString() + " - GRID " + gridx.ToString() + "," +
```

```
            gridy.ToString();

        if (radioDrawMode.Checked)
        {
            int index = gridy * mapSize + gridx;
            txtTileNum.Text = tilemap[index].tilenum.ToString();
            txtData1.Text = tilemap[index].data1;
            txtData2.Text = tilemap[index].data2;
            txtData3.Text = tilemap[index].data3;
            txtData4.Text = tilemap[index].data4;
            chkCollidable.Checked = tilemap[index].collidable;
            chkPortal.Checked = tilemap[index].portal;
            txtPortalX.Text = tilemap[index].portalx.ToString();
            txtPortalY.Text = tilemap[index].portaly.ToString();
            txtPortalFile.Text = tilemap[index].portalfile;
        }

        clickDrawArea(e);
    }

    private void Form1_Load(object sender, EventArgs e){}

    private void palette_MouseMove(object sender, MouseEventArgs e)
    {
        if (e.X < paletteColumns * 33)
        {
            gridx = e.X / 33;
            gridy = e.Y / 33;
            paletteIndex = gridy * paletteColumns + gridx;
            lblTileInfo.Text = "TILE #" + paletteIndex + " : " +
                gridx.ToString() + "," + gridy.ToString();
            lblSelected.Text = "SELECTED: " + selectedPaletteTile.
                ToString();
        }
    }
    private void palette_MouseClick(object sender, MouseEventArgs e)
    {
        if (e.X < paletteColumns * 33)
        {
            gridx = e.X / 33;
```

```
        gridy = e.Y / 33;

        switch (e.Button)
        {
            case MouseButtons.Left:
                selectedPaletteTile = gridy * paletteColumns + gridx;
                setSelectedTile();
                break;
        }
    }
}
```

Now, what about the next most important issue—loading and saving? After selecting and editing the tilemap, this is definitely the most significant feature of a level editor! Okay, if you have never tried to load or save data using an XML file before, then this will be helpful to you beyond just this level editor project, because working with XML in the .NET environment of Visual C# or Visual Basic is pretty common, and knowing how to read and write XML is a valuable skill. There's a couple of prerequisites here that I haven't explained yet, but they are part of the GUI—the OpenFileDialog and SaveFileDialog controls must be added to the form, and they should be called openFileDialog1 and saveFileDialog1. The key to reading an XML file is a class called XmlDocument, with help from XmlNodeList, XmlNode, and XmlElement. These classes all work together to retrieve XML data and make it easy to read.

```
//helper function for loadTilemapFile
private string getElement(string field, ref XmlElement element)
{
    string value = "";
    try
    {
        value = element.GetElementsByTagName(field)[0].InnerText;
    }
    catch (Exception e)
    {
        Console.WriteLine(e.Message);
    }
    return value;
}
```

```csharp
private void loadTilemapFile()
{
    //display the open file dialog
    openFileDialog1.DefaultExt = ".level";
    openFileDialog1.Filter = "Tilemap Files|*.level";
    openFileDialog1.Multiselect = false;
    openFileDialog1.Title = "Load Level File";
    openFileDialog1.InitialDirectory = Environment.CurrentDirectory;
    DialogResult result = openFileDialog1.ShowDialog();
    if (result != DialogResult.OK) return;
    g_filename = openFileDialog1.SafeFileName;
    this.Cursor = Cursors.WaitCursor;

    try
    {
        XmlDocument doc = new XmlDocument();
        doc.Load(g_filename);
        XmlNodeList list = doc.GetElementsByTagName("tiles");
        foreach (XmlNode node in list)
        {
            XmlElement element = (XmlElement)node;

            //read data fields
            int index = Convert.ToInt32(getElement("tile",ref element));
            tilemap[index].tilenum = Convert.ToInt32(getElement("value",
                ref element));
            tilemap[index].data1 = getElement("data1", ref element);
            tilemap[index].data2 = getElement("data2", ref element);
            tilemap[index].data3 = getElement("data3", ref element);
            tilemap[index].data4 = getElement("data4", ref element);
            tilemap[index].collidable = Convert.ToBoolean(
                getElement("collidable", ref element));
            tilemap[index].portal = Convert.ToBoolean(
                getElement("portal", ref element));
            tilemap[index].portalx = Convert.ToInt32(
                getElement("portalx", ref element));
            tilemap[index].portaly = Convert.ToInt32(
                getElement("portaly", ref element));
            tilemap[index].portalfile = "";
        }
```

```
            redrawTilemap();
        }
        catch (Exception es)
        {
            MessageBox.Show(es.Message);
        }
        this.Cursor = Cursors.Arrow;
    }
```

Saving the tilemap data into an XML file is a little more involved because we have to create the structure of the XML file while building the save data. It turns out that this is pretty easy to do, and is just a very repetitive process, so it's time consuming but not very hard. For each XML field, we create a new DataColumn object, set its DataType property to the type of variable we need to save (like string, int, float, etc.), and then add it to a DataSet object. After the structure has been defined, then we can go through all the tiles in the tilemap (all 4,096 of them) and save each one, one at a time. Finally, after all the data has been converted from the tilemap to XML, then it is saved to a file using a DataTable. Okay, so it's *not* really all that easy after all, but here's the code so whatever! I'm ready to start working on the game now!

```
    private void saveTilemapFile()
    {
        if (g_filename.Length == 0)
        {
            saveTilemapFileAs();
            return;
        }

        this.Cursor = Cursors.WaitCursor;

        try
        {
            System.Data.DataSet ds;
            ds = new DataSet();

            //create xml schema
            System.Data.DataTable table;
            table = new DataTable("tiles");
```

```
//add an autoincrement column
DataColumn column1 = new DataColumn();
column1.DataType = System.Type.GetType("System.Int32");
column1.ColumnName = "tile";
column1.AutoIncrement = true;
table.Columns.Add(column1);

//add index key
DataColumn[] keys = new DataColumn[1];
keys[0] = column1;
table.PrimaryKey = keys;

//tilemap data columns
DataColumn column2 = new DataColumn();
column2.DataType = System.Type.GetType("System.Int32");
column2.ColumnName = "value";
table.Columns.Add(column2);

DataColumn data1 = new DataColumn();
data1.DataType = System.Type.GetType("System.String");
data1.ColumnName = "data1";
table.Columns.Add(data1);

DataColumn data2 = new DataColumn();
data2.DataType = System.Type.GetType("System.String");
data2.ColumnName = "data2";
table.Columns.Add(data2);

DataColumn data3 = new DataColumn();
data3.DataType = System.Type.GetType("System.String");
data3.ColumnName = "data3";
table.Columns.Add(data3);

DataColumn data4 = new DataColumn();
data4.DataType = System.Type.GetType("System.String");
data4.ColumnName = "data4";
table.Columns.Add(data4);

DataColumn column4 = new DataColumn();
column4.DataType = System.Type.GetType("System.Boolean");
```

```
column4.ColumnName = "collidable";
table.Columns.Add(column4);

DataColumn portal = new DataColumn();
portal.DataType = System.Type.GetType("System.Boolean");
portal.ColumnName = "portal";
table.Columns.Add(portal);

DataColumn portalx = new DataColumn();
portalx.DataType = System.Type.GetType("System.Int32");
portalx.ColumnName = "portalx";
table.Columns.Add(portalx);

DataColumn portaly = new DataColumn();
portaly.DataType = System.Type.GetType("System.Int32");
portaly.ColumnName = "portaly";
table.Columns.Add(portaly);

DataColumn portalfile = new DataColumn();
portalfile.DataType = System.Type.GetType("System.String");
portalfile.ColumnName = "portalfile";
table.Columns.Add(portalfile);

//copy tilemap array into datatable
int index = 0;
for (int n=0; n<mapSize*mapSize; n++)
{
    DataRow row = table.NewRow();
    row["value"] = tilemap[index].tilenum;
    row["data1"] = tilemap[index].data1;
    row["data2"] = tilemap[index].data2;
    row["data3"] = tilemap[index].data3;
    row["data4"] = tilemap[index].data4;
    row["collidable"] = tilemap[index].collidable;
    row["portal"] = tilemap[index].portal;
    row["portalx"] = tilemap[index].portalx;
    row["portaly"] = tilemap[index].portaly;
    row["portalfile"] = tilemap[index].portalfile;
    table.Rows.Add(row);
    index++;
```

```
        }

        //save xml file
        table.WriteXml( g_filename );
        ds.Dispose();
        table.Dispose();
    }
    catch (Exception es)
    {
        MessageBox.Show(es.Message);
    }
    this.Cursor = Cursors.Arrow;
}
```

LEVEL UP!

This chapter was awesome, because it showed how to create our own custom game development tool—a level editor! You now have at least a rudimentary understanding of how a level editor should work, so that you can make changes to it as needed while creating and editing game levels. This is one of the cornerstones of the Dungeon Crawler game! What kind of RPG would we have without the ability to create game levels for the player to explore? The tilemap is the most important part of the game because it is the foundation—literally, it is *the world* on which our characters will walk. You can create a large, vast desert or a lush green world and populate it with vegetation and roads and even buildings. Of course, in a *dungeon*, there are no such luxuries! I hope you're preparing yourself to fight vile creatures in the deep places of the Earth because that's where we're headed.

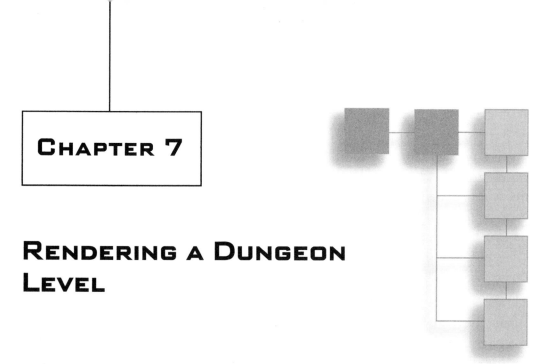

CHAPTER 7

RENDERING A DUNGEON LEVEL

We're going to take our first steps into a new world in this chapter: we will be learning how to load a game level created with the custom level editor developed in the previous chapter. This editor gives us considerable leeway in how the game will play, and we will explore some of the gameplay possibilities related to the game world in this chapter. You will learn the techniques used in tile-based scrolling, gaining an understanding of how a scrolling display is created using a "partial-tile" buffered scrolling algorithm. We'll be using level data from our custom level editor program to construct the game world. By using a small surface about the same size as the screen, the tiles are drawn to the buffer in order to produce a smooth-scrolling game world. The resulting tile scrolling engine is the foundation for the dungeon crawler game.

Here's what we'll cover in this chapter:

- Mapping the dungeon
- Loading and drawing the map/level file
- Introduction to tiled scrolling
- Scrolling a tiled game world
- Per-tile scrolling
- Per-pixel scrolling

Mapping the Dungeon

In this chapter, we'll focus on rendering the tilemap for one level and begin to interact with the level by scrolling it in the viewport. This makes it possible to travel through a large level with a much smaller viewport. The goal is to put as much functionality into the rendering and interaction of one level as possible, because that very same functionality (such as preventing the characters from passing through solid objects) extends to any level. Getting one small portion of the game world up and running means that the *entire* game world can be rendered by the game engine based solely on the level editor files.

This is what we call *data-driven* programming—where the data describes what should happen, and the source code processes the data according to known rules. So, what we're doing here is applying professional software engineering methodology to our role-playing game engine. When you want to add a new feature to the game, and that feature is added to the engine based on properties in the level file, then suddenly *every* level you create has that feature. For example, let's consider collision tiles, because that is a feature we will be addressing shortly. The level editor lets us specify which tiles are collidable, and which tiles may be passed through. The collidable tiles should block the player from moving through them. Or, put differently: the *game* should prevent the player from moving through collidable—or let us say *solid*—tiles on the map. Any tile can be made solid by setting the property in the editor. (By the way, we'll get into walking through the level and testing for collisions with the walls in the next chapter.)

Tile-Based Dungeon

The dungeon we will be creating should have a way to go up to the level above or down to the next level below, with lower levels containing increasingly more difficult monsters. So, we need to create many tilemaps with our own level editor, not just one big game world (as was the case in the sister book on Visual Basic). As you learned in the previous chapter, our tilemaps have a maximum size of 128 tiles across, and 128 tiles down, for a total *pixel* resolution of 4096x4096. What we need to focus on is the top-level "Town," which should provide the player's basic needs such as healing, weapons, armor, etc. Linked directly to the town will be the first level of the dungeon. So, the Town will be level 0, while the first dungeon level will be level 1. Within that first level of the

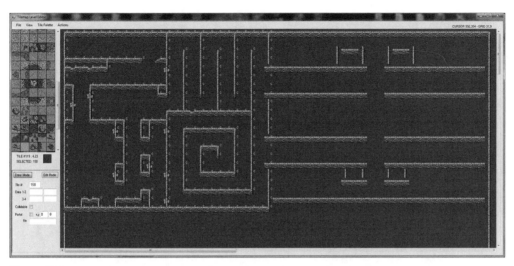

Figure 7.1
The level editor window is resizable for large widescreen displays.

dungeon will be a staircase going down to level 2. Figure 7.1 shows the level editor enlarged so that more of the first level is visible in the editor window.

However, we don't have to *actually use* that full size for every map. By defining regions with the `collidable` property, we can limit the player's movements to a smaller area surrounded by walls. Although the tilemap will remain fixed at 128x128, we can use much smaller areas, as well as combine several tilemaps (via portals) to create larger areas. The gameplay possibilities are endless! If you intend to create your own dungeon crawler game with small levels, then you could have four or more levels on a single tilemap. Note in Figure 7.2 that the tiny sample dungeon only takes up about 25 tiles across—the tilemap can handle up to 128! This gets a bit into the design realm, but I recommend increasing the size of the levels proportionally with the level number. Give the player some early success by letting him complete levels quickly and make the deeper dungeon levels larger and more dangerous! Thus, as the player's character levels up, he or she will be leveling *down* further into the depths of the dungeon. Consider also the length of gameplay in your dungeon. If there are only 20 levels, and the player can go through them each in five minutes or less, then the entire game can be beaten in about an hour and a half. Decide how much gameplay you want to give the player, and design levels accordingly.

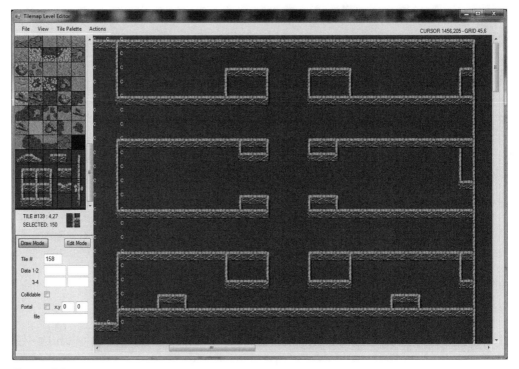

Figure 7.2
Adding details (such as wall corners) improves the realism of the dungeon level.

Figure 7.2 shows the first dungeon level with some corner tiles added to the walls to improve the realism of the level. I recommend you throw together your level designs quickly using basically just the vertical and horizontal wall tiles, and after you have the basic layout the way you want it to look, then go in and add details like this.

In addition, be mindful of the player's level as well. Do you want him to finish the game while his character is only level 3 or 4? That would deny the player the enjoyment of using higher-level abilities! Remember, this is a role-playing game, so the most important factor is giving the player an enjoyable time leveling up his character. If it all ends too quickly, then taking the time to create the character will have seemed a monumental waste of time to your players. Let them level up in proportion to the dungeon's difficulty. If necessary, recycle levels to increase the total number of levels in the dungeon.

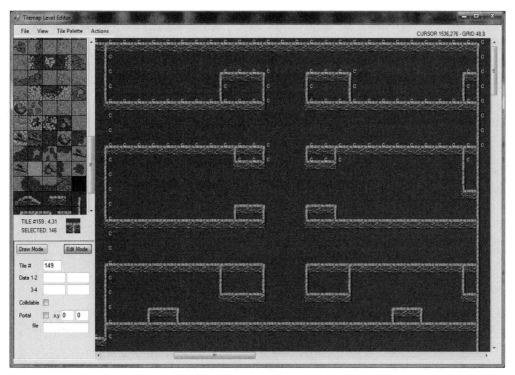

Figure 7.3
Adding a `Collidable` property to the solid wall tiles.

When all of the wall tiles have been placed, then you can go in and set the `Collidable` property for each tile. First, click the Edit Mode button on the lower-left corner of the Tilemap Level Editor window. This will switch the editor into tile editing mode. Then, check the Collidable checkbox to enable collision for any selected tile, as shown in Figure 7.3. Now, to speed things up, the Space key has been set to toggle the `Collidable` property, so just click a tile and hit Space to move quickly through the level.

I want to emphasize again that the game world truly has no limit when using level files with portal tiles (which we cover in Chapter 9). When a portal is entered, the game teleports the player to a new location. By using a portal *file* as well as the coordinates, we can even load up a new level file entirely and position the player at any location in that new file with the same technique. Furthermore, teleporting the player will be almost instantaneous. Which means, you could create a *huge* level with seamless edges by creating a strip of portal tiles along one edge so that when the player reaches that edge, the player continues to walk in the same direction, having been wrapped around to the beginning. Also, if two level files are designed with seamless edges, the player will never know he has just entered a new level file! This can create the impression of a much larger game world than what there really is (sort of like the Holodeck on Star Trek).

To quickly set the Collidable property for all solid tiles, you can use the Action menu, wherein is an option called Auto Set Collidable. First, select a tile in the palette that is the base "ground" tile, which will be skipped when the action is performed. Then, select the Auto Set Collidable item in the Action menu. This has the effect of setting the Collidable property on every tile *except* the selected one! A real time saver!

Loading and Drawing Level Files

Our custom level editor that was developed in the previous chapter produces XML files containing information about a game level. We can load the XML file

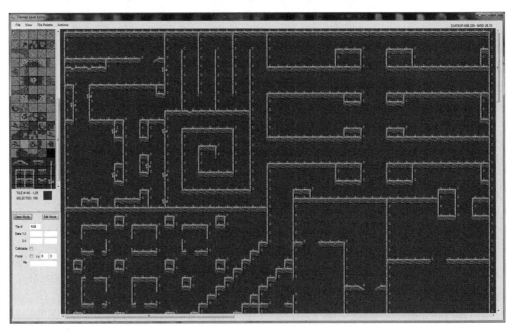

Figure 7.4
Using the Auto Set Collidable action.

using .NET classes in the System.Xml namespace—so loading is not a problem. Rendering the level is where we'll focus most of our attention. First, let's just look at loading the data from a level file and render one screen full of tiles with it as a starting point. Until now, we have only seen game levels inside the editor, but now we'll be able to render the level with C# code. To render a level, we need two things: 1) The tilemap data from the .xml file; and 2) The source tiles stored in a bitmap file. The level file describes the tile number that should be represented at each location in the game level.

Here is the source code for the Level Viewer. This example does not know how to scroll, but it's a good start. Figure 7.5 shows the result of our first attempt to render a game level.

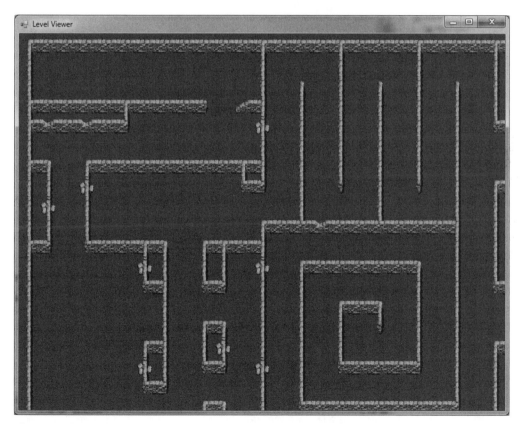

Figure 7.5
The Level Viewer demo displays just the upper-left corner of the game world.

```csharp
using System;
using System.Drawing;
using System.Text;
using System.Windows.Forms;
using System.Xml;

namespace Level_Viewer
{
    public partial class Form1 : Form
    {
        public struct tilemapStruct
        {
            public int tilenum;
            public string data1;
            public bool collidable;
        }
        const int COLUMNS = 5;
        private Bitmap bmpTiles;
        private Bitmap bmpSurface;
        private PictureBox pbSurface;
        private Graphics gfxSurface;
        private Font fontArial;
        private tilemapStruct[] tilemap;

        public Form1()
        {
            InitializeComponent();
        }

        private void Form1_Load(object sender, EventArgs e)
        {
            this.Text = "Level Viewer";
            this.Size = new Size(800 + 16, 600 + 38);

            //create tilemap
            tilemap = new tilemapStruct[128 * 128];

            //set up level drawing surface
            bmpSurface = new Bitmap(800, 600);
            pbSurface = new PictureBox();
            pbSurface.Parent = this;
```

```csharp
    pbSurface.BackColor = Color.Black;
    pbSurface.Dock = DockStyle.Fill;
    pbSurface.Image = bmpSurface;
    gfxSurface = Graphics.FromImage(bmpSurface);

    //create font
    fontArial = new Font("Arial Narrow", 8);

    //load tiles bitmap
    bmpTiles = new Bitmap("palette.bmp");

    //load the tilemap
    loadTilemapFile("level1.level");

    drawTilemap();
}

private void Form1_FormClosed(object sender, FormClosedEventArgs e)
{
    bmpSurface.Dispose();
    pbSurface.Dispose();
    gfxSurface.Dispose();
}

private void loadTilemapFile(string filename)
{
try
{
    XmlDocument doc = new XmlDocument();
    doc.Load(filename);
    XmlNodeList nodelist = doc.GetElementsByTagName("tiles");
    foreach (XmlNode node in nodelist)
    {
        XmlElement element = (XmlElement)node;
        int index = 0;
        int value = 0;
        string data1 = "";
        bool collidable = false;

        //read tile index #
```

```
            index = Convert.ToInt32(element.GetElementsByTagName(
                "tile")[0].InnerText);

            //read tilenum
            value = Convert.ToInt32(element.GetElementsByTagName(
                "value")[0].InnerText);

            //read data1
            data1 = Convert.ToString(element.GetElementsByTagName(
                "data1")[0].InnerText);

            //read collidable
            collidable = Convert.ToBoolean(element.GetElementsByTagName(
                "collidable")[0].InnerText);

            tilemap[index].tilenum = value;
            tilemap[index].data1 = data1;
            tilemap[index].collidable = collidable;
        }
    }
    catch (Exception es)
    {
        MessageBox.Show(es.Message);
    }
}

private void drawTilemap()
{
    for (int x = 0; x < 25; x++)
        for (int y = 0; y < 19; y++)
            drawTileNumber(x, y, tilemap[y * 128 + x].tilenum);
}

public void drawTileNumber(int x, int y, int tile)
{
    //draw tile
    int sx = (tile % COLUMNS) * 33;
    int sy = (tile / COLUMNS) * 33;
    Rectangle src = new Rectangle(sx, sy, 32, 32);
    int dx = x * 32;
```

```
        int dy = y * 32;
        gfxSurface.DrawImage(bmpTiles, dx, dy, src, GraphicsUnit.Pixel);

        //save changes
        pbSurface.Image = bmpSurface;
    }

    private void Form1_KeyUp(object sender, KeyEventArgs e)
    {
        if (e.KeyCode == Keys.Escape)
            Application.Exit();
    }
  }
}
```

INTRODUCTION TO TILED SCROLLING

What is scrolling? In today's gaming world, where 3D is the focus of everyone's attention, it's not surprising to find gamers and programmers who have never heard of scrolling. What a shame! The heritage of modern games is a long and fascinating one that is still relevant today, even if it is not understood or appreciated. The console industry puts great effort and value into scrolling, particularly on handheld systems such as the Nintendo DS/DSi/3DS. *Scrolling* is the process of displaying a small window of a larger virtual game world. There are three basic ways to scroll the display:

- Loading a large tiled bitmap image
- Creating a large bitmap out of tiles at runtime
- Drawing tiles directly on the screen

Figure 7.6 illustrates the concept of scrolling, which, in essence, involves the use of a large game world of which only a small portion is visible through the screen at a time.

The key to scrolling is having something in the virtual game world to display in the scroll window (or the screen). Also, I should point out that the entire screen need not be used as the scroll window. It is common to use the entire screen in scrolling-shooter games, but role-playing games often use a smaller window on the

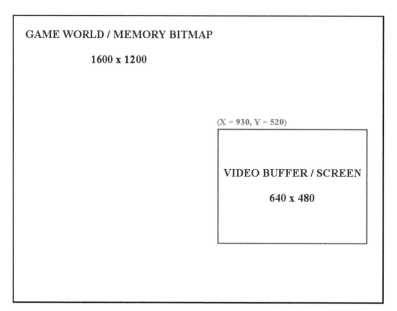

Figure 7.6
The scroll window shows a small part of a larger game world.

screen for scrolling, using the rest of the screen for gameplay (combat, inventory, and so on) and player/party information, as shown in Figure 7.7.

You could display one huge bitmap image in the virtual game world representing the current level of the game (or the *map*), and then copy a portion of that virtual world onto the screen. This is the simplest form of scrolling. Another method uses tiles to create the game world at runtime. Suppose we had a large bitmap file containing a pre-rendered image of the game world. You would then load up that large bitmap and copy a portion of it to the screen, and that portion would represent the current scroll position.

Constructing the Tiled Image

This theory of using a single large bitmap seems reasonable at first glance, but that method of scrolling has a very serious limitation. When you create a game world, the whole point is to interact with that game world. A single, large bitmap used to render the game world prevents you from actually tracking where the player is located on the map, as well as what other objects are on the map. In a tile-based game world, each tile is represented by a number, and that number

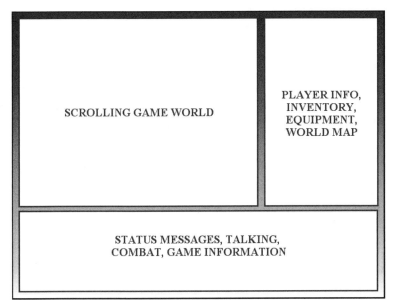

Figure 7.7
Some games use a smaller portion of the game screen for a scrolling window.

has *meaning*. A tile containing a tree is *impassable*, whereas a tile of grass can be walked on. Of course, you could create a new array or some other method to keep track of the player, various enemies, and objects in the game world, but that requires a lot of extra work. There's a better way to do it. A high-speed scrolling arcade game automatically scrolls horizontally or vertically, displaying ground-, air-, or space-based terrain below the player's vehicle (usually represented by an airplane or spaceship). The point of such games is to keep the action moving so fast that the player doesn't have a chance to rest from one wave of enemies to the next.

Tile Buffer

Tiling is a process in which there really is no background, just an array of small images that make up the background as it is drawn. In other words, it is a virtual background and takes up very little memory compared to a full bitmapped background. You are already familiar with how tiling works after learning about the level editor, but you are probably wondering: How can I load tiles and make a scrolling game world out of a level file?

Most levels in a scrolling arcade game are quite large, comprised of thousands of tiles in one orientation or the other (usually just scrolling up and down—vertically—or left to right). These types of games are called *shooters* for the most part, although the horizontally scrolling games are usually *platformers* (such as the original Mario games). Not only does your average Mario game have large scrolling levels, but those levels have parallax layers that make the background in the distance scroll by more slowly than the layer on which the player's character is walking.

When working on a new game, I find it helpful to start storing my tiles in a new image one by one as I need them, so that I can construct a new set of tiles for the game while I'm working on the game. This also helps to keep the tile numbers down to a smaller number. If you have a huge tile map with hundreds of tiles in it and you only need a few of them during the early stages of development, then you have to figure out where each tile must be drawn, and you have to work with a texture in memory.

Stepping Stones of the World

The process of drawing tiles to fill the game world reminds me of laying down stepping stones, and tiling is a perfect analogy for how this works. Basically, tiles of a larger pattern are laid down from left to right, top to bottom, in that order. The first row is added, one tile at a time, all the way across; then the next row down is filled in from left to right, and so on until the entire map is filled. A single large bitmap is just not used—that's amateur. Another possibility is that you could continue to use a single large bitmap, but *create* that bitmap at runtime, and fill it with tiles according to the map file and tile images. Although this solution would generate the game world on the fly, the resulting texture representing the game world would require several gigabytes of memory, which is not feasible.

Tile Rendering Theory

Now that you have a good understanding of what scrolling is and how we can edit tile maps and export them, let's take a look at the basic theory and code to actually draw a scrolling tile map on the screen. The problem with scrolling a large game world is that too much memory is required to create a texture in memory to contain an entire game world (even if you break the map into sections). You cannot create a single texture to hold the entire game world because most levels are far too large! It would consume so much memory that the program would not even run, and even if it did, that would be a *horrible* way to write a game. We're talking about old-school scrolling here, after all, from an era when video game systems had tiny amounts of memory—like 64 KB! Surely we can figure out how *they* did it back then.

Let's examine a method of tile rendering that supports giant maps using very little memory. In fact, all the memory required for the tiled scroller developed here is a bitmap for the tiles and an array with all of the tile values, plus a screen-sized texture. (In other words, no more memory than would be needed for a background image.) A map comprised of several million tiles can be rendered by this tile engine and will require only a small memory footprint.

Figure 7.8 shows the game world with the scroll window superimposed, so you can see how the screen represents a portion of the game world. While viewing this figure, imagine there is no image containing this game world map, just a

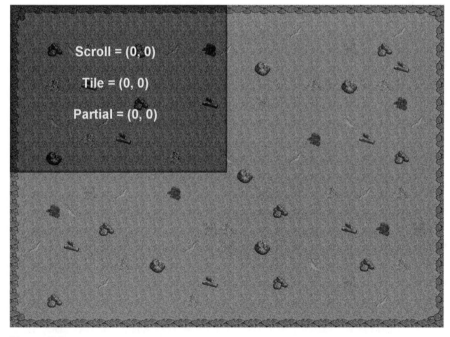

Figure 7.8
An example of a small game level.

virtual array of tile numbers. Those tiles are drawn *just* to the screen, based on what is visible in the darkened part of the figure. Do you see the rock border around the map? The border is helpful when you are developing a new tile scroller, because it shows the boundaries, allowing you to determine whether the scrolling view is being displayed at the correct location based on the scroll position. (In other words, it should stop scrolling when it reaches the edge of the "world," but should not skip any tiles.)

Now let's assume that you're using a screen resolution of 800x600, because this is a good resolution to use; it's relatively small so the screen updates quickly, but it is large enough to display a lot of details on the screen without crowding. We may even want to move up to 1024x768 at some point.

There is a simple calculation that gives you the tile number as well as the partial tile values relatively easily. Are you familiar with *modulus*? This is a mathematical operation that produces the *remainder* of a division operation. Let me give you a simple example:

$$10/5 = 2$$

This is simple enough to understand, right? What happens when you are using numbers that are not evenly divisible?

$$10/3 = 3.33333333$$

This is a problem, because the remainder is not an even number, and we're talking about pixels here. You can't deal with parts of a pixel! However, you can work with parts of a tile, because tiles are made up of many pixels. Thinking in terms of complete tiles here, let's take a look at that division again:

$$10/3 = 3, \text{ with a remainder of } 0.33333333$$

Let me now use numbers more relevant to the problem at hand:

$$800/64 = 12.5$$

This represents a calculation that returns the number of tiles that fit on a screen with a width of 800 pixels (assuming the tiles are 64 pixels wide). What does 12.5 tiles mean when you are writing a scroller? The .5 represents a *part* of a tile that must be drawn; hence, I call it *partial-tile scrolling*. Switching to 32x32 pixel tiles results in an evenly divisible screen, at least horizontally (32x32 results in 25 tiles across, 18.75 tiles down).

Here is where it gets really interesting! After you have drawn your tiles across the screen, and you want to fill in the remaining .5 of a tile, you can calculate the size of the tile like so:

$64 \times 0.5 = 32$

That is, 32 pixels of the partial tile must be drawn to handle the scrolling edge that was not lined up with a tile edge on the map. Rather than keeping track of the remainder at all, there is a simpler way to calculate the portion of the tile that must be drawn, in the measurement of pixels:

$800 \% 64 = 32$

Hint

The *modulus* operator ("%" in C#) is similar to operators like multiply, divide, add, and subtract, but it simply returns the remainder of a division, which works great for our purposes here.

Try not to think of scrolling in *screen* terms, because the whole discussion revolves around the tile map in memory (the tile data itself). The tile data is expanded to full tiles when drawn to the screen, but until that happens, these tiles might be thought of as a huge virtual game world from which the scrolling window is drawn.

Try another problem so you get the hang of calculating partial tiles before we get into the source code. Suppose the scroll position is at (700,0) on the map, and the tiles are again 64x64. Which would be the starting tile, and what is the value of the partial tile (in pixels)? To calculate first the tile position in the map data array, just drop the decimal part, which represents the remainder:

$700 / 64 = 10.9375$ (10 whole tiles plus a partial tile)

Next, you *do* want to keep the remainder, and actually drop the tile position itself, because now you're interested in pixels.

$700 \% 64 = 60$

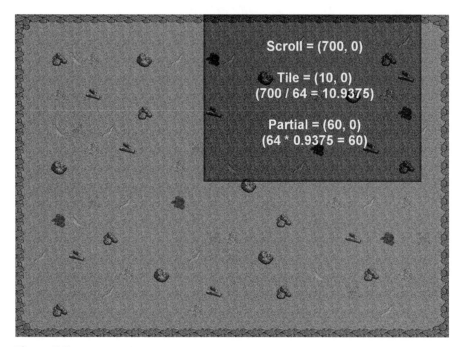

Figure 7.9
An example of how the partial tile calculation is performed at position (700,0).

To verify that this calculation is correct, you can do the following:

$$64 \times 0.9375 = 60$$

The modulus operator greatly helps with this calculation by skipping that middle step. It simply provides the remainder value directly, giving the exact number of pixels that must be drawn from the partial tile to fill in the top and left edges of the screen. I have shown the calculation in Figure 7.9, which is based on 64x64-pixel tiles.

Ready for another try at it? This time, calculate the tile numbers and partial-tile values for both the X and Y position of the scroll window at (372,489). Below is the answer, but see if you can figure it out before looking. . ..

First the X value:

$$372 / 64 = 5.8125 \text{ (tile X = 5)}$$
$$64 \times 0.8125 = 52 \text{ (pixels)}$$

Now for the Y value:

    489 / 64 = 7.640625 (tile Y = 7)

    64 × 0.640625 = 41 (pixels)

The same calculations are used for any size of tile, from 16x16 to 32x32 or any other size.

PER-TILE SCROLLING

Scrolling the level one tile at a time produces fairly good results, especially if you need extremely high performance in a very fast-paced game. Of course, a role-playing game is not a hectic, fast-paced scroller, but we do still need good performance. For an RPG, we need slower, more precise scrolling that is not possible with a full-tile scroller. What we need is sub-tile scrolling at a per-pixel rate. Let's learn the full-time method first, since that may come in handy for another game or two, and then we'll look at the sub-tile method.

Full-Tile Scrolling

For the full tile-based scroller, we'll be keeping track of the scroll position as it relates to entire tiles with a width and height of 32x32, which is the effective scroll rate (since each tile is 32 pixels across). The Level Scroller demo (shown in Figure 7.10 and listed below) does let you move around and look at the whole level but only one step at a time. There is something appealing about this scroller. I like how precise it is, moving one whole tile at a time, and think this would work great for a turn-based war game or a *Civilization* type game. We'll peruse just the *important* code for the Level Scroller demo that differs from the previous example. The loadTilemapFile() function was already shown in the previous example, so we'll just skip any functions like this that we have already seen.

To keep track of the scroll position:

```
private PointF scrollPos = new PointF(0, 0);
```

Now here is Form1_Load:

```
private void Form1_Load(object sender, EventArgs e)
{
    this.Text = "Level Scroller";
```

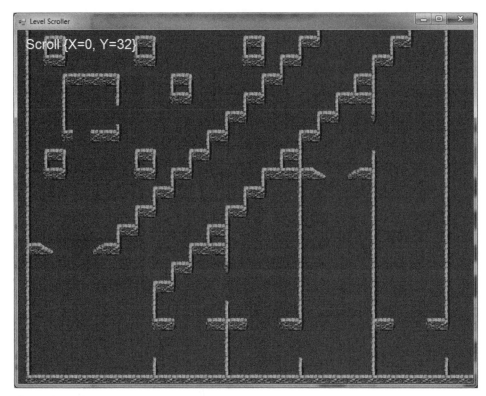

Figure 7.10
The Level Scroller demo scrolls the game world in one-tile increments.

```
this.Size = new Size(800 + 16, 600 + 38);

//create tilemap
tilemap = new tilemapStruct[128 * 128];

//set up level drawing surface
bmpSurface = new Bitmap(800, 600);
pbSurface = new PictureBox();
pbSurface.Parent = this;
pbSurface.BackColor = Color.Black;
pbSurface.Dock = DockStyle.Fill;
pbSurface.Image = bmpSurface;
gfxSurface = Graphics.FromImage(bmpSurface);
```

```
        //create font
        fontArial = new Font("Arial", 18);

        //load tiles bitmap
        bmpTiles = new Bitmap("palette.bmp");

        //load the tilemap
        loadTilemapFile("level1.level");

        drawTilemap();
    }
```

The drawTilemap() function assumes we have an 800x600 display. (800 / 32 = 25 tiles across, and 600 / 32 = 19 tiles down.)

```
    private void drawTilemap()
    {
        int tilenum, sx, sy;
        for (int x = 0; x < 25; x++)
            for (int y = 0; y < 19; y++)
            {
                sx = (int)scrollPos.X + x;
                sy = (int)scrollPos.Y + y;
                tilenum = tilemap[sy * 128 + sx].tilenum;
                drawTileNumber(x, y, tilenum);
            }

        //print scroll position
        string text = "Scroll " + scrollPos.ToString();
        gfxSurface.DrawString(text, fontArial, Brushes.White, 10, 10);
    }
```

The drawTileNumber() function uses the modulus operator to draw a tile from the tile palette image (which looks like a vertical strip of five tiles across, shown in the previous chapter). This function does not handle partial-tile scrolling as discussed, but does use the same modulus operator for a similar purpose of drawing a tile out of a source image. The same function can be found in the level editor's source code.

```
    public void drawTileNumber(int x, int y, int tile)
    {
        //draw tile
```

```
        int sx = (tile % COLUMNS) * 33;
        int sy = (tile / COLUMNS) * 33;
        Rectangle src = new Rectangle(sx, sy, 32, 32);
        int dx = x * 32;
        int dy = y * 32;
        gfxSurface.DrawImage(bmpTiles, dx, dy, src, GraphicsUnit.Pixel);

        //save changes
        pbSurface.Image = bmpSurface;
    }
```

The Form1_KeyUp() event is really the part of this program that causes things to happen. Based on user input, the tilemap is redrawn at a new scroll position. The drawTilemap() function does the work of filling in the window with tiles at the correct location of the tilemap.

```
    private void Form1_KeyUp(object sender, KeyEventArgs e)
    {
        switch (e.KeyCode)
        {
            case Keys.Escape:
                Application.Exit();
                break;

            case Keys.Up:
            case Keys.W:
                scrollPos.Y -= 1;
                if (scrollPos.Y < 0) scrollPos.Y = 0;
                drawTilemap();
                break;

            case Keys.Down:
            case Keys.S:
                scrollPos.Y += 1;
                if (scrollPos.Y > 127 - 19) scrollPos.Y = 127 - 19;
                drawTilemap();
                break;

            case Keys.Left:
            case Keys.A:
                scrollPos.X -= 1;
```

```
                    if (scrollPos.X < 0) scrollPos.X = 0;
                    drawTilemap();
                    break;

            case Keys.Right:
            case Keys.D:
                    scrollPos.X += 1;
                    if (scrollPos.X > 127 - 25) scrollPos.X = 127 - 25;
                    drawTilemap();
                    break;
        }
    }
```

Full-Tile Smooth Scrolling

The preceding example showed how to scroll the level one tile per keypress, which would work for a turn-based game but is otherwise too slow. We'll now take a look at how to scroll while a key is pressed without requiring the user to hit the key repeatedly. The main difference between this and the preceding example is that a flag is used to track the keypress and release states for the keys Up, Down, Left, and Right. As long as a key is being held, the map will continue to scroll in that direction. The Smooth Scroller demo is shown in Figure 7.11. Its code follows. Since only a few changes have been made, only the modified code is shown.

Here are the new pieces of data we need for smooth scrolling:

```
public struct keyStates
{
    public bool up, down, left, right;
}
private PointF oldScrollPos = new PointF(-1, -1);
private keyStates keyState;
private Timer timer1;
```

Here is an updated Form1_Load for the new smooth-scrolling program:

```
private void Form1_Load(object sender, EventArgs e)
{
    this.Text = "Smooth Scroller";
    this.Size = new Size(800 + 16, 600 + 38);
    fontArial = new Font("Arial", 18);
```

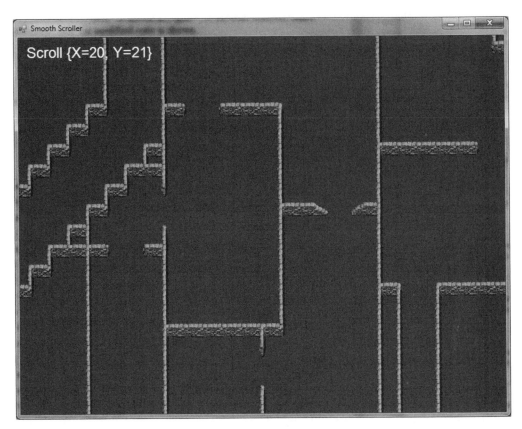

Figure 7.11
The Smooth Scroller demo scrolls the game world quickly and smoothly.

```
//set up level drawing surface
bmpSurface = new Bitmap(800, 600);
pbSurface = new PictureBox();
pbSurface.Parent = this;
pbSurface.BackColor = Color.Black;
pbSurface.Dock = DockStyle.Fill;
pbSurface.Image = bmpSurface;
gfxSurface = Graphics.FromImage(bmpSurface);

//create tilemap
tilemap = new tilemapStruct[128 * 128];
```

```
    bmpTiles = new Bitmap("palette.bmp");
    loadTilemapFile("level1.level");

    //create the timer
    timer1 = new Timer();
    timer1.Interval = 20;
    timer1.Enabled = true;
    timer1.Tick += new EventHandler(timer1_tick);
}
```

The key handling methods flag the appropriate property in the keyStates struct variable so the program will know when a key is being held or released.

```
private void Form1_KeyDown(object sender, KeyEventArgs e)
{
    switch (e.KeyCode)
    {
        case Keys.Up:
        case Keys.W:
            keyState.up = true;
            break;
        case Keys.Down:
        case Keys.S:
            keyState.down = true;
            break;
        case Keys.Left:
        case Keys.A:
            keyState.left = true;
            break;
        case Keys.Right:
        case Keys.D:
            keyState.right = true;
            break;
    }
}

private void Form1_KeyUp(object sender, KeyEventArgs e)
{
    switch (e.KeyCode)
    {
```

```
                case Keys.Escape:
                    Application.Exit();
                    break;
                case Keys.Up:
                case Keys.W:
                    keyState.up = false;
                    break;
                case Keys.Down:
                case Keys.S:
                    keyState.down = false;
                    break;
                case Keys.Left:
                case Keys.A:
                    keyState.left = false;
                    break;
                case Keys.Right:
                case Keys.D:
                    keyState.right = false;
                    break;
            }
    }
```

The "engine" behind this example is based on a Timer control called timer1, and the timer1_tick() function fires off regularly, which is what makes this a real-time program. Even if no scrolling is taking place, this function still causes the tilemap to redraw at a fast pace.

```
private void timer1_tick(object sender, EventArgs e)
{
    if (keyState.up)
    {
        scrollPos.Y -= 1;
        if (scrollPos.Y < 0) scrollPos.Y = 0;
    }
    if (keyState.down)
    {
        scrollPos.Y += 1;
        if (scrollPos.Y > 127 - 19) scrollPos.Y = 127 - 19;
    }
    if (keyState.left)
    {
```

```
        scrollPos.X -= 1;
        if (scrollPos.X < 0) scrollPos.X = 0;
    }
    if (keyState.right)
    {
        scrollPos.X += 1;
        if (scrollPos.X > 127 - 25) scrollPos.X = 127 - 25;
    }

    drawTilemap();
    string text = "Scroll " + scrollPos.ToString();
    gfxSurface.DrawString(text, fontArial, Brushes.White, 10, 10);
}
```

SUB-TILE SCROLLING

Finally, we come to sub-tile scrolling, a term that means scrolling in increments smaller than one whole tile, such as one pixel at a time. In the preceding example, the level was moved one tile at a time—that is, one whole row or column at a time. This is a good and fast way to move around the game world, and is the way I would recommend when you need to warp or jump from one location in the level to another very quickly. But for individual character movement in the game world, we need a slower, more precise form of scrolling, where only a few pixels at a time are shifted in the scroll direction. In order to accomplish this, we need a new feature—a scroll buffer. This buffer will be slightly larger than the screen, with a border around it equal to the size of the tiles. So, if our tiles are 32x32 pixels, then we need a 32-pixel border around the scroll buffer.

Sub-Tile Scrolling Theory

The key to implementing a dynamic sub-tile scrolling engine is a third buffer in memory (so called because the screen and back buffer are the first two), upon which the tiles are drawn at the current scroll position. The word *dynamic* here refers to the way the tile engine draws what is needed at that particular point in the game world, while *sub-tile* refers to the way it draws full tiles and partial tiles to fill the borders. If you think about it, the tiles are 32x32 pixels in size so without the partial-tile capability, drawing tiles directly to the screen one portion at a time results in very jumpy scrolling, where the screen is only updated whenever complete tiles can be drawn (as was the case in the preceding example).

To make this technique work, we start with a `Point` variable called `scrollPos` to keep track of the scroll position. When drawing tiles directly, these variables give a precise position at which the tiles should start drawing in a left-to-right, top-to-bottom orientation. If the scroll position is at (500,500), what does this mean, exactly? It means that the tiles specified in the map should be drawn at the upper-left corner of the screen, *from* the position of the 500x500 point in the game world. Try to keep this concept in mind when you are working on scrolling, because the screen position is always the same: the scrolling view is rendered onto the screen at the upper left, 0x0. While the scroll position changes all the time, the destination location on the screen never changes. We're drawing one screen worth of the game world at a time, from any location in that game world. At the same time, we want to render the tiles that make up that portion of the game world *dynamically,* in order to keep the scroll engine efficient.

Drawing the Scroll Buffer

After you have filled the scroll buffer with tiles for the current scroll position within the game world, the next thing you must do is actually draw the scroll buffer to the screen. This is where things get a little interesting. The scroll buffer is filled only with complete tiles, but it is from here that the partial tiles are taken into account. This is interesting because the whole tiles were drawn onto the scroll buffer, but the partial tiles are handled when drawing the scroll buffer to the screen. The `Point` variable called `subtile` is given the result of the modulus calculation, and these values are then used as the upper-left corner of the scroll buffer that is copied to the screen.

Remember, the scrolling window is just the beginning. The rest of the game still has to be developed, and that includes a lot of animated sprites for the player's character, non-player characters, plus buildings, animals, and any other objects that appear in the game. The bottom line is that the scroller needs to be as efficient as possible. (Yes, even with today's fast PCs, the scroller needs to be fast—never use the argument that PCs are fast to excuse poorly written code!)

Aligning Tiles to the Scroll Buffer

There is one factor that you must take into consideration while designing the screen layout of your game with a scrolling window. The size of the scrolling window must be evenly divisible by the size of the tiles, or you end up with a *floating overlap* at the uneven edge. This is an issue that I considered solving in the scrolling code itself. But it turns out that this is unnecessary because you can just change the destination rectangle when drawing the scroll buffer to the screen (something we'll explore later in this chapter with the "Scrolling Viewport" program).

If using a screen resolution of 800x600 with 32x32 tiles, your width is fine, but height doesn't quite line up evenly. Cut off the bottom of the scroll window at 576 (which is 18 tiles high), leaving the remaining 24 pixels unused at the bottom. This shouldn't be a problem because you can use that screen real estate for things like an in-game menu system, player status information, or perhaps in-game dialog (not to be confused with the discussion earlier about partial tiles).

We may want to limit the scrolling window to a portion of the screen as it makes more sense than displaying game information over the top of the scrolling window. This holds true unless we are doing something cool like drawing transparent windows over the top of the background. Two more options occur to me: we could just scale the buffer to fill the screen, or we could just draw the extra tile at the bottom and crop it.

Sub-Tile Scroll Buffering

Now we come to *sub-tile scrolling*, the type we need for a slow-paced RPG, in which a character walks around in the game world. This type of game requires a scroller with per-pixel granularity. In other words, scrolling at the pixel level rather than at the full tile level (which was 32 pixels at a time). I've called this method "sub-tile scroll buffering" because the game world needs to scroll slowly in any direction one pixel at a time. Some familiar techniques can be used again, but we need to modify the code quite a bit to support this more advanced form of scrolling.

To help you understand this technique better, I've created two examples. The first example (shown in Figure 7.12) just demonstrates how the scroll buffer

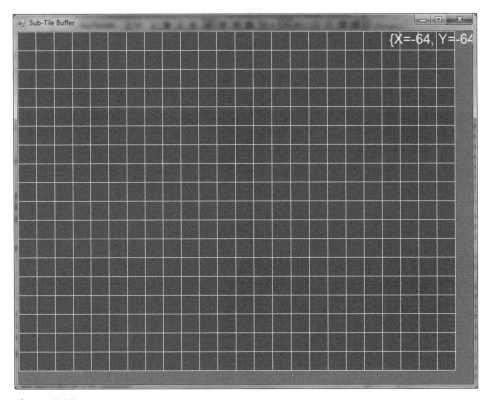

Figure 7.12
The key to dynamic sub-tile scrolling is the buffer border.

works by letting you move the scroll buffer around on the screen. The final example coming up in the next section demonstrates scrolling a game level with this technique. Again, only the key code is shown here for reference, not the complete code listing (with wasteful repeating of code). This project is called Sub-Tile Buffer demo in the chapter's resources.

These two new variables are needed for the new example:

```
Bitmap bmpScrollBuffer;
Graphics gfxScrollBuffer;
```

Here is the main source code for the demo (just the important parts for reference).

```csharp
private void Form1_Load(object sender, EventArgs e)
{
    this.Text = "Sub-Tile Buffer Demo";
    this.Size = new Size(800 + 16, 600 + 38);
    fontArial = new Font("Arial", 18);

    //set up level drawing surface
    bmpSurface = new Bitmap(800, 600);
    pbSurface = new PictureBox();
    pbSurface.Parent = this;
    pbSurface.BackColor = Color.Black;
    pbSurface.Dock = DockStyle.Fill;
    pbSurface.Image = bmpSurface;
    gfxSurface = Graphics.FromImage(bmpSurface);

    //create scroll buffer
    bmpScrollBuffer = new Bitmap(25 * 32 + 64, 19 * 32 + 64);
    gfxScrollBuffer = Graphics.FromImage(bmpScrollBuffer);

    //fill buffer border area
    gfxScrollBuffer.FillRectangle(Brushes.Gray,
        new Rectangle(0, 0, bmpScrollBuffer.Width,
        bmpScrollBuffer.Height));

    //fill buffer screen area
    gfxScrollBuffer.FillRectangle(Brushes.BlueViolet,
        new Rectangle(32, 32, 25 * 32, 19 * 32));

    for (int y = 0; y < 19; y++)
        for (int x = 0; x < 25; x++)
            gfxScrollBuffer.DrawRectangle(Pens.White, 32 + x * 32,
                32 + y * 32, 32, 32);

    gfxScrollBuffer.DrawString("SCROLL BUFFER BORDER", fontArial,
        Brushes.White, 0, 0);

    //create the timer
    timer1 = new Timer();
    timer1.Interval = 20;
    timer1.Enabled = true;
```

```
        timer1.Tick += new EventHandler(timer1_tick);
    }

    private void timer1_tick(object sender, EventArgs e)
    {
        if (keyState.down)
        {
            scrollPos.Y -= 4;
            if (scrollPos.Y < -64) scrollPos.Y = -64;
        }
        if (keyState.up)
        {
            scrollPos.Y += 4;
            if (scrollPos.Y > 0) scrollPos.Y = 0;
        }
        if (keyState.right)
        {
            scrollPos.X -= 4;
            if (scrollPos.X < -64) scrollPos.X = -64;
        }
        if (keyState.left)
        {
            scrollPos.X += 4;
            if (scrollPos.X > 0) scrollPos.X = 0;
        }

        //draw scroll buffer
        gfxSurface.DrawImage(bmpScrollBuffer, scrollPos);

        //print scroll position
        gfxSurface.DrawString(scrollPos.ToString(), fontArial,
Brushes.White, 650, 0);

        //update surface
        pbSurface.Image = bmpSurface;
    }
```

Sub-Tile Smooth Scrolling

Now for the final example of the chapter—the *sub-tile smooth scrolling*. In the
preceding example, you could see how the scroll buffer works with a border

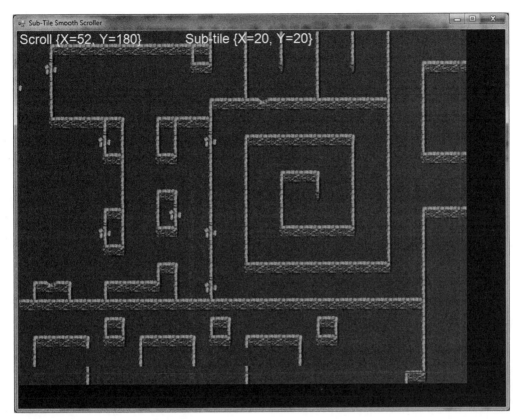

Figure 7.13
Smooth sub-tile scrolling is accomplished using an image buffer.

around the edges of the buffer to take into account the partial tiles. This produces smooth per-pixel scrolling in any direction. Figure 7.13 shows the example program that displays the right and bottom edges of the buffer so you can see how the sub-tile scroller works. (Note: there is a commented-out line of code that will render the scroll buffer smoothly without showing the partial tiles if you wish to see it, but this is more interesting as a learning experience with the tiles left in.)

This tile scroller is now finished. We have data specific to each tile for use in gameplay (such as the Collidable property), and a moving game world. However, there are optimizations that can still be made to this scroller—plus, we might want to create a reusable class to consolidate the code a bit. I think it would be nice if we could just call one function to load the tilemap, and another to draw it at any given position in the game level. This source code is found in the project called Sub-Tile Smooth Scroller in the chapter's resources.

```csharp
using System;
using System.Drawing;
using System.Text;
using System.Windows.Forms;
using System.Xml;

namespace Level_Scroller
{
    public struct tilemapStruct
    {
        public int tilenum;
        public string data1;
        public bool collidable;
    }

    struct keyStates
    {
        public bool up, down, left, right;
    }

    public partial class Form1 : Form
    {
        const int COLUMNS = 5;
        Bitmap bmpSurface;
        PictureBox pbSurface;
        Graphics gfxSurface;
        Font fontArial;
        keyStates keyState;
        Timer timer1;
        tilemapStruct[] tilemap;
        PointF subtile = new PointF(0, 0);
        Bitmap bmpTiles;
        Bitmap bmpScrollBuffer;
        Graphics gfxScrollBuffer;
        PointF scrollPos = new PointF(0, 0);
        PointF oldScrollPos = new PointF(-1, -1);

        public Form1()
```

```
{
    InitializeComponent();
}

private void Form1_Load(object sender, EventArgs e)
{
    this.Text = "Sub-Tile Smooth Scroller";
    this.Size = new Size(900, 700);
    fontArial = new Font("Arial", 18);

    //set up level drawing surface
    bmpSurface = new Bitmap(1024, 768);
    pbSurface = new PictureBox();
    pbSurface.Parent = this;
    pbSurface.BackColor = Color.Black;
    pbSurface.Dock = DockStyle.Fill;
    pbSurface.Image = bmpSurface;
    gfxSurface = Graphics.FromImage(bmpSurface);

    //create tilemap
    tilemap = new tilemapStruct[128 * 128];
    bmpTiles = new Bitmap("palette.bmp");
    loadTilemapFile("level1.level");

    //create scroll buffer
    bmpScrollBuffer = new Bitmap(25 * 32 + 64, 19 * 32 + 64);
    gfxScrollBuffer = Graphics.FromImage(bmpScrollBuffer);

    //create the timer
    timer1 = new Timer();
    timer1.Interval = 20;
    timer1.Enabled = true;
    timer1.Tick += new EventHandler(timer1_tick);
}

private void timer1_tick(object sender, EventArgs e)
{
    int steps = 4;
    if (keyState.up)
    {
```

```
        scrollPos.Y -= steps;
        if (scrollPos.Y < 0) scrollPos.Y = 0;
    }
    if (keyState.down)
    {
        scrollPos.Y += steps;
        if (scrollPos.Y > (127 - 19) * 32) scrollPos.Y =
            (127 - 19) * 32;
    }
    if (keyState.left)
    {
        scrollPos.X -= steps;
        if (scrollPos.X < 0) scrollPos.X = 0;
    }
    if (keyState.right)
    {
        scrollPos.X += steps;
        if (scrollPos.X > (127 - 25) * 32) scrollPos.X =
            (127 - 25) * 32;
    }

    //clear the ground
    //note that this is usually not needed when drawing
    //the game level but this example draws the whole buffer
    gfxSurface.Clear(Color.Black);

    //update and draw the tiles
    drawScrollBuffer();

    //print scroll position
    gfxSurface.DrawString("Scroll " + scrollPos.ToString(),
        fontArial, Brushes.White, 0, 0);
    gfxSurface.DrawString("Sub-tile " + subtile.ToString(),
        fontArial, Brushes.White, 300, 0);

    //draw a rect representing the actual scroll area
    gfxSurface.DrawRectangle(Pens.Blue, 0, 0, 801, 601);
    gfxSurface.DrawRectangle(Pens.Blue, 1, 1, 801, 601);

    //update surface
```

```
    pbSurface.Image = bmpSurface;
}

public void updateScrollBuffer()
{
    //fill scroll buffer with tiles
    int tilenum, sx, sy;
    for (int x = 0; x<26; x++)
        for (int y = 0; y < 20; y++)
        {
            sx = (int)(scrollPos.X / 32) + x;
            sy = (int)(scrollPos.Y / 32) + y;
            tilenum = tilemap[sy * 128 + sx].tilenum;
            drawTileNumber(x, y, tilenum, COLUMNS);
        }
}

public void drawTileNumber(int x, int y, int tile, int columns)
{
    int sx = (tile % columns) * 33;
    int sy = (tile / columns) * 33;
    Rectangle src = new Rectangle(sx, sy, 32, 32);
    int dx = x * 32;
    int dy = y * 32;
    gfxScrollBuffer.DrawImage(bmpTiles, dx, dy, src,
        GraphicsUnit.Pixel);
}

public void drawScrollBuffer()
{
    //fill scroll buffer only when moving
    if (scrollPos != oldScrollPos)
    {
        updateScrollBuffer();
        oldScrollPos = scrollPos;
    }

    //calculate sub-tile size
    subtile.X = scrollPos.X % 32;
    subtile.Y = scrollPos.Y % 32;
```

```
        //create the source rect
        Rectangle source = new Rectangle((int)subtile.X, (int)subtile.Y,
            bmpScrollBuffer.Width, bmpScrollBuffer.Height);

        //draw the scroll viewport
        gfxSurface.DrawImage(bmpScrollBuffer, 1, 1, source,
            GraphicsUnit.Pixel);
    }

    private void Form1_KeyDown(object sender, KeyEventArgs e)
    {
        switch (e.KeyCode)
        {
            case Keys.Up:
            case Keys.W:
                keyState.up = true;
                break;

            case Keys.Down:
            case Keys.S:
                keyState.down = true;
                break;

            case Keys.Left:
            case Keys.A:
                keyState.left = true;
                break;

            case Keys.Right:
            case Keys.D:
                keyState.right = true;
                break;
        }
    }

    private void Form1_KeyUp(object sender, KeyEventArgs e)
    {
        switch (e.KeyCode)
        {
            case Keys.Escape:
```

```
                Application.Exit();
                break;

        case Keys.Up:
        case Keys.W:
            keyState.up = false;
            break;

        case Keys.Down:
        case Keys.S:
            keyState.down = false;
            break;

        case Keys.Left:
        case Keys.A:
            keyState.left = false;
            break;

        case Keys.Right:
        case Keys.D:
            keyState.right = false;
            break;
    }
}

private void loadTilemapFile(string filename)
{
    try
    {
        XmlDocument doc = new XmlDocument();
        doc.Load(filename);
        XmlNodeList nodelist = doc.GetElementsByTagName("tiles");
        foreach (XmlNode node in nodelist)
        {
            XmlElement element = (XmlElement)node;
            int index = 0;
            int value = 0;
            string data1 = "";
            bool collidable = false;

            //read tile index #
```

```
                    index = Convert.ToInt32(element.GetElementsByTagName(
                        "tile")[0].InnerText);

                    //read tilenum
                    value = Convert.ToInt32(element.GetElementsByTagName(
                        "value")[0].InnerText);

                    //read data1
                    data1 = Convert.ToString(element.GetElementsByTagName(
                        "data1")[0].InnerText);

                    //read collidable
                    collidable = Convert.ToBoolean(element.
                        GetElementsByTagName("collidable")[0].InnerText);

                    tilemap[index].tilenum = value;
                    tilemap[index].data1 = data1;
                    tilemap[index].collidable = collidable;
                }
            }
            catch (Exception es)
            {
                MessageBox.Show(es.Message);
            }
        }

        private void Form1_FormClosed(object sender, FormClosedEventArgs e)
        {
            bmpSurface.Dispose();
            pbSurface.Dispose();
            gfxSurface.Dispose();
            bmpScrollBuffer.Dispose();
            gfxScrollBuffer.Dispose();
            fontArial.Dispose();
            timer1.Dispose();
        }

    }
}
```

Level Up!

Wow, that was a ton of great information and some killer source code! This gives us enough information to begin working on the dungeon levels! I don't know about you, but after this long wait, it feels good to have reached this point. Now that we have a level editor and a working level renderer, we can begin working on gameplay. Although the tilemap is drawing, we aren't using any of the extended data fields (such as `Collidable`), which is the topic of the next two chapters! Also, we have that really great `Game` class back in Chapter 3 that will be more useful than the clunky `Timer`, so we'll go to full-time use of the `Game` class and a `while` loop in the next chapter. Speaking of which, Chapter 8 is about adding objects to the dungeon and simulating lighting by hiding or showing things based on their distance from the player!

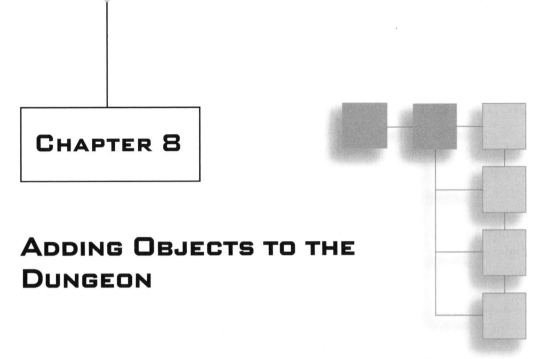

CHAPTER 8

ADDING OBJECTS TO THE DUNGEON

In this chapter we will learn how to add objects to the game world in such a way that they will show up when the viewport scrolls. This will require some coding trickery that goes a bit beyond the usual fare that we've needed so far, so if your experience with the C# language is somewhat on the light side, you will want to pay close attention to the explanations here. We will go back to using the Game class that was first introduced back in Chapter 2, "Drawing Shapes and Bitmaps with GDI+," which handles most of the "framework" code needed for a game that has been put on hold while building the level editor and testing out game levels. But now we can return to the Game class, as well as the Sprite class from Chapter 3, "Sprites and Real-Time Animation."

Here are the goods:

- Adding scenery to the game world
- A new game loop
- Level class
- Adding trees
- Adding an animated character

ADDING OBJECTS TO THE GAME WORLD

Our game level editor works great for creating tilemaps, and it has support for additional data fields and a collision property. But, there comes a point when you need more than just the tilemap data to make a real game—you need interactive objects in the game world as well. So, the first thing we're going to learn in this chapter is how to add some scenery objects, using the tilemap scrolling code developed in the previous chapter. At the same time, we need to address performance. The scrolling code takes up 100% of the processor when the scroll buffer is being refilled continuously. Even if you move the scroll position one pixel, the entire buffer is rebuilt. That is consuming huge amounts of processor time! It might not even be noticeable on a typical multi-core system today, but a laptop user would definitely notice because that tends to use up the battery very quickly. In addition to adding scenery, we'll work on a new core game loop that is more efficient.

A New Game Loop

If you open up the Sub-Tile Smooth Scroller project from the previous chapter, watch it run while looking at your processor's performance in Task Manager. To open Task Manager, you can right-click the Windows toolbar and choose Start Task Manager, or you can press Ctrl+Alt+Delete to bring up the switch user screen to find Task Manager. Figure 8.1 shows Task Manager while the aforementioned demo is running. Note how one of the cores is pretty much maxed out while the others are idle—that's because the program is running in just one thread, and it's pushing the processor pretty hard for such a seemingly simple graphics demo.

The reason for this processor abuse is the use of a timer for rendering. For reference, here is a cropped version of the `timer1_tick()` function from the previous chapter.

```
private void timer1_tick(object sender, EventArgs e)
{
    int steps = 4;
    if (keyState.up)
    {
        scrollPos.Y -= steps;
        if (scrollPos.Y < 0) scrollPos.Y = 0;
```

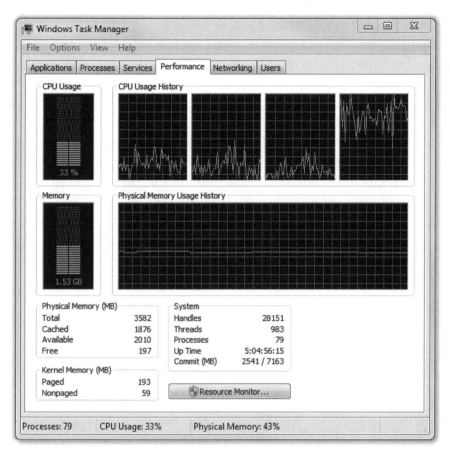

Figure 8.1
Observing processor utilization in Task Manager.

```
    }
  ...
}
```

The `timer` event began firing when the `timer1` object was created via this code in `Form1_Load`:

```
//create the timer
timer1 = new Timer();
timer1.Interval = 20;
timer1.Enabled = true;
timer1.Tick += new EventHandler(timer1_tick);
```

The Timer class was never really intended to be used as the engine for a high-speed game loop! Timers are more often used to fire off signals at regular intervals for hardware devices, to monitor a database for changes, that sort of thing. It does not have very good *granularity*, which means precision at high speed. So, we need to replace the timer with our own real-time loop. I've got just the thing—a while loop. But, Visual C# programs are graphical and forms-based, so we can't just make a loop and do what we want, because that will freeze up the form. Fortunately, there's a function that will do all of the events: Application.DoEvents(). This code can be added to the end of Form1_Load so it's the last thing that runs after everything has been loaded for the game:

```
while (!gameover)
{
    doUpdate();
}
Application.Exit();
```

Reviewing Game.cs

Somewhere in that doUpdate() function, we have to call Application.DoEvents() so the form can be refreshed. If we call it every frame, that will also be wasteful because Application.DoEvents() processes the event messages for form controls (like the Timer as well as for drawing the controls). If we call it every frame, then our game loop will be even more limited than it was with the timer! No, we need to learn just when and where to use this function and that calls for a knowledge of frame-rate timing. Do you recall the Game class from way back in Chapter 3? We will be using the Game class again in this chapter. The Game class contains the FrameRate() method. The Game.FrameRate() method gives us that value.

```
public int FrameRate()
{
    int ticks = Environment.TickCount;
    p_count += 1;
    if (ticks > p_lastTime + 1000)
    {
        p_lastTime = ticks;
        p_frames = p_count;
        p_count = 0;
    }
```

```
    return p_frames;
}
```

This function assumes that the following global variables are defined:

```
int p_count, p_lastTime, p_frames;
```

A New Game Loop

So, we want to start using the Game class again. Game is just a helper class, not an *engine* of sorts, so we do need to supply our own *pump* or *motor* in the form of a loop. Let's take a look at a new doUpdate() function, which is called from the while loop that powers our game. I'll stick with just the bare minimum for now, leaving out any code specific to one example or another, and just show you a skeleton version of the function.

```
private void doUpdate()
{
    //drawing code should be set to 60 fps
    int ticks = Environment.TickCount;
    if (ticks > drawLast + 16)
    {
        drawLast = ticks;
        game.Update();
        Application.DoEvents();
    }
    else
    {
        //throttle the cpu
        Thread.Sleep(1);
    }
}
```

Resolutions

One problem with a game based on Windows Forms and GDI+ is the lack of a fullscreen mode. Although we could extend the resolution of the game window to any desired size, it would be scaled necessarily to that target resolution, not rendered with higher detail. We could, for example, run the game at 1600x1200 by scaling the output of 800x600 by a factor of two. This would work, and the result might look pretty good since it's an even factor (odd factors tend to produce bad results when scaling graphics).

This bare minimum version of doUpdate() handles its own timing and is more action packed than it first appears. First, we need to get the frame rate from the Game class, and this needs to happen *before* the if statement, because it needs to run as fast as possible. Everything within the if statement block of code is *slowed down* code for rendering. Anything we need to draw in the game goes inside that if block.

```
if (ticks > drawLast + 16)
```

The if statement will be true once every 16 milliseconds. Where does that value come from? That is approximately 60 frames per second—a desirable goal for a game.

1 second = 1000 ms

delay = 1000 ms/60 fps

delay = 16.66667 ms

Truncating the decimal part gives our code a few free frames per second, causing the actual frame rate to clock in at around 64 fps, but that depends on the processor—it might be less than 60 on some systems. The point is, we need this uber-vital code in the game loop to keep slow stuff from bottlenecking the whole game! That's exactly what was happening in the projects in the previous chapter that had no time-limiting code.

So, we first get the current system timer value in milliseconds with Environment. TickCount, which will be some large millisecond number like 3828394918. That doesn't matter. What matters is *how many milliseconds* transpire from one frame to the next. Keeping track of that tick value in the drawLast variable allows our code to use it for comparison in the next frame. If at least 16 ms have gone by since the last time drawLast was set, then it's time to draw!

The real frame rate of a game is not the 60 fps draw rate, it's the rate at which the game is updated every frame. That includes any math and physics calculations, collision detection (which can be *very* time consuming!), A.I. for enemy movements, and so on. If we tried to do all of these things inside the 60 fps game loop, it would immediately drop to below that desired refresh rate, all the while many frames are going to waste *outside* the If statement.

Now to address the processor throttling: In the previous chapter, one thread would max out one processor core just to draw the tilemap, which seems silly for such a simple 2D demo. The problem was not the drawing code but the timer. We'll correct that now. If 16 ms have not transpired so that it's time to draw, then we tell the current thread to sleep for 1 ms. This has the effect of allowing the processor core to rest if the game is idling for that short time period. 16 ms is an extremely small amount of time in human terms, but for the computer it's enough time to read a whole book! The `else` statement in the code below kicks in if 16 ms have *not yet* transpired.

```
else
{
    Thread.Sleep(1);
}
```

New Level Class

The tilemap scrolling code has reached a level of critical mass where it's no longer possible to manage it all with global variables and methods—it's time to move all of this code into a class. This will clean up the main source code file for our projects significantly! The new `Level` class will have quite a few private variables, public properties, and public methods. All of the complex code will be hidden and the scroller will function in a turn-key fashion: simply load up a level file, and then call `Update()` and `Draw()` regularly. You will recognize all of the variables and functions present in the previous chapter's example projects, but now they are packaged nicely into the `Level.cs` file. There is *no new code* here—this is all just the same code we've already seen, organized into a class.

```
public class Level
{
    public struct tilemapStruct
    {
        public int tilenum;
        public string data1;
        public string data2;
        public string data3;
        public string data4;
        public bool collidable;
        public bool portal;
        public int portalx;
        public int portaly;
        public string portalfile;
```

```csharp
    }

    private Game p_game;
    private Size p_mapSize = new Size(0, 0);
    private Size p_windowSize = new Size(0, 0);
    private int p_tileSize;
    private Bitmap p_bmpTiles;
    private int p_columns;
    private Bitmap p_bmpScrollBuffer;
    private Graphics p_gfxScrollBuffer;
    private tilemapStruct[] p_tilemap;
    private PointF p_scrollPos = new PointF(0, 0);
    private PointF p_subtile = new PointF(0, 0);
    private PointF p_oldScrollPos = new PointF(-1, -1);

    public Level(ref Game game, int width, int height, int tileSize)
    {
        p_game = game;
        p_windowSize = new Size(width, height);
        p_mapSize = new Size(width * tileSize, height * tileSize);
        p_tileSize = tileSize;

        //create scroll buffer
        p_bmpScrollBuffer = new Bitmap(p_mapSize.Width + p_tileSize,
            p_mapSize.Height + p_tileSize);
        p_gfxScrollBuffer = Graphics.FromImage(p_bmpScrollBuffer);

        //create tilemap
        p_tilemap = new tilemapStruct[128 * 128];
    }

    public tilemapStruct getTile(PointF p)
    {
        return getTile((int)(p.Y * 128 + p.X));
    }

    public tilemapStruct getTile(int pixelx, int pixely)
    {
        return getTile(pixely * 128 + pixelx);
    }
```

```
public tilemapStruct getTile(int index)
{
    return p_tilemap[index];
}

//get/set scroll position by whole tile position
public Point GridPos
{
    get {
        int x = (int)p_scrollPos.X / p_tileSize;
        int y = (int)p_scrollPos.Y / p_tileSize;
        return new Point(x, y);
    }
    set {
        float x = value.X * p_tileSize;
        float y = value.Y * p_tileSize;
        p_scrollPos = new PointF(x, y);
    }
}

//get/set scroll position by pixel position
public PointF ScrollPos
{
    get { return p_scrollPos; }
    set { p_scrollPos = value; }
}


public bool loadTilemap(string filename)
{
    try {
        XmlDocument doc = new XmlDocument();
        doc.Load(filename);
        XmlNodeList nodelist = doc.GetElementsByTagName("tiles");
        foreach (XmlNode node in nodelist)
        {
            XmlElement element = (XmlElement)node;
            int index = 0;
            tilemapStruct ts;
            string data;
```

```
                        //read data fields from xml
                        data = element.GetElementsByTagName("tile")[0].
                            InnerText;
                        index = Convert.ToInt32(data);
                        data = element.GetElementsByTagName("value")[0].
                            InnerText;
                        ts.tilenum = Convert.ToInt32(data);
                        data = element.GetElementsByTagName("data1")[0].
                            InnerText;
                        ts.data1 = Convert.ToString(data);
                        data = element.GetElementsByTagName("data2")[0].
                            InnerText;
                        ts.data2 = Convert.ToString(data);
                        data = element.GetElementsByTagName("data3")[0].
                            InnerText;
                        ts.data3 = Convert.ToString(data);
                        data = element.GetElementsByTagName("data4")[0].
                            InnerText;
                        ts.data4 = Convert.ToString(data);
                        data = element.GetElementsByTagName("collidable")[0].
                            InnerText;
                        ts.collidable = Convert.ToBoolean(data);
                        data = element.GetElementsByTagName("portal")[0].
                            InnerText;
                        ts.portal = Convert.ToBoolean(data);
                        data = element.GetElementsByTagName("portalx")[0].
                            InnerText;
                        ts.portalx = Convert.ToInt32(data);
                        data = element.GetElementsByTagName("portaly")[0].
                            InnerText;
                        ts.portaly = Convert.ToInt32(data);
                        data = element.GetElementsByTagName("portalfile")[0].
                            InnerText;
                        ts.portalfile = Convert.ToString(data);

                        //store data in tilemap
                        p_tilemap[index] = ts;
                    }
                }
                catch (Exception es)
```

```
        {
            MessageBox.Show(es.Message);
            return false;
        }
        return true;
}

public bool loadPalette(string filename, int columns)
{
    p_columns = columns;
    try {
        p_bmpTiles = new Bitmap(filename);
    }
    catch (Exception ex)
    {
        return false;
    }
    return true;
}

public void Update()
{
    //fill the scroll buffer only when moving
    if (p_scrollPos != p_oldScrollPos)
    {
        p_oldScrollPos = p_scrollPos;

        //validate X range
        if (p_scrollPos.X < 0) p_scrollPos.X = 0;
        if (p_scrollPos.X > (127 - p_windowSize.Width) * p_tileSize)
            p_scrollPos.X = (127 - p_windowSize.Width) * p_tileSize;

        //validate Y range
        if (p_scrollPos.Y < 0) p_scrollPos.Y = 0;
        if (p_scrollPos.Y > (127 - p_windowSize.Height) * p_tileSize)
            p_scrollPos.Y = (127 - p_windowSize.Height) * p_tileSize;

        //calculate sub-tile size
        p_subtile.X = p_scrollPos.X % p_tileSize;
        p_subtile.Y = p_scrollPos.Y % p_tileSize;

        //fill scroll buffer with tiles
```

```
            int tilenum, sx, sy;
            for (int x = 0; x < p_windowSize.Width + 1; x++)
                for (int y = 0; y < p_windowSize.Height + 1; y++)
                {
                    sx = (int)p_scrollPos.X / p_tileSize + x;
                    sy = (int)p_scrollPos.Y / p_tileSize + y;
                    tilenum = p_tilemap[sy * 128 + sx].tilenum;
                    drawTileNumber(x, y, tilenum);
                }
        }
    }

    public void drawTileNumber(int x, int y, int tile)
    {
        int sx = (tile % p_columns) * (p_tileSize + 1);
        int sy = (tile / p_columns) * (p_tileSize + 1);
        Rectangle src = new Rectangle(sx, sy, p_tileSize, p_tileSize);
        int dx = x * p_tileSize;
        int dy = y * p_tileSize;
        p_gfxScrollBuffer.DrawImage(p_bmpTiles, dx, dy, src,
            GraphicsUnit.Pixel);
    }

    public void Draw(Rectangle rect)
    {
        Draw(rect.X, rect.Y, rect.Width, rect.Height);
    }

    public void Draw(int width, int height)
    {
        Draw(0, 0, width, height);
    }

    public void Draw(int x, int y, int width, int height)
    {
        Rectangle source = new Rectangle((int)p_subtile.X,
            (int)p_subtile.Y, width, height);
        p_game.Device.DrawImage(p_bmpScrollBuffer, x, y, source,
            GraphicsUnit.Pixel);
    }
}
```

Adding Trees

The first example project in this chapter will add random trees to the game level—or, at least, make it *seem* that trees have been added. Actually, the trees are just drawn over the top of the tilemap scroller at a specific location meant to *appear* to be in the level. The first step to adding interactive objects to the game world involves moving them realistically with the scroller, and drawing those objects that are in view while not drawing any object that is outside the current viewport (which is the scroll position in the level plus the width and height of the window). First, we need to make some improvements to the Sprite class, then we'll get to the random trees afterward. We can use this code to add any object to the game world or dungeon at a random location. But, more importantly, this experiment teaches us an invaluable skill: adding objects at *runtime* using a list. It's easy to add a treasure chest to a dungeon level, using tile data in the level editor, or by manually placing it, but adding treasure *at runtime* is another matter! That's what we need to learn how to do.

Modifying Sprite.cs

It turns out that we need to make some new improvements to the Sprite class introduced back in Chapter 3. The changes are needed not because of a lack of foresight back then, but because of changing needs as work on our game code progresses. Expect future needs and the changes they will require—versatility is important in software development! The Sprite class needs a new version of the Draw() method. Adding a second version of the method will *overload* Draw in the class, giving it more features, but we must be careful not to disrupt any existing code in the process. Specifically, I need to be able to draw a *copy* of a sprite, based on its current animation frame, to any location on the screen, without *changing* the sprite's position. That calls for a new Draw() function that accepts screen coordinates. For reference, here is the existing Draw() function:

```
public void Draw()
{
    Rectangle frame = new Rectangle();
    frame.X = (p_currentFrame % p_columns) * p_size.Width;
    frame.Y = (p_currentFrame / p_columns) * p_size.Height;
    frame.Width = p_size.Width;
    frame.Height = p_size.Height;
```

```
        p_game.Device.DrawImage(p_bitmap, Bounds, frame, GraphicsUnit.Pixel);
}
```

And here is the new addition:

```
public void Draw(int x, int y)
{
    //source image
    Rectangle frame = new Rectangle();
    frame.X = (p_currentFrame % p_columns) * p_size.Width;
    frame.Y = (p_currentFrame / p_columns) * p_size.Height;
    frame.Width = p_size.Width;
    frame.Height = p_size.Height;

    //target location
    Rectangle target = new Rectangle(x, y, p_size.Width, p_size.Height);

    //draw sprite
    p_game.Device.DrawImage(p_bitmap, target, frame, GraphicsUnit.Pixel);
}
```

Adding the Trees

Now that we have a new Level class and modified versions of the Game and Sprite classes, we can finally go over a new example involving interactive objects in the game world. In this example, the objects won't exactly be interactive—yet! The random trees will be visible and will seem to scroll with the tiles. The Random Tree demo program includes optimizations to the game loop, with the addition of the game level renderer (via the Level class), and a linked list of tree sprites that are scattered randomly around the upper-left corner of the game level (so we don't have to move very far to see them all—but it is very easy to scatter the trees throughout the entire level). The source image for the tree scenery objects is shown in Figure 8.2. The images used in the demo are each 64x64 pixels in size. For this demo, I've switched to a grassy level with water and some trails to take a short break from the usual dungeon walls. For the dungeon motif, we could replace the trees with stones, rubble, used torches, broken weapons, and so on.

We are going to work on an over-world level for this example because it's easier to move around on wide-open terrain and the trees illustrate the concept

Figure 8.2
The tree sprite sheet has 32 unique trees and bushes that can be used for scenery. Courtesy of Reiner Prokein.

well—although it might have been fun to fill a walled dungeon level with crates and barrels (staples of the typical dungeon crawler game genre!).

Figure 8.3 shows the Random Trees demo program running. Note the frame rate value! As you can see in the following source code listing, the trees are only randomly placed within the first 1000 pixels, in both the horizontal and vertical directions. Feel free to experiment with the code, extending the range of the trees to the entire level if you wish. Just be mindful of the *number* of objects being added. Although only the visible tree sprites are drawn, the entire list is looked at every frame, which can slow down the program quite a bit if there are too many objects. Why don't you perform a little experiment? See how many trees you can add before the frame rate drops too low to be playable?

Figure 8.3
Random trees are added to the game world.

This example requires a new function in the Game class called Random, so let's take a look at it in advance:

```
public int Random(int max)
{
    return Random(0, max);
}

public int Random(int min, int max)
{
    return p_random.Next(min, max);
}
using System;
using System.Threading;
using System.Collections.Generic;
```

```csharp
using System.Drawing;
using System.Windows;
using System.Windows.Forms;
using System.Xml;

namespace RPG
{
    public partial class Form1 : Form
    {
        public struct keyStates
        {
            public bool up, down, left, right;
        }

        Game game;
        Level level;
        keyStates keyState;
        bool gameover;
        Bitmap treeImage;
        List<Sprite> trees;
        int treesVisible;
        int drawLast;

        public Form1()
        {
            InitializeComponent();
        }

        private void Form1_FormClosed(object sender, FormClosedEventArgs e)
        {
            gameover = true;
        }
        private void Form1_Load(object sender, EventArgs e)
        {
            gameover = false;
            treesVisible = 0;
            drawLast = 0;
            this.Text = "Random Tree Demo";

            //create game object
```

```
Form form = (Form)this;
game = new Game(ref form, 800, 600);

//create tilemap
level = new Level(ref game, 25, 19, 32);
level.loadTilemap("sample.level");
level.loadPalette("palette.bmp", 5);

//load trees
treeImage = game.LoadBitmap("trees64.png");
trees = new List<Sprite>();
for (int n = 0; n< 100;n++)
{
    Sprite tree = new Sprite(ref game);
    tree.Image = treeImage;
    tree.Columns = 4;
    tree.TotalFrames = 32;
    tree.CurrentFrame = game.Random(31);
    tree.Size = new Size(64, 64);
    tree.Position = new PointF(game.Random(1000),
        game.Random(1000));
    trees.Add(tree);
}

while (!gameover)
{
    doUpdate();
}
Application.Exit();
}

private void Form1_KeyDown(object sender, KeyEventArgs e)
{
    switch (e.KeyCode)
    {
        case Keys.Escape: gameover = true; break;
        case Keys.Up:
        case Keys.W: keyState.up = true; break;
        case Keys.Down:
        case Keys.S: keyState.down = true; break;
```

```
            case Keys.Left:
            case Keys.A: keyState.left = true; break;
            case Keys.Right:
            case Keys.D: keyState.right = true; break;
        }
    }

    private void Form1_KeyUp(object sender, KeyEventArgs e)
    {
        switch (e.KeyCode)
        {
            case Keys.Up:
            case Keys.W: keyState.up = false; break;
            case Keys.Down:
            case Keys.S: keyState.down = false; break;
            case Keys.Left:
            case Keys.A: keyState.left = false; break;
            case Keys.Right:
            case Keys.D: keyState.right = false; break;
        }
    }

    private void drawTrees()
    {
        int sx,sy;
        treesVisible = 0;
        foreach (Sprite tree in trees)
        {
            sx = (int)level.ScrollPos.X;
            sy = (int)level.ScrollPos.Y;
            if (tree.X > sx && tree.X < sx + 24 * 32 && tree.Y > sy &&
                tree.Y < sy + 18 * 32)
            {
                int rx = Math.Abs(sx - (int)tree.X);
                int ry = Math.Abs(sy - (int)tree.Y);
                tree.Draw(rx, ry);
                treesVisible += 1;
            }
        }
    }
```

```
private void doUpdate()
{
    //respond to user input
    int steps = 4;
    PointF pos = level.ScrollPos;
    if (keyState.up) pos.Y -= steps;
    if (keyState.down) pos.Y += steps;
    if (keyState.left) pos.X -= steps;
    if (keyState.right) pos.X += steps;
    level.ScrollPos = pos;

    //refresh level renderer
    level.Update();

    //get the untimed core frame rate
    int frameRate = game.FrameRate();

    //drawing code should be limited to 60 fps
    int ticks = Environment.TickCount;
    if (ticks > drawLast + 16)
    {
        drawLast = ticks;

        //draw the tilemap
        level.Draw(0, 0, 800, 600);

        //draw the trees in view
        drawTrees();

        //print da stats
        game.Print(0, 0, "Scroll " + level.ScrollPos.ToString());
        game.Print(250, 0, "Frame rate " + frameRate.ToString());
        game.Print(500, 0, "Visible trees " + treesVisible.
            ToString() + "/100");

        //refresh window
        game.Update();
        Application.DoEvents();
    }
    else
```

```
        {
            //throttle the cpu
            Thread.Sleep(1);
        }
    }
  }
}
```

ADDING AN ANIMATED CHARACTER

Random trees are pretty interesting, but what is not all that fascinating any more is a scrolling game world without any characters in it. We're a little ahead of that subject at this point, which will not be covered until Part III, "Exploring the Dungeon," which begins with Chapter 10, "Creating Characters and Monsters." But, we do need an animated character to walk around and appear to begin interacting with the game world. Figure 8.4 shows the sprite sheet used for the character.

There are nine frames for each animation set and eight directions for a total of 72 frames of animation. Since the diagonal directions require two key presses (such as Up and Left), the diagonals are handled first, and then the four cardinal directions are handled with `Else` statements. The core code for this demo is in the `doUpdate()` function again, as it was in the previous demo. First, we draw the level that has the effect of also erasing the window, which saves processor cycles normally needed to clear the screen. Next, the trees are drawn if they are found within the current scroll region of the level. Finally, the hero character sprite is drawn. There is no sprite z-buffering in this demo—that is, no priority drawing of some sprites over the top of others, something that will need to be addressed in a fully featured game. Figure 8.5 shows the Walk About demo in action.

Exaggerated Dimensions

The characters in the game are clearly out of scale with the environment. In some cases, the player is taller than a full-size tree! This is fairly common in games of this type, drawing attention to the important items on the screen by highlighting them in some way. The characters will have to be somewhat larger than their surroundings so they're visible! If the game screen were rendered with all objects to scale, then characters would be only a few pixels tall compared to a tree. The game screen is a *representation* of the real world—or, at least, of some other world, anyway.

Regarding the tree artwork in this chapter: the trees are just a representation of any environment object you want in your game world. Just change the image and draw houses, signs, rocks, walls, or anything else you can imagine! Think of the trees as just placeholders for any object!

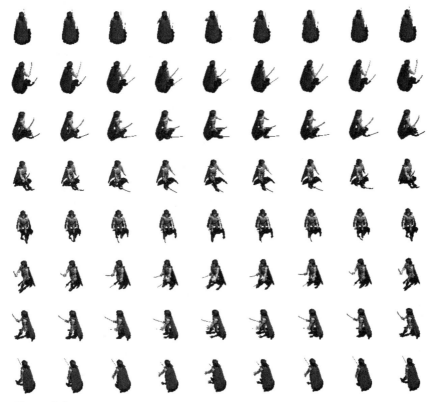

Figure 8.4
This sprite sheet is used for the animated walking character in the demo.

Since this program is very similar to the previous one, only the important code is shown here, not the complete listing. Refer to the chapter's resources for the complete Walk About demo.

```
using System;
using System.Threading;
using System.Collections.Generic;
using System.Drawing;
using System.Windows;
```

Figure 8.5
An animated character now walks in the direction that the scroller is moving.

```
using System.Windows.Forms;
using System.Xml;

namespace RPG
{
    public partial class Form1 : Form
    {
        public struct keyStates
        {
            public bool up, down, left, right;
        }

        Game game;
        Level level;
        keyStates keyState;
```

```
bool gameover = false;
Bitmap treeImage;
List<Sprite> trees;
int treesVisible = 0;
int drawLast = 0;
Sprite hero;
int heroDir = 0;

public Form1()
{
    InitializeComponent();
}

private void Form1_FormClosed(object sender, FormClosedEventArgs e)
{
    gameover = true;
}

private void Form1_Load(object sender, EventArgs e)
{
    this.Text = "Walk About Demo";

    //create game object
    Form form = (Form)this;
    game = new Game(ref form, 800, 600);

    //create tilemap
    level = new Level(ref game, 25, 19, 32);
    level.loadTilemap("sample.level");
    level.loadPalette("palette.bmp", 5);

    //load trees
    treeImage = game.LoadBitmap("trees64.png");
    trees = new List<Sprite>();
    for (int n = 0; n< 100;n++)
    {
        Sprite tree = new Sprite(ref game);
        tree.Image = treeImage;
        tree.Columns = 4;
        tree.TotalFrames = 32;
        tree.CurrentFrame = game.Random(31);
```

```
        tree.Size = new Size(64, 64);
        tree.Position = new PointF(game.Random(1000),
            game.Random(1000));
        trees.Add(tree);
    }

    //load hero
    hero = new Sprite(ref game);
    hero.Image = game.LoadBitmap("hero_sword_walk.png");
    hero.Columns = 9;
    hero.TotalFrames = 9 * 8;
    hero.Size = new Size(96, 96);
    hero.Position = new Point(400 - 32, 300 - 32);
    hero.AnimateWrapMode = Sprite.AnimateWrap.WRAP;
    hero.AnimationRate = 20;

    while (!gameover)
    {
        doUpdate();
    }
    Application.Exit();
}

private void Form1_KeyDown(object sender, KeyEventArgs e)
{
    switch (e.KeyCode)
    {
        case Keys.Escape: gameover = true; break;
        case Keys.Up:
        case Keys.W: keyState.up = true; break;
        case Keys.Down:
        case Keys.S: keyState.down = true; break;
        case Keys.Left:
        case Keys.A: keyState.left = true; break;
        case Keys.Right:
        case Keys.D: keyState.right = true; break;
    }
}

private void Form1_KeyUp(object sender, KeyEventArgs e)
```

```
    {
        switch (e.KeyCode)
        {
            case Keys.Up:
            case Keys.W: keyState.up = false; break;
            case Keys.Down:
            case Keys.S: keyState.down = false; break;
            case Keys.Left:
            case Keys.A: keyState.left = false; break;
            case Keys.Right:
            case Keys.D: keyState.right = false; break;
        }
    }

    private void drawTrees()
    {
        int sx,sy;
        treesVisible = 0;
        foreach (Sprite tree in trees)
        {
            sx = (int)level.ScrollPos.X;
            sy = (int)level.ScrollPos.Y;
            if (tree.X > sx && tree.X < sx + 24 * 32 && tree.Y > sy &&
                tree.Y < sy + 18 * 32)
            {
                int rx = Math.Abs(sx - (int)tree.X);
                int ry = Math.Abs(sy - (int)tree.Y);
                tree.Draw(rx, ry);
                treesVisible += 1;
            }
        }
    }

    private void doUpdate()
    {
        //respond to user input
        int steps = 4;
        PointF pos = level.ScrollPos;
        if (keyState.up) pos.Y -= steps;
        if (keyState.down) pos.Y += steps;
```

```
if (keyState.left) pos.X -= steps;
if (keyState.right) pos.X += steps;
level.ScrollPos = pos;

//orient the player in the right direction
if (keyState.up && keyState.right) heroDir = 1;
else if (keyState.right && keyState.down) heroDir = 3;
else if (keyState.down && keyState.left) heroDir = 5;
else if (keyState.left && keyState.up) heroDir = 7;
else if (keyState.up) heroDir = 0;
else if (keyState.right) heroDir = 2;
else if (keyState.down) heroDir = 4;
else if (keyState.left) heroDir = 6;
else heroDir = -1;

//refresh level renderer
level.Update();

//get the untimed core frame rate
int frameRate = game.FrameRate();

//drawing code should be limited to 60 fps
int ticks = Environment.TickCount;
if (ticks > drawLast + 16)
{
    drawLast = ticks;

    //draw the tilemap
    level.Draw(0, 0, 800, 600);

    //draw the trees in view
    drawTrees();

    //draw the hero
    int startFrame = heroDir * 9;
    int endFrame = startFrame + 8;
    if (heroDir > -1)
        hero.Animate(startFrame, endFrame);
    hero.Draw();
```

```
        //print da stats
        game.Print(0, 0, "Scroll " + level.ScrollPos.ToString());
        game.Print(250, 0, "Frame rate " + frameRate.ToString());
        game.Print(500, 0, "Visible trees " + treesVisible.
            ToString() + "/100");

        //refresh window
        game.Update();
        Application.DoEvents();
    }
    else
    {
        //throttle the cpu
        Thread.Sleep(1);
    }
}
}
}
```

There is one limitation to this first attempt at adding a playable character—due to the way in which the scroller works, we can't move the character all the way into the corner of the game world. The character sprite is fixed to the center of the screen. This will be remedied in the next chapter with some clever code!

LEVEL UP!

We have made quite a bit of positive progress in this chapter with some key features needed for a full-blown RPG. Although a few trees and an animated character don't seem like much to go on so far, we have laid the foundation for the interactive aspects of the game with the meager code in this chapter. Soon, we will be tapping into the data fields of the level data and positioning objects in the game world based on data entered in the level editor, which really makes for the start of a solid data-driven game. The subjects we have covered here are the core of the game that will be expanded upon even further in the next chapter.

CHAPTER 9

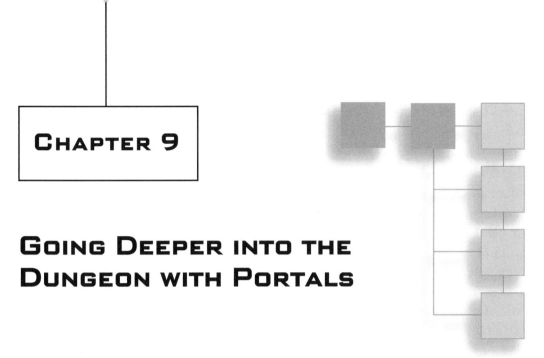

GOING DEEPER INTO THE DUNGEON WITH PORTALS

Up to this point, we have learned quite a bit about creating a game world, and we just started to interact with the game world in the previous chapter. We need to bump it up a notch now by adding to both the editor and the game project the ability to create and use *portals*. A portal is an opening that connects two worlds or allows someone to cross over from one area into another. In terms of a tiled game world, we need a portal that will teleport the player to another location on the map, as well as specify a position on a *different* level file entirely. Once the code to teleport to a new location on a map is understood, adding the ability to teleport to a new level is just a matter of loading that new level file with the Level class and then setting the scroll position to the target X,Y position. The level editor already has fields for portals built in to the tile structure, which we will learn to use in this chapter.

Here's what we'll cover in this chapter:

- Updating the level editor
- Level class modifications
- Teleporting to another dimension
- Looking for tile collisions

UPDATING THE LEVEL CLASS

We need to update the Level class to accommodate the more advanced features of the editor that have gone unused until now. The editor project is available in the chapter's resource files with the full source code, but we already covered the editor in detail back in Chapter 6, "Creating the Dungeon Editor." As you may recall, the content of a .level file is plain XML data that can be viewed and edited in a text editor. Among the tile data fields are four generic data fields that store strings, so you can put any data you want there—whole numbers, decimal numbers, names, descriptions, etc. You could use one as a searchable item name field and then add an item to the game world at that tile location, or even something as exotic as a script function name. Here are the data fields for each tile already supported by the level editor:

- Tile palette number
- Data 1
- Data 2
- Data 3
- Data 4
- Collidable
- Portal
- Portal X
- Portal Y
- Portal file

These fields are sufficient for now, but we can add new ones to meet the design goals for a new game in the future if needed. We need to make a few new changes to the Level class (Level.cs) to handle all of the data fields from a level file. First, the new data fields need to be added to the tilemapStruct structure, and then we need to add a function to return tile data at a specified index in the tilemap so that the player's character sprite can interact with the level. In other words, we need to find out where the portals are and let the character get teleported! Here is the new Level class with an expanded tilemapStruct and loadTilemap() function. The new items are highlighted in bold.

```csharp
public class Level
{
    public struct tilemapStruct
    {
        public int tilenum;
        public string data1;
        public string data2;
        public string data3;
        public string data4;
        public bool collidable;
        public bool portal;
        public int portalx;
        public int portaly;
        public string portalfile;
    }

    private Game p_game;
    private Size p_mapSize = new Size(0, 0);
    private Size p_windowSize = new Size(0, 0);
    private int p_tileSize;
    private Bitmap p_bmpTiles;
    private int p_columns;
    private Bitmap p_bmpScrollBuffer;
    private Graphics p_gfxScrollBuffer;
    private tilemapStruct[] p_tilemap;
    private PointF p_scrollPos = new PointF(0, 0);
    private PointF p_subtile = new PointF(0, 0);
    private PointF p_oldScrollPos = new PointF(-1, -1);

    public Level(ref Game game, int width, int height, int tileSize)
    {
        p_game = game;
        p_windowSize = new Size(width, height);
        p_mapSize = new Size(width * tileSize, height * tileSize);
        p_tileSize = tileSize;

        //create scroll buffer
        p_bmpScrollBuffer = new Bitmap(p_mapSize.Width + p_tileSize,
            p_mapSize.Height + p_tileSize);
        p_gfxScrollBuffer = Graphics.FromImage(p_bmpScrollBuffer);
```

```
    //create tilemap
    p_tilemap = new tilemapStruct[128 * 128];
}

public tilemapStruct getTile(PointF p)
{
    return getTile((int)(p.Y * 128 + p.X));
}

public tilemapStruct getTile(int pixelx, int pixely)
{
    return getTile(pixely * 128 + pixelx);
}

public tilemapStruct getTile(int index)
{
    return p_tilemap[index];
}

//get/set scroll position by whole tile position
public Point GridPos
{
    get
    {
        int x = (int)p_scrollPos.X / p_tileSize;
        int y = (int)p_scrollPos.Y / p_tileSize;
        return new Point(x, y);
    }
    set
    {
        float x = value.X * p_tileSize;
        float y = value.Y * p_tileSize;
        p_scrollPos = new PointF(x, y);
    }
}

//get/set scroll position by pixel position
public PointF ScrollPos
{
    get { return p_scrollPos; }
```

```
        set { p_scrollPos = value; }
}


public bool loadTilemap(string filename)
{
    try
    {
        XmlDocument doc = new XmlDocument();
        doc.Load(filename);
        XmlNodeList nodelist = doc.GetElementsByTagName("tiles");
        foreach (XmlNode node in nodelist)
        {
            XmlElement element = (XmlElement)node;
            int index = 0;
            tilemapStruct ts;
            string data;

            //read data fields from xml
            data = element.GetElementsByTagName("tile")[0].
                InnerText;
            index = Convert.ToInt32(data);
            data = element.GetElementsByTagName("value")[0].
                InnerText;
            ts.tilenum = Convert.ToInt32(data);
            data = element.GetElementsByTagName("data1")[0].
                InnerText;
            ts.data1 = Convert.ToString(data);
            data = element.GetElementsByTagName("data2")[0].
                InnerText;
            ts.data2 = Convert.ToString(data);
            data = element.GetElementsByTagName("data3")[0].
                InnerText;
            ts.data3 = Convert.ToString(data);
            data = element.GetElementsByTagName("data4")[0].
                InnerText;
            ts.data4 = Convert.ToString(data);
            data = element.GetElementsByTagName("collidable")[0].
                InnerText;
            ts.collidable = Convert.ToBoolean(data);
```

```
                data = element.GetElementsByTagName("portal")[0].
                    InnerText;
                ts.portal = Convert.ToBoolean(data);
                data = element.GetElementsByTagName("portalx")[0].
                    InnerText;
                ts.portalx = Convert.ToInt32(data);
                data = element.GetElementsByTagName("portaly")[0].
                    InnerText;
                ts.portaly = Convert.ToInt32(data);
                data = element.GetElementsByTagName("portalfile")[0].
                    InnerText;
                ts.portalfile = Convert.ToString(data);

                //store data in tilemap
                p_tilemap[index] = ts;
            }
        }
        catch (Exception es)
        {
            MessageBox.Show(es.Message);
            return false;
        }
        return true;
    }

    public bool loadPalette(string filename, int columns)
    {
        p_columns = columns;
        try
        {
            p_bmpTiles = new Bitmap(filename);
        }
        catch (Exception ex)
        {
            return false;
        }
        return true;
    }

    public void Update()
```

```
{
    //fill the scroll buffer only when moving
    if (p_scrollPos != p_oldScrollPos)
    {
        p_oldScrollPos = p_scrollPos;

        //validate X range
        if (p_scrollPos.X < 0) p_scrollPos.X = 0;
        if (p_scrollPos.X > (127 - p_windowSize.Width) * p_tileSize)
            p_scrollPos.X = (127 - p_windowSize.Width) * p_tileSize;

        //validate Y range
        if (p_scrollPos.Y < 0) p_scrollPos.Y = 0;
        if (p_scrollPos.Y > (127 - p_windowSize.Height) * p_tileSize)
            p_scrollPos.Y = (127 - p_windowSize.Height) * p_tileSize;

        //calculate sub-tile size
        p_subtile.X = p_scrollPos.X % p_tileSize;
        p_subtile.Y = p_scrollPos.Y % p_tileSize;

        //fill scroll buffer with tiles
        int tilenum, sx, sy;
        for (int x = 0; x < p_windowSize.Width + 1; x++)
            for (int y = 0; y < p_windowSize.Height + 1; y++)
            {
                sx = (int)p_scrollPos.X / p_tileSize + x;
                sy = (int)p_scrollPos.Y / p_tileSize + y;
                tilenum = p_tilemap[sy * 128 + sx].tilenum;
                drawTileNumber(x, y, tilenum);
            }
    }
}

public void drawTileNumber(int x, int y, int tile)
{
    int sx = (tile % p_columns) * (p_tileSize + 1);
    int sy = (tile / p_columns) * (p_tileSize + 1);
    Rectangle src = new Rectangle(sx, sy, p_tileSize, p_tileSize);
    int dx = x * p_tileSize;
    int dy = y * p_tileSize;
```

```
        p_gfxScrollBuffer.DrawImage(p_bmpTiles, dx, dy, src,
            GraphicsUnit.Pixel);
    }

    public void Draw(Rectangle rect)
    {
        Draw(rect.X, rect.Y, rect.Width, rect.Height);
    }

    public void Draw(int width, int height)
    {
        Draw(0, 0, width, height);
    }

    public void Draw(int x, int y, int width, int height)
    {
        Rectangle source = new Rectangle((int)p_subtile.X,
            (int)p_subtile.Y, width, height);
        p_game.Device.DrawImage(p_bmpScrollBuffer, x, y, source,
            GraphicsUnit.Pixel);
    }
}
```

IT'S A DATA-DRIVEN GAME WORLD

In the previous chapter, we learned how to create a list of tree sprites and draw them in the game world, so that when the player moves around the trees come into view within the scrolling viewport. That works well when you want to scatter random environment items like bushes, houses, coffee shops, software stores, and, well, anything you want. We can also use the level editor to position objects at a specific location, which is more useful than using randomness, especially when you need to count on a certain thing being at a certain location. For instance, you might have a quest that has the player find a certain landmark where nearby a treasure is buried.

The data fields are numbered 1 to 4, and can contain *any* type of data—numbers or strings. If we used these fields to position an item, we could use them like so:

Data 1: Item number

Data 2: Position x

Data 3: Position y

Data 4: Script function

The item number would be out of the game item database, or it could be the number or *name* of a sprite. The x,y position of the item is next in Data 2 and 3. The fourth one is a bit interesting. What is a script function? This goes a bit beyond the scope of this book, but if we wanted to *really* make this level editor and game engine interesting, we could add Lua script support to the game. Lua is an interpreted programming language—meaning, Lua source code is not compiled; it is simply stored in a text file and treated as text, and yet the Lua interpreter will *run* our script code at runtime. The ramifications for scripting are enormous. Imagine being able to edit a script *without restarting the game*. Yes, that's possible: edit the script, save it, then load and execute the script with the Lua interpreter. Like I said, this gets a bit complicated, but it adds a tremendous amount of design freedom to the game, which is otherwise bound by its data and engine. We will add Lua scripting support to the game in the next section.

Now we need to look at some code to make this all work. Among other things, we have some work to do in the `loadTilemap()` function now because of the new fields.

Creating a Portal

A portal is a doorway to another dimension. Or, in the case of our editor here, a new x,y location on the map. Or on another map file! Let's start with a series of portals on a single map and then look at how to portal to another world. Take a look at the data for the highlighted tile in Figure 9.1. The Portal flag is checked, while the x and y fields are set to coordinates (101,16). The examples here are shown using an above-ground representation of the game world instead of a dungeon level, for the sake of clarity—the dungeon levels are both smaller and harder to move around in.

The location (101,16) is on the right side of the map, shown in Figure 9.2. What we want to do is have the game jump to that location when our character walks into the portal tile. Nearby, the target location is another portal tile.

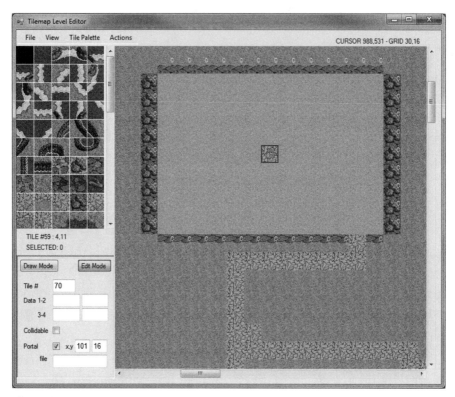

Figure 9.1
Creating a portal using the portal data fields.

In case you are wondering why the two portals aren't linked directly together, that is something you can play with if you want, but if you point one portal to a tile that contains *another* portal, then your character will teleport twice. Unless you want that kind of behavior, don't link portal squares directly—have one drop off the player nearby but not directly on another portal. Or, go ahead and do it and see for yourself what happens! In our example, you must press Space to trigger a portal, but if you use automatic teleporting then the player could be teleported repeatedly, possibly even getting stuck in a portal loop.

Teleporting to Another Dimension

The first thing we need to do to get portals working is to isolate the portion of the character sprite that is actually on the "ground," so to speak. By default, the player sprite (which is called hero in our code) is positioned on the screen in the

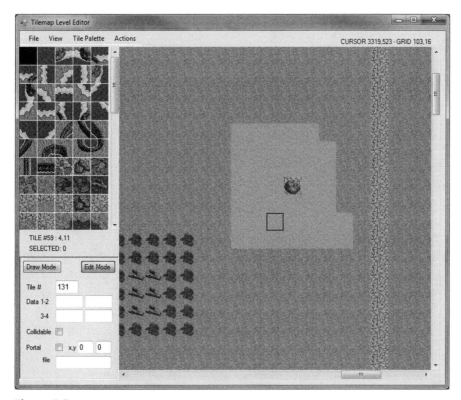

Figure 9.2
The target location of the first portal on the map is (103,16).

upper-left corner. Since the sprite is 96x96 pixels in size, there's a lot of area taken up by the sprite that is much larger than the 32x32 tiles. If we use the upper-left corner, then the player will be interacting with tiles on the ground from a position above and to the left of his or her head! That definitely won't work. So, we need to adjust the position used to determine what tile the player is walking on—we need to isolate the player's feet. Figure 9.3 shows the collision boxes for the player sprite. The blue box represents the entire character's collision box, while the small red box (and red dot) represent the walking collision box.

The small red collision box, and the red dot at its center, is what we actually want to use as a center point to determine which tile the sprite is "walking on." Thus, when the player walks onto a portal tile, it will accurately look as if the sprite's feet touched the tile before the teleport occurred. The Portal demo

Figure 9.3
Isolating the player sprite's "foot" contact with the ground.

program looks at that coordinate as a position relative to the scroll position and then retrieves the data for the tile at that location. Figure 9.4 shows information about the portal tile the player is standing on—note the message in the upper-left corner of the window.

In the game, it's up to you how the portals will work. You can make them automatically teleport the player just by merely walking on the tile, or you can require the player to take some action—perhaps using an item to trigger the

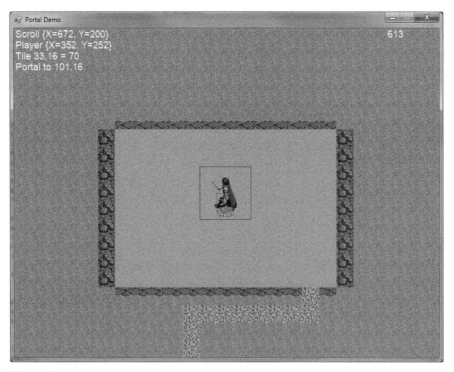

Figure 9.4
Detecting when the player walks on a portal tile.

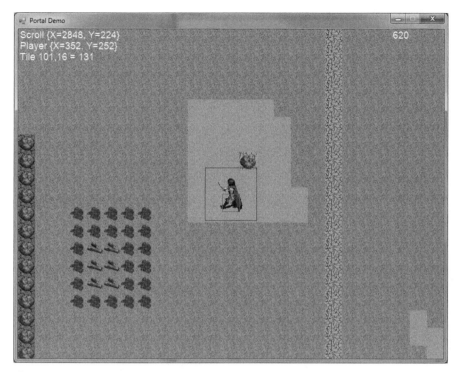

Scroll {X=2848, Y=224}
Player {X=352, Y=252}
Tile 101,16 = 131

620

Figure 9.5
The portal has sent the player across the map!

portal. In our program, the Space key is the trigger. When the portal is engaged, the player is teleported to the target coordinate (101,16), as shown in Figure 9.5.

Trick

Getting tired of the same old ground tiles in every example? Replace them! You are encouraged to use a different set of ground tiles or add new ones to this collection. I am only using these same tiles for consistency. You may replace the tiles in the level editor and in the game. The only requirement is that your tile palette image be oriented like the one presented in the book and that the tiles remain at 32x32 pixels in size. Otherwise, some coding changes will be needed.

Looking for Tile Collisions

The Portal demo program also looks for the Collidable property in tiles and reports on the screen when a collidable tile is identified. Figure 9.6 shows the message that is printed when the player walks over a collidable tile. Although the

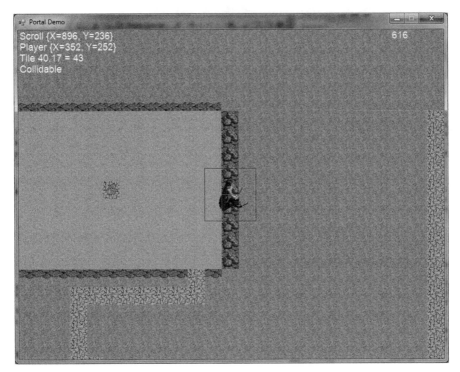

Figure 9.6
Detecting collidable tiles.

sprite doesn't respond to collidable tiles yet in this example, we can use this information to enable collision response in the next major revision to the game.

Hint

This quick example is not quite polished yet, so expect to see some jittery sprites and timing problems. The point is to get these features to work first, and then make them work *great* afterward!

Secret Doors

With the portal system working, we can now use it to create secret doors to appear to walk through walls! A portal is just a tile property that defines a target location for the player to be moved to. If you set the target for a portal to a tile just one or two spaces away, then it can appear as if the player is hopping over an obstacle. You could use this technique to get past solid objects or walls, which would be even more effective if a trigger object or key is required.

Portal Demo Program

Here is the source code for the Portal demo program.

```
using System;
using System.Collections.Generic;
using System.Threading;
using System.Data;
using System.Drawing;
using System.Windows.Forms;
using RPG;

namespace Portal_Project
{
    public partial class Form1 : Form
    {
        public struct keyStates
        {
            public bool up, down, left, right;
        }

        Game game;
        Level level;
        keyStates keyState;
        bool gameover = false;
        Sprite hero;
        int heroDir = 0;
        bool portalFlag = false;
        Point portalTarget;
        int drawLast = 0;

        public Form1()
        {
            InitializeComponent();
        }

        private void Form1_Load(object sender, EventArgs e)
        {
```

```
        this.Text = "Portal Demo";

        //create game object
        Form form = (Form)this;
        game = new Game(ref form, 800, 600);

        //create tilemap
        level = new Level(ref game, 25, 19, 32);
        level.loadTilemap("portals.level");
        level.loadPalette("palette.bmp", 5);

        //load hero
        hero = new Sprite(ref game);
        hero.Image = game.LoadBitmap("hero_sword_walk.png");
        hero.Columns = 9;
        hero.TotalFrames = 9 * 8;
        hero.Size = new Size(96, 96);
        hero.Position = new Point(400 - 48, 300 - 48);
        hero.AnimateWrapMode = Sprite.AnimateWrap.WRAP;
        hero.AnimationRate = 20;

        while (!gameover)
        {
            doUpdate();
        }
        Application.Exit();
    }

    private void Form1_KeyUp(object sender, KeyEventArgs e)
    {
        switch (e.KeyCode)
        {
            case Keys.Escape : gameover = true; break;
            case Keys.Up:
            case Keys.W : keyState.up = false; break;
            case Keys.Down:
            case Keys.S : keyState.down = false; break;
            case Keys.Left:
            case Keys.A : keyState.left = false; break;
            case Keys.Right:
```

```
            case Keys.D : keyState.right = false; break;
            case Keys.Space:
                if (portalFlag) level.GridPos = portalTarget;
                break;
        }
    }

    private void Form1_KeyDown(object sender, KeyEventArgs e)
    {
        switch (e.KeyCode)
        {
            case Keys.Up:
            case Keys.W: keyState.up = true; break;
            case Keys.Down:
            case Keys.S: keyState.down = true; break;
            case Keys.Left:
            case Keys.A: keyState.left = true; break;
            case Keys.Right:
            case Keys.D: keyState.right = true; break;
        }
    }

    private void doUpdate()
    {
        //move the tilemap scroll position
        int steps = 8;
        PointF pos = level.ScrollPos;

        //up key movement
        if (keyState.up)
        {
            if (hero.Y > 300 - 48) hero.Y -= steps;
            else
            {
                pos.Y -= steps;
                if (pos.Y <= 0) hero.Y -= steps;
            }

        }
        //down key movement
```

```
else if (keyState.down)
{
    if (hero.Y < 300 - 48)
        hero.Y += steps;
    else
    {
        pos.Y += steps;
        if (pos.Y >= (127 - 19) * 32) hero.Y += steps;
    }
}

//left key movement
if (keyState.left)
{
    if (hero.X > 400 - 48) hero.X -= steps;
    else
    {
        pos.X -= steps;
        if (pos.X <= 0) hero.X -= steps;
    }
}
//right key movement
else if (keyState.right)
{
    if (hero.X < 400 - 48) hero.X += steps;
    else
    {
        pos.X += steps;
        if (pos.X >= (127 - 25) * 32) hero.X += steps;
    }
}

//update scroller position
level.ScrollPos = pos;
level.Update();

//limit player sprite to the screen boundary
if (hero.X < -32) hero.X = -32;
else if (hero.X > 800 - 65) hero.X = 800 - 65;
if (hero.Y < -48) hero.Y = -48;
```

```
else if (hero.Y > 600 - 81) hero.Y = 600 - 81;

//orient the player in the right direction
if (keyState.up && keyState.right) heroDir = 1;
else if (keyState.right && keyState.down) heroDir = 3;
else if (keyState.down && keyState.left) heroDir = 5;
else if (keyState.left && keyState.up) heroDir = 7;
else if (keyState.up) heroDir = 0;
else if (keyState.right) heroDir = 2;
else if (keyState.down) heroDir = 4;
else if (keyState.left) heroDir = 6;
else heroDir = -1;

//get the untimed core frame rate
int frameRate = game.FrameRate();

//drawing code should be limited to 60 fps
int ticks = Environment.TickCount;
if (ticks > drawLast + 16)
{
    drawLast = ticks;

    //draw the tilemap
    level.Draw(0, 0, 800, 600);

    //draw the hero
    int startFrame = heroDir * 9;
    int endFrame = startFrame + 8;
    if (heroDir > -1) hero.Animate(startFrame, endFrame);
    hero.Draw();

    //print da stats
    game.Print(700, 0, frameRate.ToString());
    int y = 0;
    game.Print(0, y, "Scroll " + level.ScrollPos.ToString());
    y += 20;
    game.Print(0, y, "Player " + hero.Position.ToString());
    y += 20;

    Point feet = HeroFeet();
```

```
        int tilex = (int)(level.ScrollPos.X + feet.X) / 32;
        int tiley = (int)(level.ScrollPos.Y + feet.Y) / 32;
        Level.tilemapStruct ts = level.getTile(tilex, tiley);
        game.Print(0, y, "Tile " + tilex.ToString() + "," +
            tiley.ToString() + " = " + ts.tilenum.ToString());
        y += 20;
        if (ts.collidable)
        {
            game.Print(0, y, "Collidable");
            y += 20;
        }
        if (ts.portal)
        {
            game.Print(0, y, "Portal to " + ts.portalx.ToString() +
                "," + ts.portaly.ToString());
            portalFlag = true;
            portalTarget = new Point(ts.portalx - feet.X / 32,
                ts.portaly - feet.Y / 32);
            y += 20;
        }
        else
            portalFlag = false;

        //highlight collision areas around player
        game.Device.DrawRectangle(Pens.Blue, hero.Bounds);
        game.Device.DrawRectangle(Pens.Red, feet.X + 16 - 1,
            feet.Y + 16 - 1, 2, 2);
        game.Device.DrawRectangle(Pens.Red, feet.X, feet.Y, 32, 32);

        //refresh window
        game.Update();
        Application.DoEvents();
    }
    else
    {
        //throttle the cpu
        Thread.Sleep(1);
    }
}
```

```
        //return bottom center position of hero sprite
        //where feet are touching ground
        private Point HeroFeet()
        {
            return new Point((int)(hero.X + 32), (int)(hero.Y + 32 + 16));
        }
    }
}
```

LEVEL UP!

This chapter saw some dramatic improvements to both the Level class and the Dungeon Crawler game engine code, with the addition of code to detect collidable tiles, and code to make portals active, allowing us to teleport the player to a new location. Although the level editor provides the "portalfile" field to enable teleporting to a position in a *different* level file, we will reserve that feature for later. Believe it or not, we now have a game world that is suitable as an environment for the Dungeon Crawler game! That means we can shift focus from the game world and level editing over to a new subject—people and monsters!

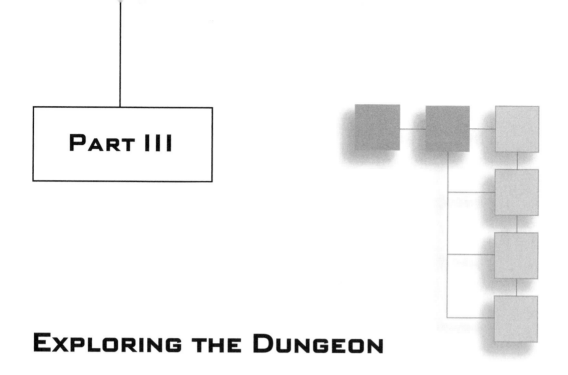

PART III

EXPLORING THE DUNGEON

This third part of the book focuses on the gameplay perspective—creating the various parts of our Dungeon Crawler game that bring it to life. Up to this point, we have been so focused on just getting something up on the screen and working as it should, we haven't had much time to explore gameplay. Now we have a game world and all of the engine-level features we need for the game. This part starts with a chapter on creating a character editor and using custom character files in the game. Chapters 11 and 12 then expand on characters by exploring a dialogue system, NPCs, and the combat side of the game. Chapters 13 and 14 develop an inventory system, making it possible to loot treasure and items. Finally, in the last two chapters, code is developed to fill the dungeon with treasure and monsters.

- Chapter 10: Creating Characters and Monsters
- Chapter 11: Dialogue: Trainers, Vendors and NPCs
- Chapter 12: Fighting Monsters, Gaining Experience, and Leveling Up
- Chapter 13: Equipping Gear and Looting Treasure
- Chapter 14: Populating the Dungeon
- Chapter 15: Deep Places of the World

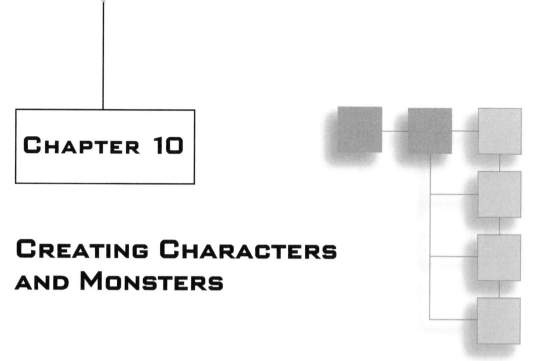

CHAPTER 10

CREATING CHARACTERS AND MONSTERS

This chapter covers character creation using a custom editor tool, and discusses the usual attributes associated with an RPG based on character race, class, and so on. You will learn how to take the designs of the character classes and make use of them in the game by applying the player character's attributes to the combat system and other aspects of any traditional RPG, such as gaining experience and leveling up. Some of these issues will be dealt with in more detail in upcoming chapters, whereas the foundation is laid here for working with character data. The character editor uses the same XML format that was used by the level editor, so we will be able to use similar code in a new Character class to load character data files in C#.

Here's what we'll cover in this chapter:

- Character classes and attributes
- Gaining experience and leveling up
- Base character classes
- Enemy and monster classes
- Loading character files in the game
- Character artwork

CHARACTER CLASSES AND ATTRIBUTES

All of the previous chapters have focused on the difficult task of getting a fully animated player to walk around in a scrolling game world. Both the animation and the movement should be semi-realistic, and tile-collision detection should prevent the player from walking through solid and impassable tiles (which still requires some work but is coming together), and using portals. Now that these basic problems have been solved, we can get into the game's design and the nuances of combat and NPC interaction.

Attributes

Attributes determine what a character is capable of doing in the game, whether it's swinging a sword, firing arrows, or defending against attacks from others. The player attributes are the most important part of the character creation process that follows.

Strength (STR)

Strength represents the character's ability to carry weight and deal damage with a melee weapon. It is generally good for the `warrior` and `paladin` classes, which use melee weapons. Strength is used to calculate the attack damage for the character if a hit is successful (see "Dexterity (DEX)" for details on the "to hit" factor). First, the player has to *hit* the target before damage is calculated. So, even an enormous amount of STR will rarely come into play if dexterity is too low. Therefore, both of these attributes are crucial for a melee fighter! STR is of little use to a priest (who favors intellect) and is of minor import to a hunter (who relies more on dexterity).

Dexterity (DEX)

Dexterity represents the agility of a character—the skillful use of one's hands. This affects the ability to wield melee weapons and shields effectively to block and parry attacks and to hit accurately with a ranged weapon such as a bow. Low DEX leads to a somewhat clumsy character, while high DEX means the character can perform complex actions (perhaps wielding two weapons). Dexterity determines the defense and the chance to hit factors in combat. See Chapter 12, "Fighting Monsters, Gaining Experience, and Leveling Up," for more details on combat calculations. The "chance to hit" value is rolled against the defender's defense value to determine if an attack is successful. Thus, it is of little use for a level 1 character to attack someone who is level 20, because he will not be able to land hits, let alone do any damage.

Stamina (STA)

Stamina represents a character's endurance, the ability to continue performing an activity for a long period of time, and it is used directly in the calculation of hit points (health). High STA provides a character with the ability to engage in lengthy battles without rest, while low STA causes a character to get tired quickly and fall in battle. Although every class benefits from stamina, it is more vital for the melee characters since they engage in "in your face" combat. Although a low STA will lead a hunter or priest to fall just as quickly, they aren't likely to take as many hits since they attack at range.

Intellect (INT)

Intellect represents the character's ability to learn, remember things, and solve problems. A very high INT is required by the `priest` class, while relatively low INT is common in fighters where brute force is more important than mental faculties. Also, INT affects the amount of experience gained for performing actions such as defeating enemies and completing quests, so a character with high INT will level up more quickly. This is important for the ranged classes since they usually have fewer battles.

Charisma (CHA)

Charisma represents the character's attractiveness, which affects how others respond to the character. High CHA attracts people, while low CHA repels them—although in the violent world of the dungeon crawler, a "pretty boy" is of little use even to the ladies. In the converse, low CHA also represents the ugliness of a monster such as an undead zombie. CHA does not represent just a character or monster's scariness, but is more related to personality and physical attractiveness. In other words, it is possible for a dangerous creature (such as a dragon) to be beautiful.

Hit Points

Hit points, or HP, represent the amount of health a character has. HP is calculated initially (at level 1) by adding a D8 roll to the character's stamina.

Then, each time the character levels, additional HP is added with another die roll. Thus, it is entirely possible to create a weakling of a warrior (by consistently rolling badly) who has less HP than even a priest. It's all left to chance, which is what makes RPGs so universally compelling. Purists will play with their rolled stats, while less serious players will re-roll their character until they get the points that they want. Generally, the class modifiers make up for bad initial rolls.

Gaining Experience and Leveling Up

One of the most rewarding aspects of an RPG is gaining experience by performing actions in the game (usually combat) and leveling up your character. When you start the game, the character is also just starting out as a level 1 with no experience. This reflects the player's own skill level with the game itself, and that is the appeal of an RPG: *You*, the player, gain experience with the game while your character gains experience at the same time in the virtual world. You grow together and become a seamless "person."

Both you and your character improve as you play the game, so you transfer some of your own identity to the character, and in some cases, younger players even assume some of the identity of their inspiring hero. This fascinating give-and-take relationship can really draw someone into your game if you design it well! Like I have said, cut back on the magic and let players really get in the game world and experience some good, solid combat to make the whole experience feel more real, and less detached. You want to do everything possible to suspend the players' disbelief that they are in a game—you want to bring them into your game world by doing things that cause them to invest emotionally in their characters.

The most common way to gain experience is through combat with monsters and enemy characters. Since there are a lot of calculations involved in the chance to hit, armor class, melee attack, ranged attack, spell attack, and other factors, I will reserve Chapter 12 for a discussion of the mechanics of combat.

The Base Character Classes

The standard, or base, classes can be used for the player as well as for the non-player characters (NPCs). You should feel free to create as many classes as you want to make your game world diversified and interesting. The classes I have described here are just the usual classes you find in an RPG, which you might consider the stock classes. Each class also has subclasses, or specialties within that class. For instance, Paladins are really just a subclass of the Knight, which may include Teutonic Knight, Crusader, and so on.

When you are designing a game, you can make it as historically accurate or as fictional as you want; don't feel compelled to make every class realistic or historically based. You might make up a fictional type of Knight subclass, such as a Dark Knight or Gothic Knight, with some dark magic abilities. However, I want to encourage you to shy away from overdoing the magic system in a game. Many RPGs have character classes that might be thought of as wizards on steroids, because the whole game boils down to upgrading spells and magic, with little emphasis on "realistic" combat.

You would be surprised by how effective an RPG can be with just a *few* magic abilities. You can really go overboard with the hocus pocus, and that tends to trivialize a well-designed storyline and render interesting characters into fireball targets. No warrior should be able to do *any* magic whatsoever. Think about it: The warriors are basically barbarians—massive, hulking fighters who use brute force to bash skulls on the battlefield (think Arnold Schwarzenegger in the *Conan* movies). This type of character can become civilized and educated, but so many games blur the line here and allow any class to develop magical abilities. (I'm just pointing out some obvious design concerns with characters. If you really want a world of magic, then go ahead and create magical characters; that sounds like a really fun game, as a matter of fact!) If you are designing a traditional RPG, then be realistic with your classes and keep the magic reasonable. Think about *The Lord of the Rings*; these stories are a source of inspiration for every RPG ever made. Everything since J.R.R. Tolkien has been derivative!

The character editor tool has the ability to apply modifiers to the basic stats, but this is a manual process. If you add new classes to the `cboClass` list in the editor, then you'll have to make changes to the modifiers manually in the code (hint: look for the code in `cboClass_SelectedIndexChanged()`).

One design consideration that we might use is the concept of class modifiers. Say you have a set of stock classes like those listed in the upcoming tables. Instead of re-creating a class from scratch using similar values, you can create a subclass based on the parent class—and modify the attributes by a small amount to produce the new class with custom attributes.

Say, for instance, that you want to create a new type of Warrior called the Berserker, which is an extremely stupid and ugly character with immense strength and stamina. Sounds a little bit scary, doesn't it? By setting the base class of the Berserker to Warrior, you can then modify the base class at any time and the Berserker automatically is changed along with the base class (Warrior). This works great for balancing the gameplay without requiring that you modify *every single* subclass that you have used in the game. Since our character class system in the dungeon crawler is based on classes, we can easily subclass the base character classes to create new types of characters in this manner.

Hint

It goes without saying that female characters are fun to play with in an RPG. Unfortunately, we have no female equivalents to the four player characters represented in the game artwork. Yes, there are some female NPCs available in the artwork from Reiner Prokein, but not for the primary character classes. If you have artwork available, I encourage you to add a gender property to the character editor. Gender is not extremely important to the gameplay, as it turns out.

Tables 10.1 to 10.4 present my idea of a character class structure that is programmed into the editor. Since this only applies to the editor, and not to any game source code, you may modify the editor to use your own preferred values and classes.

To keep your game character classes balanced, it's important to use a standard total for all modifiers so that they all add up to the same amount. I have based the following class modifiers on a total of 15 points. In testing the game, it seemed that values much lower made the hero characters less impressive (compared to, say, a peasant), while values much higher resulted in unusually powerful characters. If you want a character to have one very high attribute, then that will have to be balanced with an equally low value for another. Note also that monsters need not follow this standard—go ahead and use whatever factors you want to create unique foes. The goal of this point modifier system is to create player characters that are based on the same fixed number of attribute points.

Hint

The character class modifiers should add up to a total of 15 points. The points can be applied to any of the attributes. These mod values are then added to 2D6 rolls to come up with the total attribute values.

Warrior Class

The `warrior` class represents the strongest melee fighter who deals enormous crushing blows against his opponents, but who is not especially accurate at lower levels. Warriors are like home run hitters, in that they tend to knock it out of the park or strike out. In gameplay, a low-level warrior will miss a lot but then do massive damage when he does land a blow, which usually takes out most lower-level creatures. At higher levels, warriors gain an appreciable amount of DEX that compensates for the initial low starting value. Since the warrior is a rage-filled barbarian, he has low INT and CHA because these attributes are not important. Warriors can wear chain or plate armor, and have abilities like rage and berserk that boost his attributes during combat. Drawing from inspiration such as Tolkien, one might look to Gimli.

Table 10.1 Warrior Attributes

Attribute	Roll	Modifiers (+15)
Strength	2D6	+8
Dexterity	2D6	+3
Stamina	2D6	+4
Intellect	2D6	0
Charisma	2D6	0
Hit Points	1D8	+STA

Table 10.2 Paladin Attributes

Attribute	Roll	Modifiers (+15)
Strength	2D6	+3
Dexterity	2D6	+3
Stamina	2D6	+8
Intellect	2D6	0
Charisma	2D6	+1
Hit Points	1D8	+STA

Paladin Class

The paladin is a balanced melee fighter with massive survivability. Classically, a paladin was a melee fighter with some healing abilities, making him a cross between warrior and priest. If you want to follow this traditional view of the `paladin` class, you may do so. I have taken a simpler approach to the paladin, making him slightly less damaging than the warrior but able to take more damage. While the single point in CHA might seem like a waste, it reflects the nature of the paladin as an attractive, heroic knight. He has abilities that give a temporary boost to his weapons and armor points. Paladins can wear chain or plate armor, preferring the most brightly polished pieces of gear they can find. Drawing from popular inspiration, one might look to the Tolkien characters Baromir or Eomer.

Hunter Class

The hunter is a ranged class with no melee combat ability, but capable of dealing massive damage with a bow. Hunters are fast on their feet, wear light leather armor, and usually have many different types of arrows for their favorite bow. Hunters have a high DEX to improve ranged chance to hit, with less use for traits like STR and INT. Abilities revolve around ranged attack modifiers that improve accuracy (chance to hit). A good example from which to draw inspiration is the Tolkien character Legolas.

Table 10.3 Hunter Attributes		
Attribute	**Roll**	**Modifiers (+15)**
Strength	2D6	+2
Dexterity	2D6	+8
Stamina	2D6	+4
Intellect	2D6	0
Charisma	2D6	+1
Hit Points	1D8	+STA

Priest Class

The `priest` class represents a holy man of the cloth who has been forced to fight the rampaging undead horde that has been destroying everything in its path. A priest is unlike a traditional magic user, both unwilling and unable to call on the evil powers required to conjure magic known to traditional wizards and mages (whom he would consider opponents). A priest uses holy power to fight evil, undead creatures, never to attack other human beings. His abilities include healing and exorcism. A loose example from Tolkien's universe might be Arwen.

Table 10.4 Priest Attributes

Attribute	Roll	Modifiers (+15)
Strength	2D6	0
Dexterity	2D6	+6
Stamina	2D6	+1
Intellect	2D6	+8
Charisma	2D6	0
Hit Points	1D8	+STA

Peasants as NPCs

In addition to these player character classes, you might want to create base classes for some of the regular people in the world, like townsfolk, peasants, farmers, and so on. These non-combat NPCs might all just share the same character class (with weak combat skills, poor experience, and so on). We will need NPCs like this for the quest system coming up later. (See Table 10.5.) NPCs do not need to follow the same modifier rules reserved for player character classes (which, again, should be thought of as heroes). Note that NPCs and monsters generally have more HP than their levels imply to improve gameplay by increasing the difficulty early on—which makes the player eager to level up quickly.

The Monster Classes

We can also create fantasy creatures and monsters described in Tables 10.6 to 10.9. These creatures are unprecedented because they have no equal on the "good side." But you will not want to make all of the bad guys too powerful— save that for the unusual monsters that are rarely encountered or the game will be way too hard to play. You will generally want to have at least one type of *bad guy* for each type of *character class* available to the player, and duplicate that

Table 10.5 Peasant

Attribute	Roll	Modifiers
Strength	1D6	0
Dexterity	1D6	0
Stamina	1D6	0
Intellect	1D6	0
Charisma	1D6	0
Hit Points	1D8	+STA

character all over the game world. In addition, you must add weaker enemy characters that make good fodder for the player to help with leveling up. Another thing to remember is that monsters do not gain experience and level up, so they should start out with higher level stats than a typical level 1 player character. Since the human but otherwise *bad* characters share the same stats as the human *good guys*, we don't need to define them separately.

Remember, these are generic class types, or races, not individuals. Since we don't need to follow a modifier standard, you may get as creative as you want. Since these classes represent various level ranges, the attributes are calculated with die roll specifications *and* modifiers (both of which are supported in the character editor).

If you want to create a level 10 monster, then I recommend rolling 10D6 for its attributes. If desired level is L, then each attribute roll is LD6. The modifiers may then be used to adjust the dice rolls to ensure minimum or maximum values are reached for the monster's intended abilities. For instance, if you want to create a zombie with a minimum of 20 STR while still using the attribute roll, then add 20 to the STR roll and the result will be 20 + STR. As long as the minimums are capped to zero, it's okay to add *negative* modifiers. If you want to specify a monster's level specifically in the editor data, go ahead and add it as a new property—I just prefer to get away from the numbers game and let the player learn each monster's abilities by fighting them (in the interest of improving the suspense of disbelief!).

As a final note, there is no reason to roll the charisma attribute for monsters so I have set CHA to 0 in these tables. If you have some purpose for this attribute in your own game, by all means go ahead and use it!

Skeleton Warrior

Skeleton warriors are the mainstay of the undead horde army, and as such, they can be found *almost everywhere* in the game world. At level 4, these guys are pretty tough for a new player but are soon dealt with handily once the player goes up a few levels. The skeleton warrior has high strength and stamina, and a lot of hit points!

Table 10.6	Level 4 Skeleton Warrior	
Attribute	**Roll**	**Modifiers**
Strength	4D6	+10
Dexterity	4D6	+6
Stamina	4D6	+8
Intellect	4D6	0
Charisma	0	0
Hit Points	4D8	+STA

Skeleton Archer

Skeleton archers were once support units for some unknown army before they became undead, so there aren't as many archers as there are warriors and berserkers but they tend to be better trained and hit much harder—at range. Despite their undead condition, they retain their original skills in battle—they are crack shots with their arrows so be sure to close in fast and take them out before they get too many shots off.

Table 10.7	Level 8 Skeleton Archer	
Attribute	**Roll**	**Modifiers**
Strength	8D6	+14
Dexterity	8D6	+20
Stamina	8D6	+16
Intellect	8D6	0
Charisma	0	0
Hit Points	8D8	+STA

Berserker

Berserkers are lost explorers who have gone insane while trying to find their way out of the dungeon, and pose a threat to the player and other explorers. Bereft of most of their original equipment (as well as their sanity), Berserkers roam the passageways of the dungeon's many levels, no longer remembering what their purpose was, but still feeling a longing to go *somewhere*. That somewhere is back to the top level and out of the dungeon, but having lost their minds, they do not remember that goal any longer and simply fight everything that comes near them.

Table 10.8 Level 12 Berserker

Attribute	Roll	Modifiers
Strength	12D6	+20
Dexterity	12D6	+18
Stamina	12D6	+16
Intellect	12D6	0
Charisma	0	0
Hit Points	12D8	+STA

Zombie

Zombies are the mainstay of the undead horde you will find in the depths of the dungeon. A combination of lost adventurers and foolhardy peasants who were

Table 10.9 Level 16 Zombie

Attribute	Roll	Modifiers
Strength	16D6	+22
Dexterity	16D6	+12
Stamina	16D6	+28
Intellect	16D6	0
Charisma	0	0
Hit Points	16D8	+STA

unlucky enough to fall into a pit above the dungeon or (worse) were grabbed by other zombies and dragged down into the depths, a zombie is a mindless killer with a hunger for human brains. As a result, zombies are confused about their existence and believe they still need to *feed*. They carry no weapons or armor. Despite having no weapons, zombies are extremely dangerous because they can take an extraordinary amount of damage before they fall.

THE CHARACTER EDITOR

The character editor is a Visual Basic program designed to create and edit game characters. I know what you're thinking—*Basic*? We do not need to reinvent the wheel when it comes to tools programming just because of the *language*! The character editor was developed over a period of several weeks and has reached a level of refinement that works exceptionally well with the codebase for our dungeon crawler engine. I considered porting it to C# just for this chapter but I would rather spend that time working on the game instead of re-inventing the editor just for the sake of the programming language. C# and Basic are partners and almost interchangeable anyway due to the .NET Framework library. Each character will be stored in its own file with an extension of .char, although this data is also just XML like the level editor data. Figure 10.1 shows the Character Editor program running.

I generally do not see the point of sharing source for a complex form-based application like this editor, because you can't create the editor from just this source code and it's too complex to list the properties for every control in an attempt to build it, tutorial style. The full source code for the character editor tool is included in the chapter resource files if you're interested in learning how the tool works.

Hint

The "DROP GOLD" and "DROP ITEMS" fields are not used yet, but reserved for Chapter 13, "Equipping Gear and Looting Treasure." When we have the code to work with these data fields, then we can edit monster character files and specify what we want them to drop, but first we need an item editor.

Table 10.10 provides a list of fields stored in a character data file.

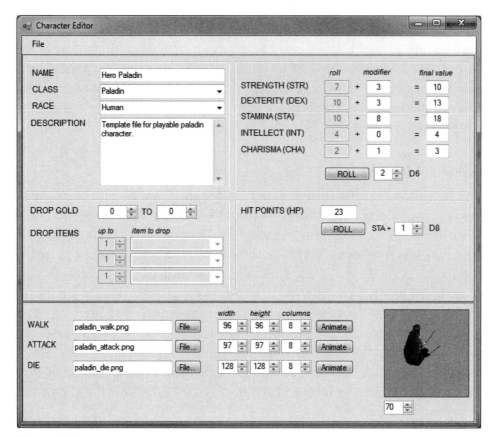

Figure 10.1
The character editor tool.

LOADING CHARACTER FILES

You know what type of data you want to use in the game based on the descriptions of the various classes discussed so far, and that data is now editable with the new character editor tool. How, then, do you make use of these character files in the game? We already have a very convenient Level class that makes the game world scroll very easily with code like this:

```
Level level = new Level(game, 25, 19, 32);
level.loadTilemap("sample.level");
level.loadPalette("palette.png", 5);
```

After loading the level, we can scroll and draw the level with simple properties based entirely on the data inside the .level file! I want the same kind of

Table 10.10 Character Data Fields

Field Name	Description
name	Character's full name
class	Character's class (warrior, etc.)
race	Character's race (human, etc.)
desc	Short description of this character
str	Strength attribute
dex	Dexterity attribute
sta	Stamina attribute
int	Intellect attribute
cha	Charisma attribute
hitpoints	Hit points (health)
anim_walk_filename	Walk animation filename
anim_walk_width	Walk animation frame width
anim_walk_height	Walk animation frame height
anim_walk_columns	Walk animation sheet columns
anim_attack_filename	Attack animation filename
anim_attack_width	Attack animation frame width
anim_attack_height	Attack animation frame height
anim_attack_columns	Attack animation sheet columns
anim_die_filename	Die animation filename
anim_die_width	Die animation frame width
anim_die_height	Die animation frame height
anim_die_columns	Die animation sheet columns
dropgold1	Minimum drop gold
dropgold2	Maximum drop gold

functionality for game characters as well! We have a great character editor available, but it uses a *lot* of data to define a character with unique properties, so we need a class to handle characters as well. I want to be able to load a .char file and have the class automatically load up the three sprite sheets (for walking, attacking, and dying). The class should also keep track of which "state" it's in, and draw the appropriate sprite animation automatically based on the animation state and all of the animation properties, completely wrapped up in a single Draw() routine. Here's an example:

```
Character hero = new Character(ref game);
hero.Load("paladin.char");
```

```
hero.Position = new Point(400, 300);
...
hero.Draw();
```

The Character Class

The Character class is the biggest class of the entire book so far, but that doesn't mean it's overly complex, it just has a lot of data to keep track of and makes use of a *lot* of convenient properties. This is a very user-friendly class, but that means there's a lot of code up front in the class. The end result is a lot of code now in the class definition, but *much less* code in our game required to work with characters. This class will necessarily require changes in the upcoming chapters to accommodate features that we haven't covered yet, like gaining experience and leveling (which are not found in the class yet!). Not to worry, our characters will gain experience and level up—and loot treasure and go on quests too!

```
using System;
using System.Collections.Generic;
using System.Xml;
using System.Drawing;
using System.Windows;
using System.Windows.Forms;

namespace RPG
{
    class Character
    {

        public enum AnimationStates
        {
            Walking = 0,
            Attacking = 1,
            Dying = 2
        }

        private Game p_game;
        private PointF p_position;
        private int p_direction;
        private AnimationStates p_state;
```

```csharp
//character file properties;
private string p_name;
private string p_class;
private string p_race;
private string p_desc;
private int p_str;
private int p_dex;
private int p_sta;
private int p_int;
private int p_cha;
private int p_hitpoints;
private int p_dropGold1;
private int p_dropGold2;
private string p_walkFilename;
private Sprite p_walkSprite;
private Size p_walkSize;
private int p_walkColumns;
private string p_attackFilename;
private Sprite p_attackSprite;
private Size p_attackSize;
private int p_attackColumns;
private string p_dieFilename;
private Sprite p_dieSprite;
private Size p_dieSize;
private int p_dieColumns;

public Character(ref Game game)
{
    p_game = game;
    p_position = new PointF(0, 0);
    p_direction = 1;
    p_state = AnimationStates.Walking;

    //initialize loadable properties
    p_name = "";
    p_class = "";
    p_race = "";
    p_desc = "";
    p_str = 0;
    p_dex = 0;
```

```
                p_sta = 0;
                p_int = 0;
                p_cha = 0;
                p_hitpoints = 0;
                p_dropGold1 = 0;
                p_dropGold2 = 0;
                p_walkSprite = null;
                p_walkFilename = "";
                p_walkSize = new Size(0, 0);
                p_walkColumns = 0;
                p_attackSprite = null;
                p_attackFilename = "";
                p_attackSize = new Size(0, 0);
                p_attackColumns = 0;
                p_dieSprite = null;
                p_dieFilename = "";
                p_dieSize = new Size(0, 0);
                p_dieColumns = 0;

        }

        public string Name
        {
            get { return p_name; }
            set { p_name = value; }
        }

        public string PlayerClass
        {
            get { return p_class; }
            set { p_class = value; }
        }

        public string Race
        {
            get { return p_race; }
            set { p_race = value; }
        }

        public string Description
```

```
{
    get { return p_desc; }
    set { p_desc = value; }
}

public int STR
{
    get { return p_str; }
    set { p_str = value; }
}

public int DEX
{
    get { return p_dex; }
    set { p_dex = value; }
}

public int STA
{
    get { return p_sta; }
    set { p_sta = value; }
}

public int INT
{
    get { return p_int; }
    set { p_int = value; }
}

public int CHA
{
    get { return p_cha; }
    set { p_cha = value; }
}

public int HitPoints
{
    get { return p_hitpoints; }
    set { p_hitpoints = value; }
}
```

```csharp
public int DropGoldMin
{
    get { return p_dropGold1; }
    set { p_dropGold1 = value; }
}

public int DropGoldMax
{
    get { return p_dropGold2; }
    set { p_dropGold2 = value; }
}

public Sprite GetSprite
{
    get {
        switch (p_state)
        {
            case AnimationStates.Walking:
                return p_walkSprite;
            case AnimationStates.Attacking:
                return p_attackSprite;
            case AnimationStates.Dying:
                return p_dieSprite;
            default:
                return p_walkSprite;
        }
    }
}

public PointF Position
{
    get { return p_position; }
    set { p_position = value; }
}

public float X
{
    get { return p_position.X; }
    set { p_position.X = value; }
}
```

```
public float Y
{
    get { return p_position.Y; }
    set { p_position.Y = value; }
}

public int Direction
{
    get { return p_direction; }
    set { p_direction = value; }
}

public AnimationStates AnimationState
{
    get { return p_state; }
    set { p_state = value; }
}

public void Draw()
{
    int startFrame, endFrame;
    switch (p_state)
    {
        case AnimationStates.Walking:
            p_walkSprite.Position = p_position;
            if (p_direction > -1)
            {
                startFrame = p_direction * p_walkColumns;
                endFrame = startFrame + p_walkColumns - 1;
                p_walkSprite.AnimationRate = 30;
                p_walkSprite.Animate(startFrame, endFrame);
            }
            p_walkSprite.Draw();
            break;

        case AnimationStates.Attacking:
            p_attackSprite.Position = p_position;
            if (p_direction > -1)
            {
                startFrame = p_direction * p_attackColumns;
```

```
                        endFrame = startFrame + p_attackColumns - 1;
                        p_attackSprite.AnimationRate = 30;
                        p_attackSprite.Animate(startFrame, endFrame);
                    }
                    p_attackSprite.Draw();
                    break;

                case AnimationStates.Dying:
                    p_dieSprite.Position = p_position;
                    if (p_direction > -1)
                    {
                        startFrame = p_direction * p_dieColumns;
                        endFrame = startFrame + p_dieColumns - 1;
                        p_dieSprite.AnimationRate = 30;
                        p_dieSprite.Animate(startFrame, endFrame);
                    }
                    p_dieSprite.Draw();
                    break;
            }
        }

        private string getElement(string field, ref XmlElement element)
        {
            string value = "";
            try
            {
                value = element.GetElementsByTagName(field)[0].InnerText;
            }
            catch (Exception ex)
            {
                Console.WriteLine(ex.Message);
            }
            return value;
        }


        public bool Load(string filename)
        {
            try
            {
```

```
//open the xml file
XmlDocument doc = new XmlDocument();
doc.Load(filename);
XmlNodeList list = doc.GetElementsByTagName("character");
XmlElement element = (XmlElement)list[0];

//read data fields
string data;
p_name = getElement("name", ref element);
p_class = getElement("class", ref element);
p_race = getElement("race", ref element);
p_desc = getElement("desc", ref element);

data = getElement("str", ref element);
p_str = Convert.ToInt32(data);

data = getElement("dex", ref element);
p_dex = Convert.ToInt32(data);

data = getElement("sta", ref element);
p_sta = Convert.ToInt32(data);

data = getElement("int", ref element);
p_int = Convert.ToInt32(data);

data = getElement("cha", ref element);
p_cha = Convert.ToInt32(data);

data = getElement("hitpoints", ref element);
p_hitpoints = Convert.ToInt32(data);

data = getElement("anim_walk_filename", ref element);
p_walkFilename = data;

data = getElement("anim_walk_width", ref element);
p_walkSize.Width = Convert.ToInt32(data);

data = getElement("anim_walk_height", ref element);
p_walkSize.Height = Convert.ToInt32(data);
```

```
                data = getElement("anim_walk_columns", ref element);
                p_walkColumns = Convert.ToInt32(data);

                data = getElement("anim_attack_filename", ref element);
                p_attackFilename = data;

                data = getElement("anim_attack_width", ref element);
                p_attackSize.Width = Convert.ToInt32(data);

                data = getElement("anim_attack_height", ref element);
                p_attackSize.Height = Convert.ToInt32(data);

                data = getElement("anim_attack_columns", ref element);
                p_attackColumns = Convert.ToInt32(data);

                data = getElement("anim_die_filename", ref element);
                p_dieFilename = data;

                data = getElement("anim_die_width", ref element);
                p_dieSize.Width = Convert.ToInt32(data);

                data = getElement("anim_die_height", ref element);
                p_dieSize.Height = Convert.ToInt32(data);

                data = getElement("anim_die_columns", ref element);
                p_dieColumns = Convert.ToInt32(data);

                data = getElement("dropgold1", ref element);
                p_dropGold1 = Convert.ToInt32(data);

                data = getElement("dropgold2", ref element);
                p_dropGold2 = Convert.ToInt32(data);
            }
            catch (Exception ex)
            {
                MessageBox.Show(ex.Message);
                return false;
            }

            //create character sprites
```

```
        try
        {
            if (p_walkFilename != "")
            {
                p_walkSprite = new Sprite(ref p_game);
                p_walkSprite.Image = LoadBitmap(p_walkFilename);
                p_walkSprite.Size = p_walkSize;
                p_walkSprite.Columns = p_walkColumns;
                p_walkSprite.TotalFrames = p_walkColumns * 8;
            }

            if (p_attackFilename != "")
            {
                p_attackSprite = new Sprite(ref p_game);
                p_attackSprite.Image = LoadBitmap(p_attackFilename);
                p_attackSprite.Size = p_attackSize;
                p_attackSprite.Columns = p_attackColumns;
                p_attackSprite.TotalFrames = p_attackColumns * 8;
            }

            if (p_dieFilename != "")
            {
                p_dieSprite = new Sprite(ref p_game);
                p_dieSprite.Image = LoadBitmap(p_dieFilename);
                p_dieSprite.Size = p_dieSize;
                p_dieSprite.Columns = p_dieColumns;
                p_dieSprite.TotalFrames = p_dieColumns * 8;
            }
        }

    catch (Exception ex)
    {
        MessageBox.Show(ex.Message);
        return false;
    }
    return true;
}

private Bitmap LoadBitmap(string filename)
{
```

```
              Bitmap bmp=null;
              try
              {
                  bmp = new Bitmap(filename);
              }
              catch (Exception ex){}
              return bmp;
          }


      }
}
```

The Animated Character Artwork

Now I'd like to discuss how you can prepare a sprite for use in this game. Each sprite is somewhat different in the number of frames it uses for each type of animation, as well as the types of animation available. All of the character sprites that I'm using in the game have the full eight-direction walking animation sequences, as well as frames for attacking with a weapon. Some sprites have a death animation, and some have running and falling. Normally, to keep the game as uniform as possible, you would use character sprites that have the exact same number of animation frames for the key animation that takes place in the game so that it's easy to switch character classes without changing any source code. But since our editor stores the sprite data in the character data files, we don't need to worry about keeping the animations all uniform. Figure 10.2 shows the walking animation sprite sheet for the paladin character.

The source artwork from Reiner's Tilesets does not come in this format, but it comes with each frame of animation stored in a separate bitmap file. The easiest way to combine these frames into a sprite animation sheet is with Cosmigo's Pro Motion sprite animation program. Because Pro Motion works best with single animation strips, I decided to import each group of bitmaps for the character's walking animation in all eight directions. Using Pro Motion, I converted all 64 frames of animation into a single sprite sheet.

Nothing beats experimentation, so it is up to you to use the freely available sprites provided by Reiner's Tilesets (and other sources) to enhance the Dungeon Crawler game to suit your own needs. We can only accomplish so

Figure 10.2
Walking animation for the paladin sprite.

much in this book, so I want to give you as many tools, tips, and tricks as I can possibly squeeze in at this time. There are thousands of sprites and tiles available at www.reinerstilesets.de that you can use for your own games! There is a sprite for everything you can possibly imagine adding to an RPG!

All of the characters and monsters discussed in this chapter have been chosen very carefully because we have artwork available for them. Generally, when a game is being designed from the ground up, the game designer will not limit himself to what artwork is available, because none exists before the game goes into development. But in our case, we have all of this artwork provided by Reiner Prokein (www.reinerstileset.de). I strongly recommend that you start

Figure 10.3
The warrior sprite sheets for walking, attacking, and dying.

with artwork and design your game characters around that instead of designing first and looking for artwork later (unless you know a talented artist who can do the work!).

All of the sprite sheets used in the game were significantly manipulated from their original sources provided by Reiner Prokein. All of the sprites arranged in columns and rows in a sprite sheet and transparent regions have been converted to an alpha channel in each file, which is saved in the Portable Network Graphics (PNG) file format. When you visit Reiner's website, you will not find sprite sheets like these, as they are provided in individual bitmaps. Just be aware that additional work will be required on your part to add new characters or animations to your game. Figure 10.3 shows the three sheets used for the warrior character—note the different number of columns for each sheet, which is handled by the character editor and the Character class!

Character Demo

Let's take the new Character class and artwork for a spin. The Character demo program is not much different, functionally, from the Portal demo in Chapter 9. However, *all* of the character code is now transferred over to the Character class, which knows how to load a .char file (created by the character editor tool), parse the XML fields, and create the three sprites needed for each character. In addition, the three animation states can be changed using the standard numeric

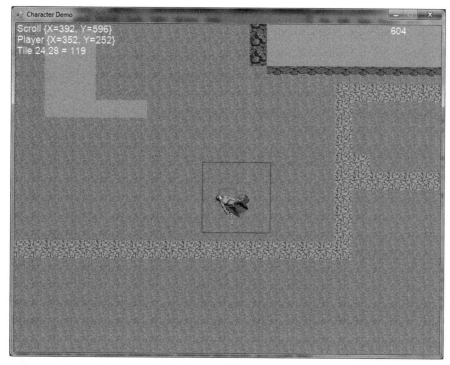

Scroll {X=392, Y=596}
Player {X=352, Y=252}
Tile 24,28 = 119

604

Figure 10.4
We can now kill the player character—wait, is that a good thing?

keys 1, 2, and 3. The result is shown in Figure 10.4. The demo looks a little bit goofy since you have to move in order to show the attack and die animations, but that's okay, as those animations will not be used during normal walking, only when another action is triggered. The point is, the Character class works!

Since the code for the Character demo is derived from Chapter 9's example, I will instead just show you the relevant sections of code related to the new Character class, and let you open the project to see the complete sources. Since the Character class mimics some of the Sprite class' properties and also makes available the current sprite object via the GetSprite() function, we can replace most of the Sprite-specific code in this demo with Character-based code without making significant changes.

First, we declare a new `Character` variable:

```
Character hero;
```

Next, we create the `hero` object and set its initial position.

```
hero = new Character(ref game);
hero.Load("paladin.char");
hero.Position = new Point(400 - 48, 300 - 48);
```

In the `Form1_KeyUp()` event, the `AnimationState` property is changed with the 1, 2, and 3 keys, to test the three different character states (which are `Walking`, `Attacking`, and `Dying`).

```
private void Form1_KeyUp(object sender, KeyEventArgs e)
{
    switch (e.KeyCode)
    {
        case Keys.Escape: gameover = true; break;
        case Keys.Up:
        case Keys.W: keyState.up = false; break;
        case Keys.Down:
        case Keys.S: keyState.down = false; break;
        case Keys.Left:
        case Keys.A: keyState.left = false; break;
        case Keys.Right:
        case Keys.D: keyState.right = false; break;
        case Keys.Space:
            if (portalFlag) level.GridPos = portalTarget;
            break;
        case Keys.D1:
            hero.AnimationState = Character.AnimationStates.Walking;
            break;
        case Keys.D2:
            hero.AnimationState = Character.AnimationStates.Attacking;
            break;
        case Keys.D3:
            hero.AnimationState = Character.AnimationStates.Dying;
            break;
    }
}
```

Tip

Press the keys 1, 2, 3 to change the player sprite's animation.

In the main loop function, doUpdate(), we simply call hero.Draw(), which both animates *and* draws the character sprite. This Draw() function is so smart that it even figures out automatically which sprite to draw based on the Animation State. Notice how very little the code has changed! This is due to the similarities between the Sprite and Character classes (which were intentional!).

```
int ticks = Environment.TickCount;
if (ticks > drawLast + 16)
{
    drawLast = ticks;

    //draw the tilemap
    level.Draw(0, 0, 800, 600);

    //draw the hero
    hero.Draw();
    ...
}
```

This is not the *entire* code listing to the Character demo project, which must be omitted due to length. Please open the complete project (www.courseptr.com/downloads) and peruse the source code for this program.

LEVEL UP!

The new character editor tool and the Character class that knows how to work with the new .char files have together dramatically improved our game's potential gameplay with even more data-driven features! It is now possible to design a totally new character or monster, edit the sprite sheet images, and save the new character to a data file, then load it up inside the game and have the new character moving around in a matter of minutes, with only a few lines of code! Not solely to be used for player characters, we will also use the Character class for monsters and NPCs as well! This is really getting exciting, because it means you aren't stuck with just what the designer has put into a game (at least, a game based on these tools). If you want to tweak a character, you won't have to edit any source code, you'll just open the file in the character editor, make the changes, save it, then try it out in the game again. That's the beautiful thing about game editor tools, and why this is such a hot topic in the game industry, with skilled tool programmers in high demand.

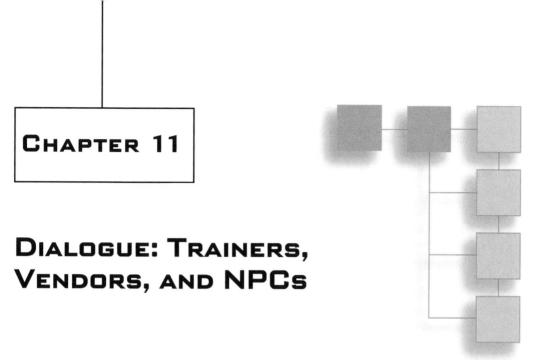

CHAPTER 11

DIALOGUE: TRAINERS, VENDORS, AND NPCS

The purpose of this chapter is to build a dialogue system for the game so that the player's character can talk with non-player characters (NPCs). This is important, because a dialogue system will allow players to sell items and treasures they pick up in the dungeon and buy new gear items to improve their attack and defense strengths. The dialogue system developed in this chapter will be used to communicate with the player in many more ways beyond the single purpose of focus in this chapter. In future chapters, this system will be used for combat and looting as well.

Here's what we'll cover in this chapter:

- Creating the "Vendor" NPC
- Starting a conversation
- Dialogue choices
- Making eye contact
- Positioning the dialogue window
- Dialogue GUI
- Complete `Dialogue` class

TALKING WITH NPCs

For a dialogue system to work well in the game, the first step is to allow the player to get the attention of an NPC, who will either be walking around or staying in a certain location, usually in a town, in a shop, or on the street. Talking with NPCs usually involves walking up close to them and hitting a "talk" button. In console games, that is usually one of the non-combat buttons (like the X or Y button on an Xbox 360 controller, for instance). Until you are in range of the NPC, you cannot talk with them. So, we'll need to use the distance function to find out if we're close enough to an NPC. Interestingly enough, this distance code will be used for combat in the next chapter as well—you know, so that you can only hit an enemy if you're close enough to it.

Creating the "Vendor" NPC

Our example in this chapter has just one NPC—the vendor character. Normally, we would see many NPCs in a level file with a town in it, not just one character. But, this demo will be on the simple side so you can study the code and understand how this one NPC works. Adding more characters will then be no problem. We need to treat the NPCs like any other object in the game, and render them appropriately. Do you recall the Tree demo back in Chapter 8, "Adding Objects to the Dungeon"? The same sort of code will be used now to draw the NPC, although we won't use an array or list this time because there's only one object. If you want to see a full-blown NPC system with many characters, scenery objects, and monsters, see the finished game in the last chapter!

We will use the character editor again to create the vendor character, which is shown in Figure 11.1. You'll see in the figure that the vendor has no real attributes worthy of note. That is because the vendor cannot fight, and cannot even be attacked. Note also that only one image is used for the vendor's so-called "animation" sheets, and the columns property is set to 1 for all three. This character doesn't need to animate or move, which keeps things simple in the art requirement!

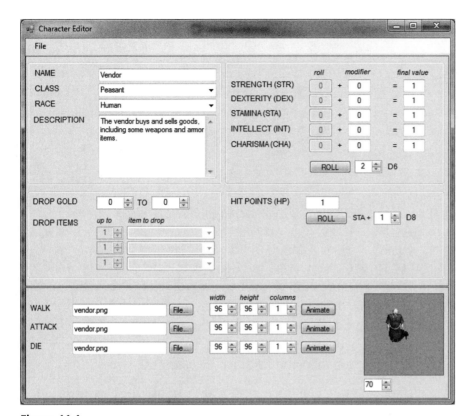

Figure 11.1
The vendor character in the editor.

Starting a Conversation

Since both the player and the NPC are based on the Character class, we know that they both have the same properties, including a Position property that returns a PointF (which is like a regular Point structure but containing floats instead of ints). So, how do we use the position of the two characters to find the distance between them? First, we treat the position of each character as the endpoint of a line between them, as shown in Figure 11.2.

Hint

The properties were left out of the Character class in the previous chapter to save space. Some of the properties are mentioned in this chapter, which may be a surprise. Please open the project to see the complete source code.

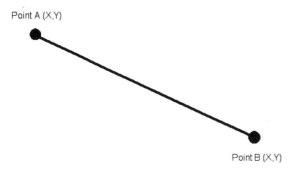

Point A (X,Y)

Point B (X,Y)

Figure 11.2
The center points of two sprites are used to calculate the distance between them.

When using distance to determine whether two sprites are colliding, what we must do is calculate the center point of each sprite, calculate the radius of the sprite (from the center point to the edge), and then check the distance between the two center points. If the distance is less than the two radii combined, then you know the sprites are overlapping. Why? The radius of each sprite, when added together, should be less than the distance between the two sprites.

To calculate the distance between any two points, we can use the classic distance formula. Any two points can be converted into a right triangle by treating them as the end points of the two sides of that triangle, as shown in Figure 11.3. Take the delta value of the X and Y of each point, square each delta value, add them

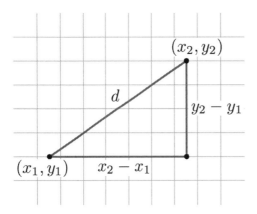

Figure 11.3
A triangle is used to calculate the distance between two points. Image courtesy of Wikipedia.

together, then take the square root, and you have the distance between the two points. Here is the formula written as pseudo-code:

```
delta_x = x2 - x1
delta_y = y2 - y1
delta_x_squared = delta_x * delta_x
delta_y_squared = delta_y * delta_y
distance = square root ( delta_x_squared + delta_y_squared)
```

Here is a function that will meet our needs for calculating distance. This Distance() function would be most reusable if added to the Game class along with some overloaded parameters. We may also need a more specific function suited for the player's standing position (returning the distance to another Character), so it might be helpful to also add a helper function to the Character class that *also* calculates distance.

```
public double Distance(PointF first, PointF second)
{
    float deltaX = second.X - first.X;
    float deltaY = second.Y - first.Y;
    double dist = Math.Sqrt(deltaX * deltaX + deltaY * deltaY);
    return dist;
}
```

But, we don't want to just use the player's raw X,Y position for the comparison. Remember back in Chapter 9, "Going Deeper into the Dungeon with Portals," we had to compare the player's *foot position* to see if he's walking on a portal or not? The raw position gives the upper-left corner of the player sprite's collision box. We need to use the same HeroFeet() function that returns an adjusted Point containing the coordinates of the player's feet, as if the sprite is really walking on the tiled ground.

```
private Point HeroFeet()
{
    return new Point((int)hero.X + 32, (int)hero.Y + 32 + 16);
}
```

After deciding whether the player is close enough to an NPC to talk with it, the next step is to trigger a new dialogue mode in the game. We will want the rest of the game to pause while talking so nothing happens that the player would be unable to respond to in the game (like being attacked). This pause mode can be handled with a flag that causes some parts of the game to stop updating, but we

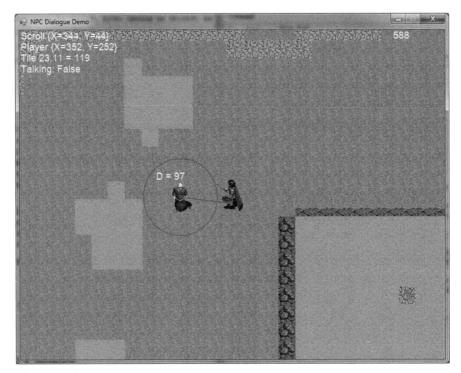

Figure 11.4
If the NPC is in range, then the player can begin a dialogue.

will want them to be drawn. While that is happening, we do want to allow dialogue to happen, so this probably calls for a Dialogue class. But what should the class do?

The first example for this chapter, Dialogue demo 1, shows how to calculate the distance between the hero and an NPC, displays the distance, and draws a "talk radius" circle around the NPC so you can see when the character is in range. By pressing the Space key when in range, a "talking" flag is triggered. Figure 11.4 shows the example. (The code to load the vendor and player characters will be shown in the second example later in this chapter.)

Without getting too deep into the complete source code listing, here is the key code from the first demo (there are three for this chapter). If the player is in range then the circle is drawn in blue to show that the player is in range. A line connecting both characters shows visually what the distance looks like from the precise locations from which is it calculated.

```
private void doVendor()
{
    float relativeX=0, relativeY=0;
    int talkRadius = 70;
    Pen color;

    //draw the vendor sprite
    if (vendor.X > level.ScrollPos.X &&
        vendor.X < level.ScrollPos.X + 23 * 32 &&
        vendor.Y > level.ScrollPos.Y &&
        vendor.Y < level.ScrollPos.Y + 17 * 32)
    {
        relativeX = Math.Abs(level.ScrollPos.X - vendor.X);
        relativeY = Math.Abs(level.ScrollPos.Y - vendor.Y);
        vendor.GetSprite.Draw((int)relativeX, (int)relativeY);
    }

    //get center of hero sprite
    PointF heroCenter = HeroFeet();
    heroCenter.X += 16;
    heroCenter.Y += 16;
    game.Device.DrawRectangle(Pens.Red, heroCenter.X - 2,
        heroCenter.Y - 2, 4, 4);

    //get center of NPC
    PointF vendorCenter = new Point((int)relativeX, (int)relativeY);
    vendorCenter.X += vendor.GetSprite.Width / 2;
    vendorCenter.Y += vendor.GetSprite.Height / 2;
    game.Device.DrawRectangle(Pens.Red, vendorCenter.X - 2,
        vendorCenter.Y - 2, 4, 4);

    double dist = Distance(heroCenter, vendorCenter);
    //draw line connecting player to vendor
    if (dist < talkRadius)
        color = new Pen(Brushes.Blue, 2.0f);
    else
        color = new Pen(Brushes.Red, 2.0f);
    game.Device.DrawLine(color, heroCenter, vendorCenter);

    //print distance
```

```
game.Print((int)relativeX, (int)relativeY,
    "D = " + dist.ToString("N0"), Brushes.White);

//draw circle around vendor to show talk radius
float spriteSize = vendor.GetSprite.Width / 2;
float centerx = relativeX + spriteSize;
float centery = relativeY + spriteSize;
RectangleF circleRect = new RectangleF(centerx - talkRadius,
    centery - talkRadius, talkRadius * 2, talkRadius * 2);
game.Device.DrawEllipse(color, circleRect);

//is playing trying to talk to this vendor?
if (dist < talkRadius)
{
    if (talkFlag) talking = true;
}
else talking = false;
}
```

Tip

The complete source code for the Dialogue demo is found later in the chapter. We'll skip through the code in the meantime while exploring how the dialogue system works.

Dialogue Choices

If our game had a mystery plot that required the player to interview dozens or perhaps hundreds of NPCs to find out "who dunnit," then we would absolutely need another game editor to handle all of the complex interactions with these NPCs, with branching dialogue trees and variables so that the NPCs remember past conversations—or at least *seem* to remember them. We don't want this level of complexity for our Dungeon Crawler game. Basically, on each major area of the game, we want to have several NPCs that help the player: buying drop items, selling better gear, healing the player, and so on. These are pretty simple interactions. Since the inventory system and item editor won't be coming along for a couple more chapters, we can't offer up actual gear for the player to use, nor can we let the player sell drop items to the town vendors (yet). But we *can* get the framework in place so that these things *are* possible. In other words, we need a generic dialogue system with options that the player can select.

The graphical user interface (GUI) for a game is a complex subject. GUI programmers are in high demand in the game industry, as are tool programmers! So you are learning a bit of both high-demand skills here!

Continuing to think through the design considerations of our dialogue system, one assumption I'll make now is that we will not have any complex graphical controls like scrolling lists, drop-down lists, or even anything like a scrollbar. The level of complexity for our GUI will end with *buttons*, and there will be a limited number of them. However, with the use of a *state variable*, we can create multiple levels for the dialogue system. Let's say, first of all, there are two dialogue choices for a vendor:

- BUY
- SELL

If you choose the "BUY" option, then a variable is set so that a list of items for sale is displayed next. Then we just recycle the same dialogue with a different set of options (a limited list of items for sale).

- Dagger
- Short Sword
- Barbarian Hammer
- Leather Armor
- Chain Armor
- Plate Armor
- More...

There are some limitations to this system, but with creative use of state variables you could offer an unlimited number of items by making the last button a More button that brings up a second page, and so on. One design consideration that you might want to consider is abandoning any sort of Back button in the dialogue system. I know it seems reasonable to let the player go back one level or page, but that tends to complicate things. It is easy enough to just end the dialogue and start it up again with the character, and I have seen many games take this approach.

CREATING THE DIALOGUE SYSTEM

Now that we can determine whether the player is close enough to an NPC to talk with it, the next step is to bring up a dialogue window and let the user interact with the NPC. First, we'll incorporate the new dialogue helper functions and properties into the classes to make more effective use of them.

Making Eye Contact

We can still use the distance function to find out when the player is close to an NPC, but Distance() is obviously so reusable that it *must* be moved into the Game class. I'll go a step further by adding an overload. Feel free to add any other variations of the core Game functions or properties that you would find useful. This new version works with individual coordinate values for the two points passed as parameters. This new Distance function along with the previous version have been added to the Game class starting with the Dialogue demo 2 project.

```
public double Distance(float x1, float x2, float y1, float y2)
{
    PointF first = new PointF(x1, x2);
    PointF second = new PointF(x2, y2);
    return Distance(first, second);
}
```

The HeroFeet() function will work again, but it is becoming tiresome. Simple, yes, but it is not very reusable. I want a more generic version of this code actually built into the Character class. We have to make some more assumptions about the tile size used in the game, but at this point we're set on 32x32 so I won't be concerned with that now. The HeroFeet() function has become the Character. FootPos property. This property is also now part of the Character class (beginning with the Dialogue demo 2 project).

```
public PointF FootPos
{
    get { return new Point((int)this.X + 32, (int)this.Y + 32 + 16); }
}
```

Another helpful property that would greatly help to simplify our code is a CenterPos property for the Character class. The center of a character is its X,Y position plus its width and height, each divided by two.

```
public PointF CenterPos
{
    get
    {
        PointF pos = this.Position;
        pos.X += this.GetSprite.Width / 2;
        pos.Y += this.GetSprite.Height / 2;
        return pos;
    }
}
```

Next, we'll incorporate the distance calculations right inside the Character class while taking into account both the foot position and the center position of the character. Some parameters are objects passed by reference, not because changes are made to them, but to avoid having the object copied to the function every time (a reference is just a pointer to the object in memory).

```
public double FootDistance(ref Character other)
{
    return p_game.Distance(this.FootPos, other.FootPos);
}

public double FootDistance(PointF pos)
{
    return p_game.Distance(this.FootPos, pos);
}

public double CenterDistance(ref Character other)
{
    return p_game.Distance(CenterPos, other.CenterPos);
}

public double CenterDistance(PointF pos)
{
    return p_game.Distance(this.CenterPos, pos);
}
```

I'm going to use the CenterPos property this time, rather than FootPos, to simplify the example code a bit and show that both techniques work equally well when you just want to know if the player is close enough to an NPC to talk to it.

When the player character is within range of the NPC and the talk radius circle turns blue, then press the Space key to begin talking.

Dialogue GUI

What do we want this dialogue system to look like? It needs to be simple and positioned in such a way that it doesn't block out a large portion of the screen, but at the same time, it would be helpful to draw the dialogue interface as a window at a certain location every time. What about drawing the window at one of the four corners of the game window, depending on where the player character is located? It would be unfortunate to draw the dialogue window over the top of the player! That affects the user's suspension of disbelief. The player wants to *see* his character while talking with an NPC, not interact in some sort of disembodied way. Let's start by figuring out where the player is located and then drawing a box in an opposing corner—whichever corner is farthest from the player.

The `Dialogue` class will be reusable and serve many roles beyond just talking with NPCs. This will be our de facto way to communicate with the player, with either just simple messages requiring the click of an OK button to a more complex message with many choices. The `Dialogue` class will be self-contained, requiring very little from other classes except for `Game.Device`, which is needed to draw. We're going to need to use a smaller font than the default font in the `Game` class. Although we have `Game.SetFont()` for changing that font, it will be too much of a pain to change the font back and forth after showing the dialogue text, so the dialogue system will use its own font. The dialogue window will be set up using properties and then drawn with a `Draw()` function, which will pause the game until the player chooses one of the options. Figure 11.5 shows a dialogue window positioned at the lower left with a size of one-quarter the screen (400x300).

Positioning the Dialogue Window

In my opinion, this window size is a bit too large, even if we give it some transparency with an alpha channel. While I would enjoy working on a resizable dialogue window, I'm not willing to get into the complexity of drawing button controls onto a variable-sized window—no, we need to keep this simple and enhance it as needed for each game. Let's try a slightly smaller window with that

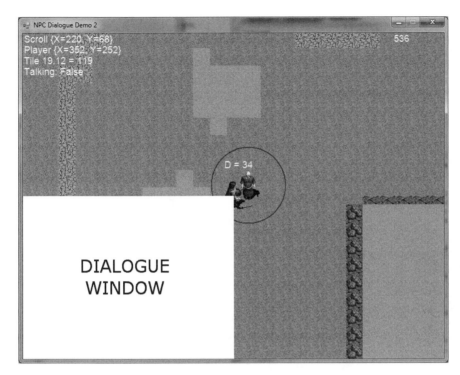

Figure 11.5
A possible dialogue window position.

alpha channel, shown in Figure 11.6. This screen mock-up shows the slightly smaller dialogue window (360x280) in the four corners. A border and shadow would certainly improve its appearance, but it already looks usable.

Hint

To create your own dialogue window with whatever level of transparency you want, use a graphic editor like GIMP or Paint.Net, create a window with the resolution you want, and then use the Opacity slider or Layer, Mask menu option to change the alpha level of the image. An alpha level of 60% looks pretty good. However, we can also just draw a filled rectangle with whatever alpha level we want at runtime so that's probably the best solution (although it's a bit slower).

To automatically move the dialogue to one of the corners based on the player's position, we'll use an enumeration:

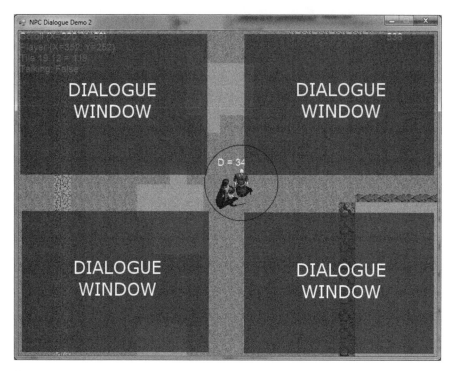

Figure 11.6
Positioning the dialogue window at any of the four corners.

```
public enum Positions
{
    UpperLeft,
    LowerLeft,
    UpperRight,
    LowerRight
}
```

Now, based on the player's current position, the dialogue window will automatically reposition itself to one of the four corners farthest away from the player.

```
switch (p_corner)
{
    case Positions.UpperLeft:
        p_position = new PointF(10, 10);
        break;
    case Positions.LowerLeft:
```

```
            p_position = new PointF(10, 600 - p_size.Y - 10);
            break;
        case Positions.UpperRight:
            p_position = new PointF(800 - p_size.X - 10, 10);
            break;
        case Positions.LowerRight:
            p_position = new PointF(800 - p_size.X - 10,
                600 - p_size.Y - 10);
            break;
    }
}
```

In our main game code, the automatic positioning of the dialogue window is handled. This could easily be moved inside the Dialogue class itself if you prefer.

```
if (hero.CenterPos.X < 400)
{
    if (hero.CenterPos.Y < 300)
        dialogue.setCorner(Dialogue.Positions.LowerRight);
    else
        dialogue.setCorner(Dialogue.Positions.UpperRight);
} else {
    if (hero.CenterPos.Y < 300)
        dialogue.setCorner(Dialogue.Positions.LowerLeft);
    else
        dialogue.setCorner(Dialogue.Positions.UpperLeft);
}
```

Drawing the window is done with a call to Graphics.FillRectangle(). The trick here is to create a color that contains an alpha channel at the percentage of transparency that we want. Since the color values fall in the range of 0 to 255, one easy way to calculate the alpha level is to just multiply 255 by the desired percentage like so:

```
Pen pen = new Pen(Color.FromArgb((int)(255 * 0.6), 255, 255, 255));
p_game.Device.FillRectangle(pen.Brush, p_position.X,
    p_position.Y, p_size.X, p_size.Y);
```

The color manipulation code is a bit tricky, because FillRectangle() doesn't accept just a normal Color parameter, it must be a Brush. Since Pen can convert to a Brush, we can use a Pen with the desired Color components to arrive at a white rectangle with 60% alpha. The result is shown in Figure 11.7. See the example Dialogue demo 2 to see the next step.

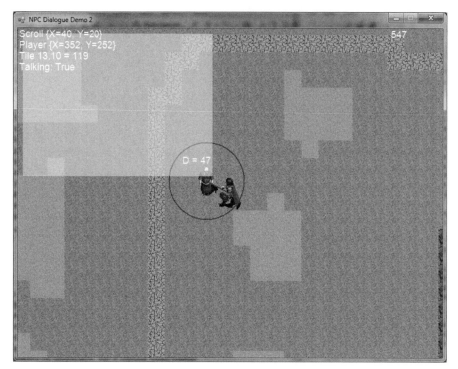

Figure 11.7
The dialogue automatically moves based on the player's location.

Hint

If the dialogue window is too small for your needs, you could make a much taller window and just cause it to stay in place or allow it to automatically move from left to right instead of jumping among the four corners. A window of this type could be used for the player's inventory system, for instance. For the dialogue system, I was thinking about keeping it smaller and using a small font.

Drawing the Dialogue Window

I think that's all we need to build the dialogue window at this point. All of the items on the window will be positioned relative to the window's position so that everything gets drawn in the right place even when the window moves. As for the interface, there will be a title, message text, and ten buttons, as shown in the design mock-up in Figure 11.8.

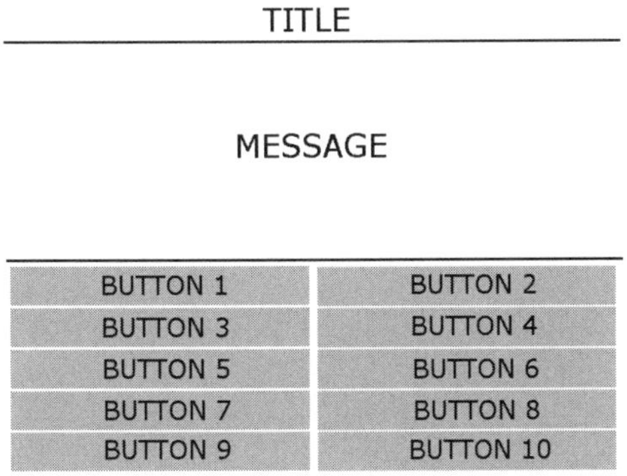

TITLE

MESSAGE

BUTTON 1	BUTTON 2
BUTTON 3	BUTTON 4
BUTTON 5	BUTTON 6
BUTTON 7	BUTTON 8
BUTTON 9	BUTTON 10

Figure 11.8
A mock-up of the dialogue user interface.

Drawing the Title

Let's begin with the title. It should display the name of the character with whom you're talking. The Title property, p_title, will be displayed in the Draw() function. To center the title on the dialogue window, we use a function called Graphics.MeasureString(), which returns the width and height of text according to the specified string and font. Using this information, we can get the width of the text and center it on the window.

```
SizeF size = p_game.Device.MeasureString(p_title, p_fontTitle);
int tx = (int)(p_position.X + p_size.Width / 2 - size.Width / 2);
int ty = (int)p_position.Y + 6;
p_game.Device.DrawString(p_title, p_fontTitle, Brushes.Gold, tx, ty);
```

Drawing the Message with Word Wrapping

Next up is the message text. This is the information an NPC wants to communicate to the player, be it for a quest or an introduction or any other purpose. We have quite a bit of room here for a lengthy message given the Arial-12 font. If you want to change the font for the title or the message, that could be done via properties. We again use Graphics.MeasureString(), but this time it is used to position multi-line text within a bounded region specified in the SizeF property layoutArea. Using the supplied dimensions, MeasureString() provides the minimum width and height needed to render the message with the specified font. It's a very cool function!

```
SizeF layoutArea = new SizeF(p_size.Width, 80);
```

```
int lines = 4;
int length = p_message.Length;
size = p_game.Device.MeasureString(p_message, p_fontMessage, layoutArea,
    null, out length, out lines);
RectangleF layoutRect = new RectangleF(p_position.X + 4, p_position.Y + 34,
    size.Width, size.Height);
p_game.Device.DrawString(p_message, p_fontMessage, Brushes.White,
    layoutRect);
```

Drawing the Buttons

Now we come to the buttons, and the most difficult aspect of the user interface. However, by making some assumptions we can keep the problem under control. First of all, let me state that there is a *huge* amount of variation in what you could potentially do with the dialogue buttons. With the right options in the form of enumeration values and some creative code, this could be an even more versatile dialogue system than planned. But, I don't want to go all out with it at this point—keep it functional and simple, with the knowledge that it can handle more at a later time if needed.

A helper structure is needed to manage and draw the buttons. We don't need to be concerned with the *position* of each button, because they are simply enumerated and drawn in order, based on the dialogue's properties. (A future enhancement to the user interface might require a position property for the buttons, though.) In fact, the Dialogue.Button structure doesn't really resemble a button at all! There is no positional or dimensional information in the structure, just a text property. What gives?!

The structure is in place for future needs (such as the aforementioned features). We don't need anything more than the text property, but putting it in a structure allows for much easier changes later.

For the *first time* we are actually going to use the mouse in our game code! That's quite a statement now that we're so heavily invested into 11 chapters, but until now we have not needed the mouse. The main form is covered up by the PictureBox that is created by the Game class and attached to the form, so we have to modify the PictureBox control in the Game class to support mouse input, oddly enough.

```
private Point p_mousePos;
private MouseButtons p_mouseBtn;
```

A new event handler is needed to support mouse input. This new function is added to the Game class and handles the events for MouseMove and MouseDown, which are both needed to get mouse movement and button clicks. The mouse event handler is created in the Game constructor with these two lines:

```
p_pb.MouseMove += new MouseEventHandler(p_pb_MouseInput);
p_pb.MouseDown += new MouseEventHandler(p_pb_MouseInput);
```

Here is the new mouse event handler in the Game class:

```
void p_pb_MouseInput(object sender, MouseEventArgs e)
{
    p_mousePos.X = e.X;
    p_mousePos.Y = e.Y;
    p_mouseBtn = e.Button;
}
```

In support of the new mouse handler are these two new properties in the Game class.

```
public Point MousePos
{
    get { return p_mousePos; }
    set { p_mousePos = value; }
}

public MouseButtons MouseButton
{
    get { return p_mouseBtn; }
    set { p_mouseBtn = value; }
}
```

Three private variables are needed to handle the buttons on the dialogue window.

```
private Button[] p_buttons;
private int p_numButtons;
private int p_selection;
```

The following code will cause the buttons to come to life when the mouse hovers over each button, and causes the Dialogue class to report which button was clicked.

```
public int NumButtons
{
    get { return p_numButtons; }
    set { p_numButtons = value; }
}

public void setButtonText(int index, string value)
{
    p_buttons[index].Text = value;
}

public string getButtonText(int index)
{
    return p_buttons[index].Text;
}

public Rectangle getButtonRect(int index)
{
    int i = index - 1;
    Rectangle rect = new Rectangle((int)p_position.X,
        (int)p_position.Y, 0, 0);
    rect.Width = p_size.Width / 2 - 4;
    rect.Height = (int)(p_size.Height * 0.4 / 5);
    rect.Y += (int)(p_size.Height * 0.6 - 4);
    switch (index)
    {
        case 1:
        case 3:
        case 5:
        case 7:
        case 9:
            rect.X += 4;
            rect.Y += (int)(Math.Floor((double)i / 2) *
                rect.Height);
            break;
        case 2:
        case 4:
        case 6:
        case 8:
        case 10:
```

```
            rect.X += 4 + rect.Width;
            rect.Y += (int)(Math.Floor((double)i / 2) *
                rect.Height);
            break;
    }
    return rect;
}

public int Selection
{
    get { return p_selection; }
    set { p_selection = value; }
}
```

Now we come to the Draw() function again. Previously, we have already added the code to draw the title and message onto the dialogue window. Now we need to write the code that draws the buttons and detects mouse movement and selection. This code is primarily based around the getButtonRect() function, which returns a Rectangle that represents the position and dimensions of the virtual button. This is then used to both draw the button and to look for mouse activity within its region.

```
//draw the buttons
for (int n = 1; n < p_numButtons; n++)
{
    Rectangle rect = getButtonRect(n);

    //draw button background
    Color color;
    if (rect.Contains(p_mousePos))
    {
        //clicked on this button?
        if (p_mouseBtn == MouseButtons.Left)
            p_selection = n;
        else
            p_selection = 0;

        color = Color.FromArgb(200, 80, 100, 120);
        p_game.Device.FillRectangle(new Pen(color).Brush, rect);
    }
```

```
    //draw button border
    p_game.Device.DrawRectangle(Pens.Gray, rect);

    //print button label
    size = p_game.Device.MeasureString(p_buttons[n].Text,
        p_fontButton);
    tx = (int)(rect.X + rect.Width / 2 - size.Width / 2);
    ty = rect.Y + 2;
    p_game.Device.DrawString(p_buttons[n].Text, p_fontButton,
        Brushes.White, tx, ty);
}
```

Final Example

I promised to go over the source code for a complete example before ending this chapter, so we'll do that now. There are three Dialogue demo projects that go with this chapter that you can open and study one step at a time, from the initial code to calculate distance between the characters to the opening and positioning of the dialogue window to the full user interface. Figure 11.9 shows the final GUI for the dialogue window with all of the buttons filled with sample items for purchase, while Figure 11.10 shows that the game responds to the selection after the dialogue window is closed. To save space, the using statements and the namespace will be omitted since they are now redundant.

```
public partial class Form1 : Form
{
    public struct keyStates
    {
        public bool up, down, left, right;
    }

    Game game;
    Level level;
    keyStates keyState;
    bool gameover = false;
    Character hero;
    Character vendor;
    bool talkFlag = false;
    bool talking = false;
    int drawLast = 0;
```

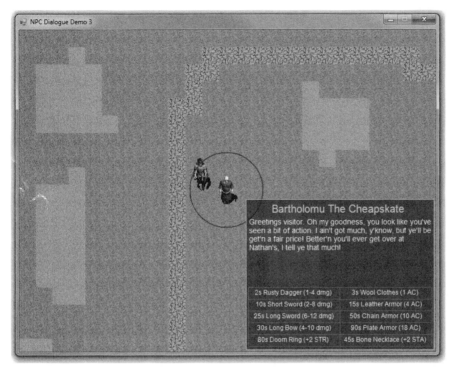

Figure 11.9
The final Dialogue demo program responds to user choices.

Figure 11.10
Displaying the item selected in the dialogue.

```
Dialogue dialogue;
string purchase = "";

public Form1()
{
    InitializeComponent();
}

private void Form1_Load(object sender, EventArgs e)
{
    this.Text = "NPC Dialogue Demo 3";

    //create game object
    Form form = (Form)this;
    game = new Game(ref form, 800, 600);

    //create tilemap
    level = new Level(ref game, 25, 19, 32);
    level.loadTilemap("sample.level");
    level.loadPalette("palette.bmp", 5);

    //load hero
    hero = new Character(ref game);
    hero.Load("paladin.char");
    hero.Position = new Point(400 - 48, 300 - 48);

    //load vendor
    vendor = new Character(ref game);
    vendor.Load("vendor.char");
    vendor.Position = new Point(600, 300);

    //create dialogue
    dialogue = new Dialogue(ref game);

    while (!gameover)
    {
        doUpdate();
    }
    Application.Exit();
}
```

```csharp
private void Form1_KeyDown(object sender, KeyEventArgs e)
{
    switch (e.KeyCode)
    {
        case Keys.Up:
        case Keys.W : keyState.up = true; break;
        case Keys.Down:
        case Keys.S : keyState.down = true; break;
        case Keys.Left:
        case Keys.A : keyState.left = true; break;
        case Keys.Right:
        case Keys.D : keyState.right = true; break;
        case Keys.Space : talkFlag = true; break;
    }
}

private void Form1_KeyUp(object sender, KeyEventArgs e)
{
    switch (e.KeyCode)
    {
        case Keys.Escape : gameover = true; break;
        case Keys.Up:
        case Keys.W : keyState.up = false; break;
        case Keys.Down:
        case Keys.S : keyState.down = false; break;
        case Keys.Left:
        case Keys.A : keyState.left = false; break;
        case Keys.Right:
        case Keys.D : keyState.right = false; break;
        case Keys.Space : talkFlag = false; break;
    }
}

private void doUpdate()
{
    int frameRate = game.FrameRate();
    int ticks = Environment.TickCount;
    if (ticks > drawLast + 16)
    {
        drawLast = ticks;
```

```
            doScrolling();
            doHero();
            doVendor();
            doDialogue();
            if (purchase != "")
            {
                game.Print((int)hero.Position.X, (int)hero.Position.Y,
                    purchase, Brushes.White);
            }

            game.Update();
            Application.DoEvents();
        }
        else Thread.Sleep(1);
    }

    private void doScrolling()
    {
        //move the tilemap scroll position
        int steps = 4;
        PointF pos = level.ScrollPos;

        //up key movement
        if (keyState.up)
        {
            if (hero.Y > 300 - 48) hero.Y -= steps;
            else
            {
                pos.Y -= steps;
                if (pos.Y <= 0) hero.Y -= steps;
            }
        }
        //down key movement
        else if (keyState.down)
        {
            if (hero.Y < 300 - 48) hero.Y += steps;
            else
            {
                pos.Y += steps;
                if (pos.Y >= (127 - 19) * 32) hero.Y += steps;
```

```
            }
        }

        //left key movement
        if (keyState.left)
        {
            if (hero.X > 400 - 48) hero.X -= steps;
            else
            {
                pos.X -= steps;
                if (pos.X <= 0) hero.X -= steps;
            }
        }

        //right key movement
        else if (keyState.right)
        {
            if (hero.X < 400 - 48) hero.X += steps;
            else
            {
                pos.X += steps;
                if (pos.X >= (127 - 25) * 32) hero.X += steps;
            }
        }

        //update scroller position
        level.ScrollPos = pos;
        level.Update();

        //draw the tilemap
        level.Draw(0, 0, 800, 600);
    }

    private void doHero()
    {
        //limit player sprite to the screen boundary
        if (hero.X < -32) hero.X = -32;
        else if (hero.X > 800 - 65) hero.X = 800 - 65;

        if (hero.Y < -48) hero.Y = -48;
```

```
        else if (hero.Y > 600 - 81) hero.Y = 600 - 81;
        //orient the player in the right direction
        if (keyState.up && keyState.right) hero.Direction = 1;
        else if (keyState.right && keyState.down) hero.Direction = 3;
        else if (keyState.down && keyState.left) hero.Direction = 5;
        else if (keyState.left && keyState.up) hero.Direction = 7;
        else if (keyState.up) hero.Direction = 0;
        else if (keyState.right) hero.Direction = 2;
        else if (keyState.down) hero.Direction = 4;
        else if (keyState.left) hero.Direction = 6;
        else hero.Direction = -1;

        //draw the hero
        hero.Draw();
    }

    private void doVendor()
    {
        float relativeX=0, relativeY=0;
        int talkRadius = 70;
        Pen color;

        //draw the vendor sprite
        if (vendor.X > level.ScrollPos.X &&
            vendor.X < level.ScrollPos.X + 23 * 32 &&
            vendor.Y > level.ScrollPos.Y &&
            vendor.Y < level.ScrollPos.Y + 17 * 32)
        {
            relativeX = Math.Abs(level.ScrollPos.X - vendor.X);
            relativeY = Math.Abs(level.ScrollPos.Y - vendor.Y);
            vendor.GetSprite.Draw((int)relativeX, (int)relativeY);
        }

        //get center of hero sprite
        PointF heroCenter = hero.FootPos;
        heroCenter.X += 16;
        heroCenter.Y += 16;
        game.Device.DrawRectangle(Pens.Red, heroCenter.X - 2,
            heroCenter.Y - 2, 4, 4);
```

```
    //get center of NPC
    PointF vendorCenter = new Point((int)relativeX, (int)relativeY);
    vendorCenter.X += vendor.GetSprite.Width / 2;
    vendorCenter.Y += vendor.GetSprite.Height / 2;
    game.Device.DrawRectangle(Pens.Red, vendorCenter.X - 2,
        vendorCenter.Y - 2, 4, 4);

    double dist = game.Distance(heroCenter, vendorCenter);

    //get distance to the NPC and draw a line
    if (dist < talkRadius)
        color = new Pen(Brushes.Blue, 2.0f);
    else
        color = new Pen(Brushes.Red, 2.0f);
    game.Device.DrawLine(color, heroCenter, vendorCenter);

    //print distance
    game.Print((int)relativeX, (int)relativeY,
        "D = " + dist.ToString("NO"), Brushes.White);

    //draw circle around vendor to show talk radius
    float spriteSize = vendor.GetSprite.Width / 2;
    float centerx = relativeX + spriteSize;
    float centery = relativeY + spriteSize;
    RectangleF circleRect = new RectangleF(centerx - talkRadius,
        centery - talkRadius, talkRadius * 2, talkRadius * 2);
    game.Device.DrawEllipse(color, circleRect);

    //is playing trying to talk to this vendor?
    if (dist < talkRadius)
    {
        if (talkFlag) talking = true;
    }
    else talking = false;
}

private void doDialogue()
{
    if (!talking) return;
```

```
//prepare the dialogue
dialogue.Title = "Bartholomu The Cheapskate";
dialogue.Message = "Greetings visitor. Oh my goodness, you look " +
    "like you've seen a bit of action. I ain't got much, y'know, " +
    "but ye'll be get'n a fair price! Better'n you'll ever get " +
    "over at Nathan's, I tell ye that much!";
dialogue.setButtonText(1, "2s Rusty Dagger (1-4 dmg)");
dialogue.setButtonText(2, "3s Wool Clothes (1 AC)");
dialogue.setButtonText(3, "10s Short Sword (2-8 dmg)");
dialogue.setButtonText(4, "15s Leather Armor (4 AC)");
dialogue.setButtonText(5, "25s Long Sword (6-12 dmg)");
dialogue.setButtonText(6, "50s Chain Armor (10 AC)");
dialogue.setButtonText(7, "30s Long Bow (4-10 dmg)");
dialogue.setButtonText(8, "90s Plate Armor (18 AC)");
dialogue.setButtonText(9, "80s Doom Ring (+2 STR)");
dialogue.setButtonText(10, "45s Bone Necklace (+2 STA)");

//reposition dialogue window
if (hero.CenterPos.X < 400)
{
    if (hero.CenterPos.Y < 300)
        dialogue.setCorner(Dialogue.Positions.LowerRight);
    else
        dialogue.setCorner(Dialogue.Positions.UpperRight);
} else {
    if (hero.CenterPos.Y < 300)
        dialogue.setCorner(Dialogue.Positions.LowerLeft);
    else
        dialogue.setCorner(Dialogue.Positions.UpperLeft);
}

//draw dialogue and look for selection
dialogue.updateMouse(game.MousePos, game.MouseButton);
dialogue.Draw();
if (dialogue.Selection > 0)
{
    talking = false;
    purchase = "You bought " + dialogue.getButtonText(
        dialogue.Selection);
    dialogue.Selection = 0;
```

```
        }
        else purchase = "";
    }
}
```

LEVEL UP!

This was a heavy-hitting chapter that covered some tough new material, but it was absolutely necessary and we ended up with a powerful new user interface class that can be used for many different parts of the Dungeon Crawler game. Speaking of which, in the very next chapter, it will be time to learn about fighting, gaining experience, and leveling! We have a few minor things to fix by the time we get to the final game in the last chapter, such as character sprites jumping a bit as we near the edge of the level, but it's nothing that a little extra code won't fix.

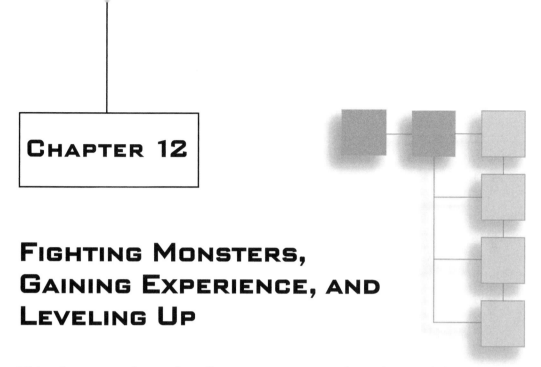

CHAPTER 12

FIGHTING MONSTERS, GAINING EXPERIENCE, AND LEVELING UP

This chapter explores the all-important topic of combat and how gaining experience affects the player's character. Chapter 11 gave us some tools that will be useful again now, such as code to figure out when the player is close to an enemy. This applies solely to melee fights, of course, and not to attacks at range, which will require a bit of extra effort. The simplest form of melee combat occurs when the player is close enough to an enemy and hits the attack button, similar to the way in which dialogue was engaged. One additional requirement for combat is that we must ensure the player is facing toward the enemy in order to deal any damage. In this chapter, we will explore these techniques and the random attack dice rolls needed to make realistic combat that even an RPG purist will appreciate.

Here's what we'll cover in this chapter:

- Preparing for combat
- Character animation templates
- Creating the combat system
- Attack and damage rolls
- Facing your enemies
- State-based combat
- Dealing permanent damage

PREPARING FOR COMBAT

In a normal game, hostile NPCs will be guarding locations or wandering around in the environment, usually following a series of waypoints or just walking back and forth between two points. For our first few examples of combat, the hostile NPCs will be positioned in the level randomly and will *not move*. We will give them movement behavior later, but for now I just want to show you how to engage an enemy in order to attack them. There are several ways we could go about handling combat in the game. In a real-time game, there is never a pause in the action: when the player engages one enemy, there may be other nearby enemies who charge into the battle as well. A variation is a partial real-time game where the player can move freely through the game but each round of combat causes the game to pause while it is resolved.

A second type of combat is turn-based. Although our game allows the player to roam the world freely in real time, I have decided to use a turn-based system with rounds to resolve combat. This choice comes after much play testing of a fully real-time combat system that just seemed to happen too quickly. With the player and hostile NPC swinging weapons at each other, basically as fast as the attacks are allowed to go, the HP for each slowly goes down until one falls or retreats. This form of combat works great for a game like *Diablo* and *Baldur's Gate*, and our own pending Dungeon Crawler game. The combat system for our game can be either real time or turn-based with a few simple flags in the code.

Starting an Attack

The code to draw the monsters is the same code used in previous chapters to draw objects with a global position within the scrolling level. Before drawing objects, we must get its relative position with respect to the scroll position and then draw it at the relative position.

```
//is monster in view?
if (monsters[n].X > level.ScrollPos.X &&
    monsters[n].X < level.ScrollPos.X + 23 * 32 &&
    monsters[n].Y > level.ScrollPos.Y &&
    monsters[n].Y < level.ScrollPos.Y + 17 * 32)
```

If the object is within the viewport at the current scroll position, then we can figure out its relative position on the screen and draw it.

```
relativePos = new PointF(
    Math.Abs(level.ScrollPos.X - monsters[n].X),
    Math.Abs(level.ScrollPos.Y - monsters[n].Y));
monsterCenter = relativePos;
monsterCenter.X += monsters[n].GetSprite.Width / 2;
monsterCenter.Y += monsters[n].GetSprite.Height / 2;
```

Distance is calculated from the center of the NPC's sprite to the center of the PC's sprite.

```
dist = hero.CenterDistance(monsterCenter);
if (dist < ATTACK_RADIUS)
```

As you can see, most of this code was developed previously. We first learned how to calculate relative position back in Chapter 8, "Adding Objects to the Dungeon," and then how to calculate distance to an NPC in Chapter 11. When the PC is within range of an NPC, its radius circle will change from red to blue, and then the Space key will trigger an attack. In this first demo, nothing happens beyond printing out the attack flag status. We'll evolve this initial code as the chapter proceeds.

Combat Demo 1

The first Combat demo project shows how to calculate the attack radius around each NPC and the logic to determine when the player is in range to attack. At this point, the NPCs do not move or react to the player and combat isn't working yet. We will build on this example while building a combat system. See Figure 12.1. In the truncated source code listing below, the sections related to the radius and combat are highlighted in bold. For the complete source code listing of each sample in this chapter, see the chapter resources or the final example at the end of the chapter.

```
private void doMonsters()
{
    PointF relativePos;
    Pen color;
    PointF heroCenter;
    PointF monsterCenter;
    double dist=0;
    float spriteSize;
    Point center;
```

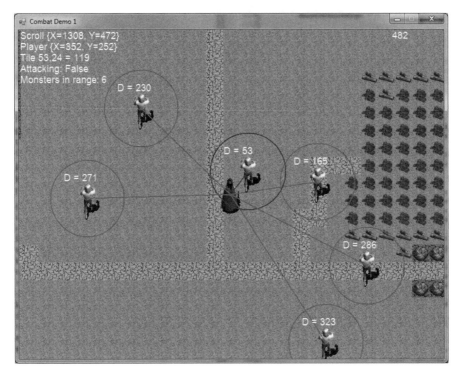

Figure 12.1
A circle around each hostile NPC show its combat radius.

```
RectangleF circleRect;

//get center of hero sprite
heroCenter = hero.CenterPos;
game.Device.DrawRectangle(Pens.Red, heroCenter.X - 2,
    heroCenter.Y - 2, 4, 4);

monstersInRange = 0;
for (int n = 1; n < NUM_MONSTERS; n++)
{
    //is monster in view?
    if (monsters[n].X > level.ScrollPos.X &&
        monsters[n].X < level.ScrollPos.X + 23 * 32 &&
        monsters[n].Y > level.ScrollPos.Y &&
        monsters[n].Y < level.ScrollPos.Y + 17 * 32)
    {
```

```
monstersInRange += 1;
relativePos = new PointF(
    Math.Abs(level.ScrollPos.X - monsters[n].X),
    Math.Abs(level.ScrollPos.Y - monsters[n].Y));

//draw the monster sprite
monsters[n].GetSprite.Draw((int)relativePos.X,
    (int)relativePos.Y);

//get center of NPC
monsterCenter = relativePos;
monsterCenter.X += monsters[n].GetSprite.Width / 2;
monsterCenter.Y += monsters[n].GetSprite.Height / 2;
game.Device.DrawRectangle(Pens.Red, monsterCenter.X - 2,
    monsterCenter.Y - 2, 4, 4);

//get distance to the NPC
dist = hero.CenterDistance(monsterCenter);

//draw line to NPCs in view
if (dist < ATTACK_RADIUS)
    color = new Pen(Brushes.Blue, 2.0f);
else
    color = new Pen(Brushes.Red, 2.0f);
game.Device.DrawLine(color, heroCenter, monsterCenter);

//print distance
game.Print((int)relativePos.X, (int)relativePos.Y,
    "D = " + dist.ToString("N0"), Brushes.White);

//draw circle around monster to show attack radius
spriteSize = monsters[n].GetSprite.Width / 2;
center = new Point((int)(relativePos.X + spriteSize),
    (int)(relativePos.Y + spriteSize));
circleRect = new RectangleF(
    center.X - ATTACK_RADIUS, center.Y - ATTACK_RADIUS,
    ATTACK_RADIUS * 2, ATTACK_RADIUS * 2);
game.Device.DrawEllipse(color, circleRect);
}
```

```
            //is player trying to attack to this monster?
            if (dist < ATTACK_RADIUS)
            {
                if (attackFlag) attacking = true;
            }
            else attacking = false;
        }
    }
```

CHARACTER TEMPLATES

We have come to the point where additional artwork is needed to make any more progress with the Dungeon Crawler game, so in this section we will look at most of the character art planned for the game, including sprites for the player character and NPCs. Real characters will be created out of these templates in the final chapter when the game is fully realized. So, you'll want to look at these character descriptions and animation artwork as mere templates of actual character classes, not characters themselves. Let's take a short break from working on the combat system to look at the artwork. As you continue into the combat system in this chapter, begin thinking about which of these sprites you plan to use in the game.

Animations: Player Characters (PCs)

For the last two chapters, we have been using the paladin character file generated back in Chapter 10, "Creating Characters and Monsters." That character has good animations and is representative of the PC for a dungeon crawler, but we have three additional sets of artwork available and need to bring them into the game world. Technically, we aren't supposed to pre-roll a player character. Part of the fun factor of playing an RPG—one might even argue that it's the *most important* part of the gameplay—is creating your own character. I don't want to take away that joy from players by pre-rolling them with the character editor. This tool is meant to be used to create NPCs, but we use it to manage the artwork for the PC classes. The final game project includes a character generator! Let's create random PC classes for use in this chapter. You have already seen the paladin, so we'll roll the other three classes.

I will provide animation sets so that it is easy for you to add new characters to the game without requiring much extra work. The monsters need attack animations. I won't focus on the player character classes here, but rather on what artwork is available for use in creating characters—because we have more artwork than we need for just the four classes (Warrior, Paladin, Hunter, and Priest). Feel free to use the animation sets specified in these template .char files for any unique classes of your own design. The purpose behind the .char file, at least for player characters, is to define the animation properties.

Hint

In the final game, these character templates will be used to create real game characters. The complete sets of animation and character editor data files are included for each one in this chapter's resource files which can be downloaded from www.courseptr.com/downloads or from www.jharbour.com/forum.

Hero (Axe)

The hero sprite animations that show the character carrying an axe (Figure 12.2) are usually variations of the warrior, who may also carry a single sword, and is generally different from a paladin because he doesn't have a shield.

Hero (Sword)

This hero sprite has a single sword and is often a variation of the warrior class (along with the axe sprite) (Figure 12.3).

Hero (Axe & Shield)

We have already seen the paladin character back in Chapter 11, but the actual character is not all that important prior to the player actually creating a player character at the start of a new game (Figure 12.4).

Hero (Sword & Shield)

The hero sprite animation featuring both a sword and shield (Figure 12.5) is also usually associated with the paladin class, but this is a loose interpretation that you are welcome to change if you wish!

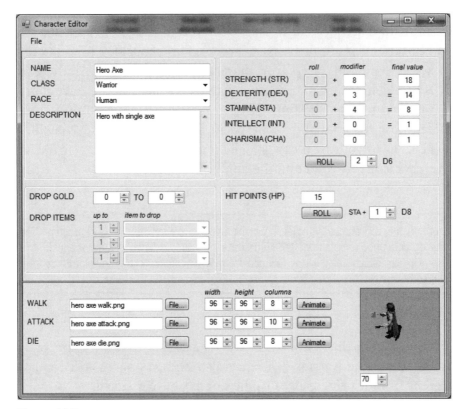

Figure 12.2
Hero sprite wielding a single axe.

Hero (Bow)

The hero sprite with bow animations (Figure 12.6) is obviously associated with a hunter, archer, or scout class, but you may invent any name for the class using these animation sets.

Hero (Staff)

The staff-wielding hero character (Figure 12.7) usually represents a cloth wearing mage, wizard, or priest. To show how these animations are created, I've included a screenshot of the priest sprite as it appeared in Pro Motion (the sprite animation software—see www.cosmigo.com for a trial copy). The sprite sheet produced by Pro Motion is shown next to it. Pro Motion saves the file as a .bmp file, so it must be converted to a .png with an alpha channel, and I prefer to

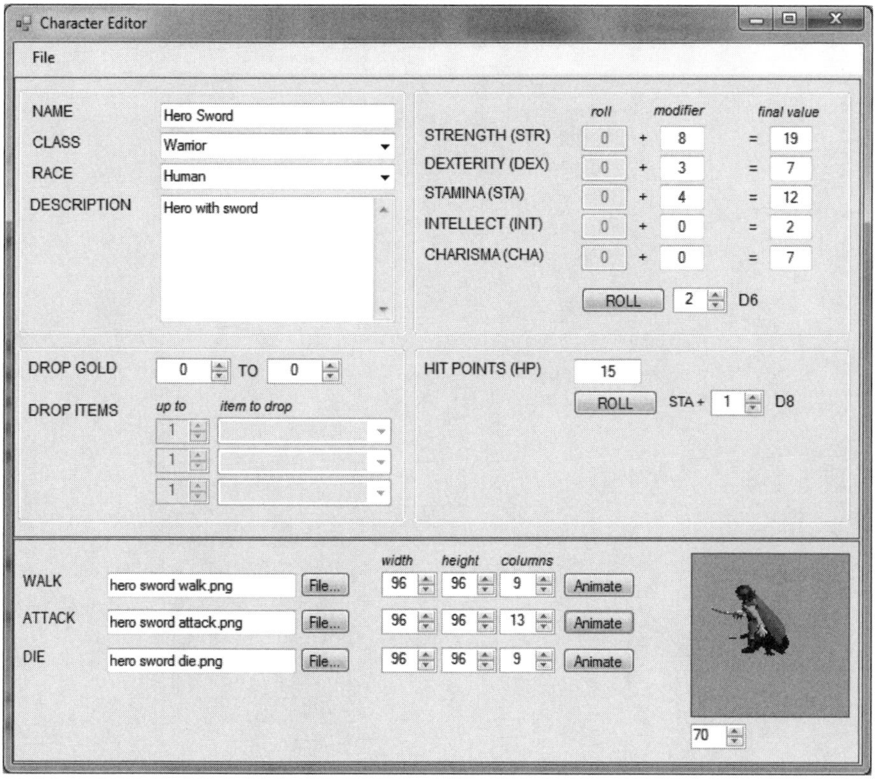

Figure 12.3
Hero sprite wielding a single sword.

use GIMP for that step. It's easy to use the Color Select tool to highlight the background color and convert it to a Layer Mask.

Hero (Unarmed)

The hero sprite animation with *no weapon or shield* (Figure 12.8) still has unarmed animations, with a kick attack, which might be fun to explore in a game. How about a Kung Fu character?

Animations: Hostile NPCs

The hostile NPC character sheets show just what is possible with these animation sets, but you are encouraged to create characters of your own design

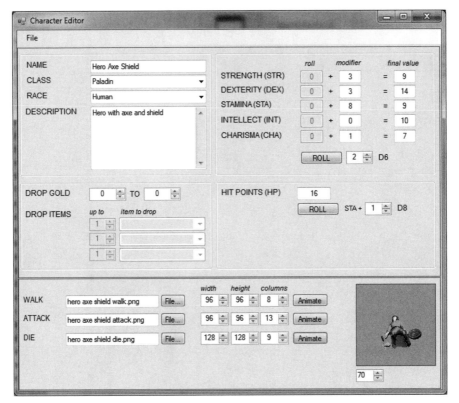

Figure 12.4
Hero sprite wielding an axe and shield.

with the character editor using these template files as a starting point (with the animations already in place).

Skeleton (Bow)

The skeleton animation set with a bow (Figure 12.9) is an undead archer or hunter.

Skeleton (Sword & Shield)

The sword & shield animation set for the undead skeleton (Figure 12.10) can be used for a typical *former* warrior or paladin turned undead, with any number of actual characters derived from it. Since there is no other variation of an undead

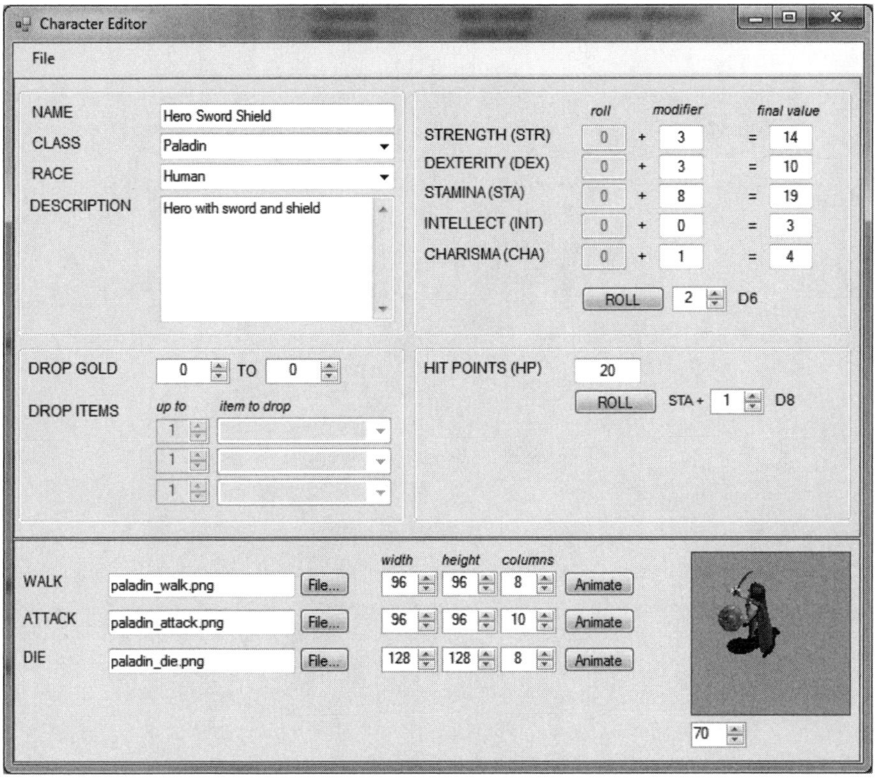

Figure 12.5
Hero sprite wielding a sword and shield.

melee character, this one will be reused. The image here shows the sprite animation as it appears in Pro Motion, along with the saved sprite sheet.

Skeleton (Unarmed)

The unarmed undead skeleton sprite (Figure 12.11) is a good general-purpose template for lower-level enemy characters, which may be good for early leveling by player characters.

Zombie (Unarmed)

This undead zombie sprite (Figure 12.12) has no weapon, but that is traditionally accurate of zombies in popular culture (namely, zombie films). With an appetite for gray matter, the player would do well to take them out at range!

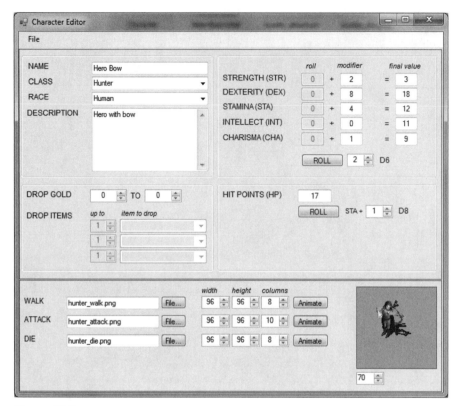

Figure 12.6
Hero sprite wielding a bow.

CREATING THE COMBAT SYSTEM

Melee combat occurs when opponents fight each other with hand-held weapons (while unarmed combat occurs when no weapons are used, as in a martial art). The game engine already has *support* for melee combat, but it's just not put into place yet. First, we must determine when the player is near an enemy, then cause the enemy to turn toward the player, and then allow combat to ensue. Fortunately, the sprites available from Reiner's Tilesets (www.reinerstilesets. de) also include the attack and falling animations. We already have the first step working. Next, we'll work on causing sprites to face each other and attack.

Combat requires another layer of logic added to the state engine that controls the characters. Although higher-level interaction with characters would make the game more realistic, we'll just be treating this like an old-style hack-and-slash

Figure 12.7
Hero sprite wielding a staff, shown here with animation assembled with Pro Motion.

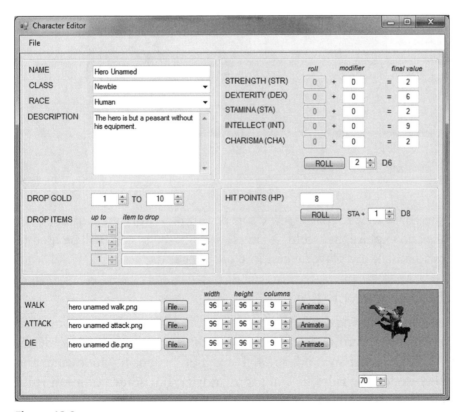

Figure 12.8
Hero sprite wielding only fists of fury!

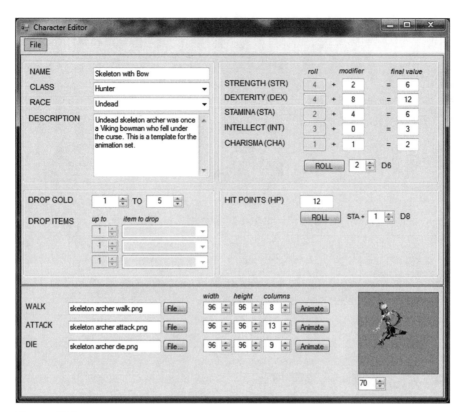

Figure 12.9
Undead skeleton sprite with bow.

game where the goal is not to follow some sort of complex storyline, but rather to gain experience and explore the world. A simple state-based system will be used to cause enemies to attack the player when in close range.

Making Up Our Own Rules

There are many role-playing game systems that we can emulate for our own games, or we can just borrow ideas from many different games and come up with totally unique gameplay and rules. I am not proposing following any particular franchise for the rules in Dungeon Crawler, but some common rules will be familiar to an experienced RPG player.

The current project at this point is a template game that has most of the functionality you need to create an RPG, but is lacking most of the finer details.

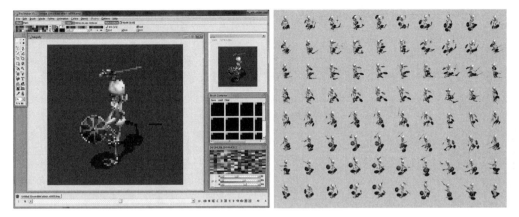

Figure 12.10
Undead skeleton sprite with sword & shield.

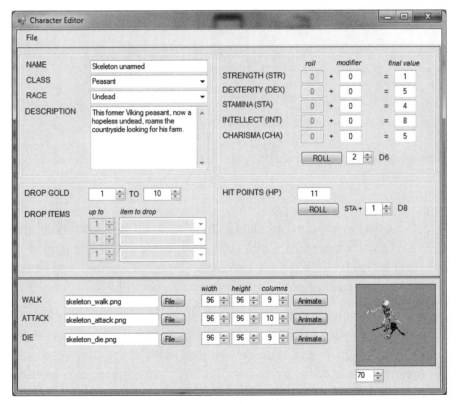

Figure 12.11
This undead skeleton sprite has no weapon.

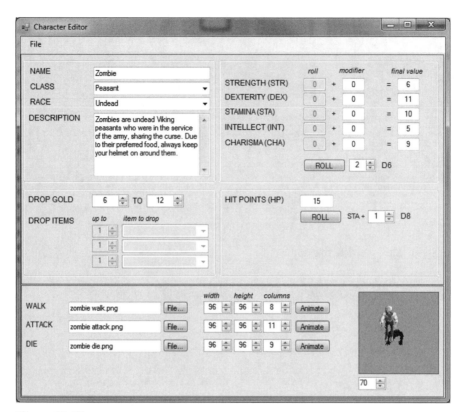

Figure 12.12
The zombie is undead—but what else could it be?

There is just an enormous amount of detail that must be put into even the simplest of RPGs. We will create a fun hack-and-slash game where the goal is to gain experience and go up levels, with the corresponding new abilities and skills, but there won't be an overriding plot or story—that's your job!

Chapter 11 developed the ability for the player to have encounters with NPCs, which is an important first step in the game's NPC interaction. From this point, you can engage the NPCs in dialogue or combat, and the game responds appropriately. A higher level of behavior over the NPCs is also needed to turn this skeleton game into a polished game, a system of behavior that causes NPCs to seek out and engage the player, rather than always *responding* to the player. At the very least, you can add the ability for NPCs to fight back.

Spawning Enemy NPCs

A non-player character (NPC) can be friendly or hostile—we might refer to them as "friendly NPCs" or "hostile NPCs"—but they are still grouped together as "not the player," for the sake of discussion. We're going to combine the work done already to create random monsters that will react to the player with, well, *hostility*.

When you are fighting with an NPC and kill that character, there should be a death animation. These are not always possible in every case, due to a limited number of sprites. You are limited overall by the availability of artwork, without which you have to get creative with your sprites. Rather than dealing with a whole slew of death animations for each NPC, I have seen some games use the fade effect, where a character blinks out of existence or fades away. You might use the alpha color parameter in the sprite class to cause a character to fade out of existence after dying rather than using a death animation. The important thing is that you recycle your sprites in the game, which means recycling the NPCs. You don't want the NPCs to just respawn at the same place every time, because then the player can see the spawning taking place (which seriously ruins the realism of the game). In addition, if a player learns where some of the NPCs are respawning on the map, he or she will be able to spawn camp (which refers to hiding out near a spawn point and killing new players that appear) and rack up a ridiculous amount of experience, which also ruins the game.

Attack Rolls

What really happens when you attack another character in the game? That is the basis of the game's combat system, and it has to do with each player's attributes, including weapon and armor class. Usually, the defender's defensive value is compared to the attacker's attack value, and a simulated "roll" of dice is made to determine if the attack succeeded (before calculating damage). All of the attributes are available already from the character editor files.

If the attack value is less than the defense value, then basically you can do no damage to your opponent! So, say you are a new warrior with an axe that does +10 damage, and you attack a level 10 zombie with 93 defense points. What happens in this situation? You can stand there and bang against this monster all day long with your pathetic little axe and do *no damage* to him! In a situation like this, you are helplessly outclassed by the monster, which swiftly and easily kills you with a single blow.

This is called the "to-hit roll" and it adds a nice layer of realism to the game (as opposed to some games where just swinging your sword kills enemies nearby). Knowing that not every swing does damage requires you to use some tactics in your fighting method, and this gives players the ability to be somewhat creative in how they fight enemies. You can swing and run or swing several times in a row, hoping to get a hit. It's a hit-or-miss situation. Figure 12.13 shows an example of several types of dice.

Many RPGs allow the player to equip modifiers such as rings and special weapons with bonuses for the to-hit value. These modifiers increase your chances of scoring a hit when you attack. Not only is it essential for a good RPG, but working with miscellaneous items as well as different types of swords, shields, armor, helmets, and so on, is an extremely fun part of the game! Our Character class will be modified over the next two chapters to add support for gear such as the weapon, armor, and other items that the player can equip, and you have an opportunity to use these special items to customize characters. You may even allow the player to pick up items found in the world and equip them.

Armor Class (AC)

A character's armor class determines whether an attack made against him will succeed or not. If the attack fails, then no damage is applied at all. Usually, regardless of the AC, an attack to-hit roll of 1 is an *epic fail* and does not hit. Here's one possible way to calculate AC:

```
AC = DEX + Armor Points + Shield Points
```

Figure 12.13
Six different dice with 4, 6, 8, 10, 12, and 20 sides. Image courtesy of Wikipedia.

where `Armor Points` represent the sum total of all armor items and `Shield Points` represent the defense value of an equipped shield. I say *possible way* because this is not the *only way* to perform the calculation. Some game systems do not allow a DEX bonus for plate armor wearers because that represents a slow-moving character, whereas high DEX represents high agility. To keep the rules simple in Dungeon Crawler, I just apply the full DEX and full AP to the calculation.

Based on the type of gear available in your game, you may want to add a modifier to the AC calculation to help balance the gameplay a bit if it seems that too many attack rolls are an instant hit. I would expect about half of all attacks to fail when rolled against a foe at the same level. If you find that significantly more than half of all attacks are succeeding, then that's a sign you need to add a modifier to the AC (such as +5).

Melee "Chance To-Hit" Rolls

The mechanics of combat for any game is entirely up to the designer. The important thing is not that your game works like many other RPGs out there, only that combat is balanced within your own game system. In other words, as long as the PC and hostile NPCs attack with the same set of rules, then the game is playable. One thing you really don't want to happen is for combat to end too quickly. It's generally necessary to artificially raise the hit points (HP) of monsters at the lower levels so they don't fall with one hit. You want the player to feel as if real combat is taking place, not that they're just walking around taking out enemies with a single blow as if they're using a lightsaber. We do want the player's attributes to play an important role in the to-hit roll as well as the damage done in an attack.

For Dungeon Crawler, I'm going to use a D20 (a 20-sided die) as the basis for the to-hit roll. In RPG lingo, a D20 roll of 1 is an *epic fail* while a roll of 20 is a *critical hit*, which usually means a definite hit (ignoring the defender's AC).

```
Melee Chance To-Hit = STR + D20
```

Ranged "Chance To-Hit" Rolls

Ranged attacks with a bow or spell are similar to melee with a D20 roll, but with DEX instead of STR as a modifier. The character's agility contributes to his ability to hit accurately at a distance, where his strength has little or no effect.

```
Ranged Chance To-Hit = DEX + D20
```

Rolling for Damage

If the to-hit roll results in a hit, the next step is to roll again to determine how much damage was done to the target. This is where the weapon attributes come into play. If the game features real items that you can give your character to use in combat, then it makes a big difference in the gameplay. For one thing, you can scatter treasure chests around the game world that contain unique quest items (like magical swords, shields, and armor), as well as valuable jewels and gold. (These types of items are all modeled and available in the sprites provided in the Reiner's Tileset collection.)

Melee "Damage" Rolls

The melee damage value is calculated primarily from STR and weapon damage with a 1D8 roll added to the mix. This damage factor is then reduced by the defender's AC to come up with a total damage, which goes against the defender's HP.

```
Melee Damage = D8 + STR + Weapon Damage - Defender's AC
```

Some games apply a different die roll based on the type of weapon, such as a 2D6 for a two-handed sword, 2D8 for a two-handed mace, and 1D10 for a bow. You may use modifiers such as this if you want, but it adds an additional bit of information to the item database. I found it easier to use a base random die roll (D8) and the weapon damage as an *additional* die roll. The result is very nearly the same, but it results in more reasonable weapon damage factors. For instance, we wouldn't expect a rusty short sword to deal 12–16 damage where normally it should be 1–4. By using the D8 roll in addition to the weapon damage range, the damage factors will be more reasonable.

Ranged "Damage" Rolls

The ranged damage value is calculated primarily from DEX and weapon damage with a 1D8 roll added for some randomness. A range penalty is then subtracted from the total to arrive at a new attack value, which is further reduced by the defender's AC. The final value is the total damage dealt against the defender's HP.

```
Ranged Damage = D8 + DEX + weapon damage - range penalty - Defender's AC
```

Ranged damage differs slightly from melee due to the range penalty, but it's a reasonable subtraction, because without it the player would be nearly invincible, able to deal out full damage at long range where no monster would ever be able to catch him before being cut down.

Critical Hits ("Crit")

If the chance to-hit roll of the D20 results in a 20, then the attack is a *critical hit* and incurs additional damage! You may add whatever modifier you want to the attack damage factor, such as a 2x roll factor. So, if the damage was calculated with 1D8, then the critical damage will be 2D8. Optionally, you may just double the 1D8 damage roll. Remember, your system doesn't have to mimic the combat mechanic of any other system—be creative and unique!

Attack Roll Example

Let's simulate one half of an attack round where just one player attacks and the other defends, to see how the calculations are done and what results we get. First of all, we'll give the player these attributes:

- STR: 18
- DEX: 12
- STA: 9
- Weapon: 2–8 dmg
- Armor: 10
- HP: 14

The monster will have these attributes:

- STR: 15
- DEX: 14
- STA: 16
- Weapon: 1–6 dmg
- Armor: 12
- HP: 16

Armor Class

First, we'll calculate the AC for the monster:

```
AC = DEX + Armor Points + Shield Points
AC = 14 + 12 + 0
AC = 26
```

Attack Roll

Now, we'll calculate the attacker's attack chance to-hit:

```
To-Hit = Attack Roll (STR + D20) - Defender's AC
Attack roll = STR + D20
Attack roll = 18 + 9 (roll) = 27
```

Did the attack succeed?

```
To-Hit = Attack Roll (27) - AC (26) = 1 (Hit!)
```

Damage Roll

Since our attack succeeded, but was not a critical hit, we calculate normal damage.

```
Damage = D8 + STR + Weapon Damage - Defender's AC
Damage = roll (1-8) + 18 + roll (2-8) - 26
Damage = roll (3) + 18 + roll (7) - 26
Damage = 3 + 18 + 7 - 26 = 2
```

Had the attack been a critical hit with an attack roll of 20, then critical damage would be calculated with a factor of 2 as follows:

```
Damage = D8 * 2 + STR + Weapon Damage - Defender's AC
Damage = roll (1-8) * 2 + 18 + roll (2-8) - 26
Damage = roll (3) * 2 + 18 + roll (7) - 26
Damage = 6 + 18 + 7 - 26 = 5
```

Hit Points

The monster's HP is reduced by the total damage until it reaches zero (which is death):

```
HP = 16 - 2 = 14 (normal damage)
HP = 16 - 5 = 11 (critical damage)
```

As you can see from these results, the die rolls are *crucial*! After all those many calculations, our hero only dealt 2 points of damage to the monster, and the monster then gets to strike back at the player. This continues round after round until one or the other loses all their HP or flees.

Dealing with the Player's Death

One drawback to combat is that you can die. It's a cold, hard, truth, I realize, but it can happen. What should you do, as the game's designer and programmer, when the *player's character (PC)* dies? That is a tough decision that requires some thought and should be based on the overall design of your game. You might let the player save and load the game, but that takes away from the suspension of disbelief. You want the player to be completely immersed in the game and unaware of a file system, an operating system, or even of the computer. You want your players to be mesmerized by the content on the screen, and something as cheesy as a load/save feature takes away from that. I'll admit, though, most players abuse the save/load game feature and complain if you don't have one. After all, you want the player to be able to quit at a moment's notice without going through any hassle. Let's face it: Sometimes the real world asserts itself into the reverie you are experiencing in the game, and you have to quit playing.

But just for the sake of gameplay, what is the best way to deal with the player character's death, aside from having a save/load feature? I recommend just re-spawning the PC at the starting point of a level file. The location of a re-spawn is up to you as the game's designer. Do you want to make it too easy for the player to die and come back too quickly, or do you want to make them work a little bit before resuming the fight they were in previously? Re-spawning too close to the last fight might make the game too easy, so a spawn point at a central hub town or other location might be better, and then the player must walk and portal to get back to the location where they were at prior to dying.

Combat Demo 2

The second Combat demo shows how to make these calculations for an attack against an NPC (Figure 12.14). This demo uses the `Dialogue` class to show the results of attack rolls with each part of the calculation shown for you to study. This scene, for instance, shows a critical attack roll that dealt 14 damage to a target NPC. Most RPG purists will enjoy seeing this information, whereas casual RPG fans will prefer to just hurry up and kill the monster so they can loot its corpse for items and gold. It's up to you to decide how much information you want to share with the player.

On the one hand, it might be impressive to see what all is involved in an attack with the various rolls and calculations, since the casual player might just assume your combat system uses a simple attack roll versus defense roll system. If you don't show any information, and just show damage dealt (as in games like *Baldur's Gate*), the player might assume just a random attack roll is all there is to it. Every attribute is important and affects the outcome of combat, and every player knows this intuitively, but it's easy to forget if combat tends to happen very quickly. One advantage to turn-based combat is that it will reflect a pencil-and-paper game, which is at the root of every computer RPG. On the other

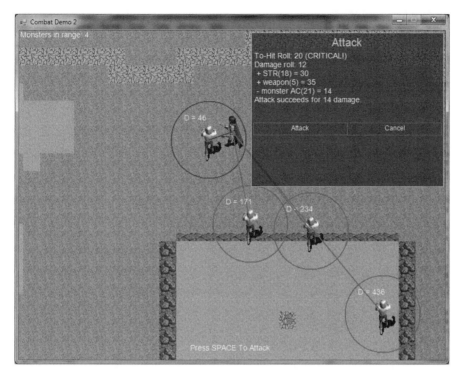

Figure 12.14
Demonstration of an attack roll against a hostile NPC.

hand, some players might get annoyed with the slow pace of combat and give up on your game. You have to decide on the best balance between information overload (TMI) and dumbed-down gameplay.

Turn-based Combat

When a turn-based combat system is the way to go, we need to make a few minor changes to the input system. In the previous example, we used the Space key to trigger a flag called attackFlag, which was set to false when the Space key was released. That works for a real-time combat system, but not for a turn-based one. For turn-based combat, we need to wait until the user *releases* the attack key. Otherwise, some sort of timing mechanism must be used and that can get messy. So, here is the new keyboard code—note how attackFlag is now handled.

```
private void Form1_KeyDown(object sender, KeyEventArgs e)
{
    switch (e.KeyCode)
    {
        case Keys.Escape: gameover = true; break;
        case Keys.Up:
        case Keys.W: keyState.up = true; break;
        case Keys.Down:
        case Keys.S: keyState.down = true; break;
        case Keys.Left:
        case Keys.A: keyState.left = true; break;
        case Keys.Right:
        case Keys.D: keyState.right = true; break;
    }
}
private void Form1_KeyUp(object sender, KeyEventArgs e)
{
    switch (e.KeyCode)
    {
        case Keys.Up:
        case Keys.W: keyState.up = false; break;
        case Keys.Down:
        case Keys.S: keyState.down = false; break;
        case Keys.Left:
        case Keys.A: keyState.left = false; break;
        case Keys.Right:
        case Keys.D: keyState.right = false; break;
        case Keys.Space: attackFlag = true; break;
    }
}
```

More Dialogue

We need the Dialogue class again to show the results of an attack. You can now see how useful Dialogue is beyond its original intended use as a way to talk with NPCs! Granted, the window is not very attractive yet. We will need to add some more configuration options to it so the buttons look better and the height is adjusted automatically to the number of buttons in use. But, the important thing is, we have a way to interact with the player. Before using it, we need to add some new features to the Dialogue class. See, I warned you that this was likely to happen! But, we can't possibly foresee in the future what new things we'll need to do with our code, so this is to be expected.

As you'll recall, the Dialogue class will display the dialogue window until a button is clicked, and then set the Selection property equal to the button number. Previously, the Dialogue class did not hide itself after a selection was made or reset any of its properties. The new feature we need to add is a Visible property.

```
private bool p_visible;
public bool Visible
{
    get { return p_visible; }
    set { p_visible = value; }
}
```

The Draw() function will check p_visible before drawing anything. Now we will have the ability to continually update the Dialogue object and have it display whatever we want to the player, and selectively show it as needed.

```
public void Draw()
{
    if (!p_visible) return;
    ...
}
```

Back to our main source code for Combat demo 2. Here is the new doUpdate() function, which now handles scrolling, hero, monsters, attacking, and dialogue.

```
private void doUpdate()
{
    int frameRate = game.FrameRate();
    int ticks = Environment.TickCount;
    if (ticks > drawLast + 16)
    {
        drawLast = ticks;
        doScrolling();
        doHero();
        doMonsters();
        doAttack();
        doDialogue();
```

```
        game.Print(0, 0, "Monsters in range: " +
            monstersInRange.ToString());
        game.Print(320, 570, "Press SPACE to Attack");
        game.Update();
        Application.DoEvents();
    }
    else Thread.Sleep(1);
}
```

The doDialogue() function does not automatically move, but you may use that feature if you want (see Chapter 15 for details). I want the combat dialogue to stay in the same place.

```
private void doDialogue()
{
    dialogue.updateMouse(game.MousePos, game.MouseButton);
    dialogue.setCorner(Dialogue.Positions.UpperRight);
    dialogue.Draw();
    if (dialogue.Selection > 0)
    {
        dialogue.Visible = false;
        dialogue.Selection = 0;
    }
}
```

The doDialogue() function is called continuously from the main loop, and properties determine what it should do. To trigger a dialogue to "pop up," we can call on this new showDialogue() function, which automatically formats the dialogue with two buttons:

```
private void showDialogue(string title, string message,
    string button1, string button2)
{
    dialogue.Title = title;
    dialogue.Message = message;
    dialogue.NumButtons = 2;
    dialogue.setButtonText(1, button1);
    dialogue.setButtonText(2, button2);
    dialogue.Visible = true;
}
```

Attack!

The doAttack() function handles a single round of combat. Well, technically, it's just one-half of a round since the NPC doesn't fight back yet. Study the calculations in this function to learn more about how the armor class, attack roll, and damage roll are related.

```
private void doAttack()
{
    const int DEF_ARMOR = 10;
    const int DEF_SHIELD = 0;
    const int WEAPON_DMG = 5;
    bool hit = false;
    bool critical = false;
    bool fail = false;
    int roll = 0;
    int AC = 0;
    int damage = 0;
    string text="";

    if (!attacking) return;

    //calculate target's AC
    AC = monsters[target].DEX + DEF_ARMOR + DEF_SHIELD;

    //calculate chance to-hit for PC
    roll = game.Random(1, 20);
    text += "To-Hit Roll: " + roll.ToString();
    if (roll == 20)
    {
        //critical hit!
        hit = true;
        critical = true;
        text += " (CRITICAL!)\n";
    }
    else if (roll == 1)
    {
        fail = true;
        text += " (EPIC FAIL!)\n";
    }
    else
```

```
{
    //normal hit
    roll += hero.STR;
    if (roll > AC) hit = true;
    text += " + STR(" + hero.STR.ToString() + ") = " +
        roll.ToString() + "\n";
}

//did attack succeed?
if (hit)
{
    //calculate base damage
    damage = game.Random(1, 8);

    //add critical
    if (critical) damage *= 2;

    text += "Damage roll: " + damage.ToString() + "\n";

    //add STR
    damage += hero.STR;
    text += " + STR(" + hero.STR.ToString() + ") = " +
        damage.ToString() + "\n";

    //add weapon damage (usually a die roll)
    damage += WEAPON_DMG;
    text += " + weapon(" + WEAPON_DMG.ToString() + ") = " +
        damage.ToString() + "\n";

    //subtract AC
    damage -= AC;
    text += " - monster AC(" + AC.ToString() + ") = " +
        damage.ToString() + "\n";

    //minimal hit
    if (damage < 1) damage = 1;

    //show result
    text += "Attack succeeds for " + damage.ToString() +
        " damage.";
```

```
    }
    else
        text += "Attack failed.\n";

    showDialogue("Attack", text, "Attack", "Cancel");
}
```

FACING YOUR ENEMIES

It goes without saying that attacking an enemy who is behind you is kind of silly. No, it's *ridiculous*. No one can swing a sword accurately behind them, let alone shoot an arrow backward. So, the game shouldn't allow it either! What's worse, we can deal damage to a monster without even swinging *at it*. The code that figures out the direction to a target is like the code that sets the player's animation based on its direction. The `getTargetDirection()` function will "point" a character from its current angle toward a target. This is also useful for pitting NPCs against each other, or for having NPCs face the player when you talk to them. Figure 12.15 shows the Combat demo 3 running with new code to cause sprites to face toward each other.

Hint

Note: the code in these examples is not meant to be based on step-by-step modifications to the first example, but only to show the most relevant code as the chapter example is developed. You will want to open the complete project for each example and observe it running as you study the text. These projects *do* evolve toward a final, working combat system, but the complete code at each step is not listed.

Which Way Did He Go?

The logic behind figuring out the direction from one point to another is really just about brute-force If statements. First, we look at the X position of both points to find out whether the target is left, right, or directly in line with the source. Then, it checks the Y position to figure out whether the target is above, below, or right in line with the source. Based on these conditions, we set the source in a direction that will most closely match the target's location (within the limits of the 8-way directions for our animations).

```
private int getTargetDirection(PointF source, PointF target)
{
```

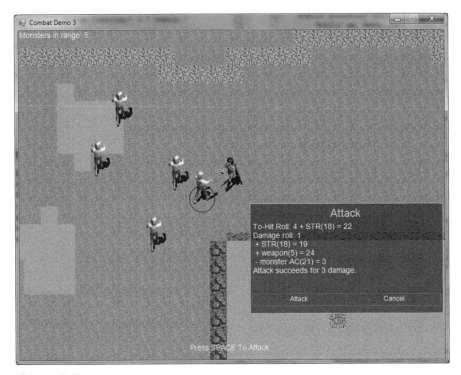

Figure 12.15
This demo shows how to cause sprites to face toward each other in order to fight.

```
int direction = 0;
if (source.X < target.X - 16)
{
    //facing eastward
    if (source.Y < target.Y - 8)
        direction = 3; //south east
    else if (source.Y > target.Y + 8)
        direction = 1; //north east
    else
        direction = 2; //east
}
else if (source.X > target.X + 16)
{
    //facing westward
    if (source.Y < target.Y - 8)
        direction = 5; //south west
```

```
        else if (source.Y > target.Y + 8)
            direction = 7; //north west
        else
            direction = 6; //west
    }
    else
    {
        //facing north or south
        if (source.Y < target.Y - 8)
            direction = 4; //south
        else if (source.Y > target.Y + 8)
            direction = 0; //north
    }
    return direction;
}
```

Using this function, we can modify doMonsters() and force the PC and NPC to face each other when the player triggers an attack! The result is much improved over the previous example.

```
//is player trying to attack this monster?
if (dist < ATTACK_RADIUS)
{
    game.Device.DrawEllipse(new Pen(Brushes.Blue, 2.0f),
        monsterCenter.X - 24, monsterCenter.Y, 48, 48);
    if (attackFlag)
    {
        attacking = true;
        target = n;
        attackFlag = false;

        //make PC and NPC face each other
        int dir = getTargetDirection(monsterCenter, hero.CenterPos);
        monsters[target].Direction = dir;
        monsters[target].Draw();

        dir = getTargetDirection(hero.CenterPos, monsterCenter);
        hero.Direction = dir;
        hero.Draw();

        break;
```

```
        }
    }
```

A Change of Character

A minor change is required in the Character class to support the feature of forcing sprites to face toward each other. The original single Character.Draw() function is replaced with these three versions:

```
public void Draw()
{
    Draw((int)p_position.X, (int)p_position.Y);
}
public void Draw(PointF pos)
{
    Draw((int)pos.X, (int)pos.Y);
}
public void Draw(int x, int y)
{
    int startFrame, endFrame;
    switch (p_state)
    {
        case AnimationStates.Walking:
            p_walkSprite.Position = p_position;
            if (p_direction > -1)
            {
                startFrame = p_direction * p_walkColumns;
                endFrame = startFrame + p_walkColumns - 1;
                p_walkSprite.AnimationRate = 30;
                p_walkSprite.Animate(startFrame, endFrame);
            }
            p_walkSprite.Draw(x,y);
            break;
        case AnimationStates.Attacking:
            p_attackSprite.Position = p_position;
            if (p_direction > -1)
            {
                startFrame = p_direction * p_attackColumns;
                endFrame = startFrame + p_attackColumns - 1;
                p_attackSprite.AnimationRate = 30;
                p_attackSprite.Animate(startFrame, endFrame);
```

```
            }
            p_attackSprite.Draw(x,y);
            break;
        case AnimationStates.Dying:
            p_dieSprite.Position = p_position;
            if (p_direction > -1)
            {
                startFrame = p_direction * p_dieColumns;
                endFrame = startFrame + p_dieColumns - 1;
                p_dieSprite.AnimationRate = 30;
                p_dieSprite.Animate(startFrame, endFrame);
            }
            p_dieSprite.Draw(x,y);
            break;
    }
}
```

STATE-BASED COMBAT

The combat system is now complex enough to require a state variable. Previously, a bool variable, attacking, kept track of just whether combat was supposed to happen. Now, we need to involve several steps for combat:

1. Player triggers an attack

2. Attack introduction

3. Attack commences

4. Report the attack results

This enumeration will handle the four states in the combat system:

```
public enum AttackStates
{
    ATTACK_NONE,
    ATTACK_TRIGGER,
    ATTACK_ATTACK,
    ATTACK_RESULT,
}
```

This is the variable we will be using to keep track of the current state of the combat system:

Figure 12.16
The new state-based combat system slows down and improves the gameplay.

```
AttackStates attackState = AttackStates.ATTACK_NONE;
```

By the time we're done adding state to the combat engine for this Combat demo 4 project, shown in Figure 12.16, the game will allow you to make distinct, individual attacks against an enemy with a click of the Attack button.

Dialogue Improvements

Now that we're using a state-based system for combat, we need to modify other parts of the game code to also work correctly: namely, the `Dialogue` class. Previously, we just looked for a mouse click to trigger a button selection event. Now, that will not work because the dialogue will be repeatedly updated so a mouse click will be seen as *many clicks* while the button is being held. No matter how fast you press and release the mouse button, it will pick up several events because the loop is running at 60 fps. What we need to do is look for a button *release* event instead. A new variable is needed:

```
private MouseButtons p_oldMouseBtn;
```

When updating the mouse, we also need to keep track of the previous click state:

```
public void updateMouse(Point mousePos, MouseButtons mouseBtn)
{
    p_mousePos = mousePos;
    p_oldMouseBtn = p_mouseBtn;
    p_mouseBtn = mouseBtn;
}
```

And this change has been made to the `Dialogue.Draw()` function:

```
//clicked on this button?
if (p_mouseBtn == MouseButtons.None && p_oldMouseBtn == MouseButtons.Left)
    p_selection = n;
else
    p_selection = 0;
```

Plugging in Attack State

I will not go over every line of the next example, but suffice it to say there were a lot of changes made to move the combat system over to a state-based system. The most important changes were made to doMonsters() and doCombat(), which mainly involved just checking the current state and acting appropriately. For instance, in doMonsters(), rather than simply setting the target to whatever monster the player is close to without regard for any previously targeted monster, the code now checks to see if the player isn't already in a fight.

```
if (attackState == AttackStates.ATTACK_NONE)
{
    if (attackFlag)
    {
        attackState = AttackStates.ATTACK_TRIGGER;
        target = n;
        attackFlag = false;
        dialogue.Visible = true;

        //make PC and NPC face each other
        int dir = getTargetDirection(monsterCenter, hero.CenterPos);
        monsters[target].Direction = dir;
        monsters[target].Draw();
```

```
            dir = getTargetDirection(hero.CenterPos, monsterCenter);
            hero.Direction = dir;
            hero.Draw();

            break;
        }
    }
```

Also, after all of the monsters have been processed in the loop, then we need to reset combat if the player has walked away or cancelled combat. The new attackText variable is defined in Form1 as a string.

```
    if (monstersInRange == 0)
    {
        target = 0;
        attackText = "";
        dialogue.Visible = false;
        attackState = AttackStates.ATTACK_NONE;
    }
```

Likewise, some serious changes have been made to doAttack() to support the new state-based combat system. Here is the new code for the function. All of the previous code in doAttack() is now contained solely inside the ATTACK_ATTACK state condition.

```
    private void doAttack()
    {
        const int DEF_ARMOR = 10;
        const int DEF_SHIELD = 0;
        const int WEAPON_DMG = 5;
        bool hit = false;
        bool critical = false;
        bool fail = false;
        int roll = 0;
        int AC = 0;
        int damage = 0;
        string text="";

        if (dialogue.Selection == 2)
        {
            attackState = AttackStates.ATTACK_NONE;
            return;
```

```
    }

switch (attackState)
{
    case AttackStates.ATTACK_NONE:
        break;

    case AttackStates.ATTACK_TRIGGER:
        if (target > 0)
        {
            text = "You are facing a " + monsters[target].Name +
                ". " + monsters[target].Description;
            showDialogue("Prepare to Attack", text, "ATTACK",
                "CANCEL");
        }
        if (dialogue.Selection == 1)
            attackState = AttackStates.ATTACK_ATTACK;
        break;

    case AttackStates.ATTACK_ATTACK:
        //calculate target's AC
        AC = monsters[target].DEX + DEF_ARMOR + DEF_SHIELD;

        //calculate chance to-hit for PC
        roll = game.Random(1, 20);
        text += "To-Hit Roll: " + roll.ToString();
        if (roll == 20)
        {
            //critical hit!
            hit = true;
            critical = true;
            text += " (CRITICAL!)\n";
        }
        else if (roll == 1)
        {
            fail = true;
            text += " (EPIC FAIL!)\n";
        }
        else
        {
```

```
        //normal hit
        roll += hero.STR;
        if (roll > AC) hit = true;
        text += " + STR(" + hero.STR.ToString() + ") = " +
            roll.ToString() + "\n";
    }

    //did attack succeed?
    if (hit)
    {
        //calculate base damage
        damage = game.Random(1, 8);

        //add critical
        if (critical) damage *= 2;

        text += "Damage roll: " + damage.ToString() + "\n";

        //add STR
        damage += hero.STR;
        text += " + STR(" + hero.STR.ToString() + ") = " +
            damage.ToString() + "\n";

        //add weapon damage (usually a die roll)
        damage += WEAPON_DMG;
        text += " + weapon(" + WEAPON_DMG.ToString() +
            ") = " + damage.ToString() + "\n";

        //subtract AC
        damage -= AC;
        text += " - monster AC(" + AC.ToString() + ") = " +
            damage.ToString() + "\n";

        //minimal hit
        if (damage < 1) damage = 1;

        //show result
        text += "Attack succeeds for " + damage.ToString() +
            " damage.";
    }
```

```
        else
            text += "Attack failed.\n";

        attackText = text;
        attackState = AttackStates.ATTACK_RESULT;
        break;

    case AttackStates.ATTACK_RESULT:
        showDialogue("Attack Roll", attackText, "ATTACK AGAIN",
            "CANCEL");
        if (dialogue.Selection == 1)
            attackState = AttackStates.ATTACK_ATTACK;
        break;
    }
}
```

DEALING PERMANENT DAMAGE

The final step to complete the combat system is to give the player experience after defeating a monster. This will require some new fields in the `Character` class since we did not account for experience or leveling when originally designing the class. Some additional code will be required in this final example, Combat demo 5, to allow the animation for the killed monsters to stay on the screen after they fall. Figure 12.17 shows the result. The amount of experience awarded is a random value from 50 to 100, which is just an arbitrary range that I made up as filler. How should we award experience in the real game? It should be a factor that involves the monster's level, which is not something we're currently using in the character editor files. What would you do with this design decision: add a level field, or a pair of fields that define how much experience the player receives? Something to ponder between now and the final chapter.

Tip

Even this last Combat demo 5 project is not quite polished, but it is meant to serve as a working example of combat. For a production game, you would want the player to walk over the corpses and stop them from "bobbing" as the scroller moves. These issues are easily fixed as the final version of the game demonstrates.

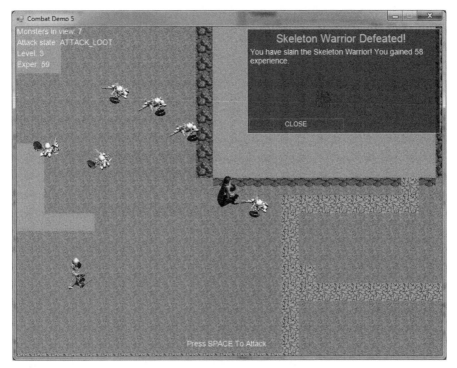

Figure 12.17
The skeletons don't get a free ride anymore!

These few changes are needed in the doAttack() function to add the ability to kill monsters, gain experience, and level up. Portions of the code that have not changed that we have already recently covered are omitted. There are two states involved when a battle is concluded: ATTACK_RESULT and ATTACK_LOOT. The former tallies the experience, kills the monster, and displays the dialogue message. The latter is simply used to hold the dialogue window up until the player has acknowledged the information by clicking the "CLOSE" button.

Note: some variables in this code will be new; refer to the source code in the finished project to see the variable declarations.

```
switch (attackState)
{
    case AttackStates.ATTACK_NONE:
        hero.AnimationState = Character.AnimationStates.Walking;
        dialogue.Visible = false;
```

```
        break;

case AttackStates.ATTACK_TRIGGER:
    if (target > 0)
    {
        text = "You are facing a " + monsters[target].Name +
            ". " + monsters[target].Description;
        showDialogue("Prepare to Attack", text, "ATTACK",
            "CANCEL");
    }
    if (dialogue.Selection == 1)
        attackState = AttackStates.ATTACK_ATTACK;

    break;

case AttackStates.ATTACK_ATTACK:
    //calculate target's AC
    AC = monsters[target].DEX + DEF_ARMOR + DEF_SHIELD;

    //calculate chance to-hit for PC
    roll = game.Random(1, 20);
    text += "To-Hit Roll: " + roll.ToString();
    if (roll == 20)
    {
        //critical hit!
        hit = true;
        critical = true;
        text += " (CRITICAL!)\n";
    }
    else if (roll == 1)
    {
        fail = true;
        text += " (EPIC FAIL!)\n";
    }
    else
    {
        //normal hit
        roll += hero.STR;
        if (roll > AC) hit = true;
        text += " + STR(" + hero.STR.ToString() + ") = " +
```

```
            roll.ToString() + "\n";
}

//did attack succeed?
if (hit)
{
    //calculate base damage
    damage = game.Random(1, 8);

    //add critical
    if (critical) damage *= 2;

    text += "Damage roll: " + damage.ToString() + "\n";

    //add STR
    damage += hero.STR;
    text += " + STR(" + hero.STR.ToString() + ") = " +
        damage.ToString() + "\n";

    //add weapon damage (usually a die roll)
    damage += WEAPON_DMG;
    text += " + weapon(" + WEAPON_DMG.ToString() +
        ") = " + damage.ToString() + "\n";

    //subtract AC
    damage -= AC;
    text += " - monster AC(" + AC.ToString() + ") = " +
        damage.ToString() + "\n";

    //minimal hit
    if (damage < 1) damage = 1;

    //show result
    text += "Attack succeeds for " + damage.ToString() +
        " damage.";
}
else
    text += "Attack failed.\n";

attackText = text;
```

```
        attackState = AttackStates.ATTACK_RESULT;
        break;

    case AttackStates.ATTACK_RESULT:
        hero.AnimationState = Character.AnimationStates.Walking;

        //is monster dead?
        if (monsters[target].HitPoints <= 0)
        {
            monsters[target].Alive = false;
            int xp = game.Random(50, 100);
            addExperience(xp);
            text = monsters[target].Name + " Defeated!";
            attackText = "You have slain the " + monsters[target].Name +
                "! You gained " + xp.ToString() + " experience.";
            showDialogue(text, attackText, "CLOSE");
            attackState = AttackStates.ATTACK_LOOT;
        }
        else
        {
            showDialogue("Attack Roll", attackText, "ATTACK AGAIN",
                "CANCEL");
            if (dialogue.Selection == 1)
                attackState = AttackStates.ATTACK_ATTACK;
        }
        break;

    case AttackStates.ATTACK_LOOT:
        hero.AnimationState = Character.AnimationStates.Walking;
        if (dialogue.Selection == 1)
        {
            attackState = AttackStates.ATTACK_NONE;
            target = 0;
        }
        break;
}
```

Gaining Experience

A helper function called addExperience() will take care of granting the player experience and leveling up. At this early stage of development, leveling up is a trivial affair meant only to demonstrate that it can be done. In the finished game, we will want to grant the player new attribute points (to STR, DEX, etc.) to reflect the fact that their new level makes them stronger. This function is just a stopgap for the time being to demonstrate experience and leveling, while a more permanent solution will be offered in the final chapter.

```
private void addExperience(int xp)
{
    hero.Experience += xp;
    if (hero.Experience > 200)
    {
        hero.Level += 1;
        hero.Experience -= 200;
    }
}
```

The Character class needs some new features to accommodate the requirements for gaining experience and leveling up the character.

```
private int p_experience;
public int Experience
{
    get { return p_experience; }
    set { p_experience = value; }
}

private int p_level;
public int Level
{
    get { return p_level; }
    set { p_level = value; }
}
```

We will also add a new Character.Alive property to make it easier to flag monsters as they are killed and prevent the code from updating those characters.

```
private bool p_alive;
public bool Alive
{
    get { return p_alive; }
    set { p_alive = value; }
}
```

The death animation will require a new item in the `Character.AnimationStates` enumeration so that when the animation finishes one cycle, the sprite will remain on the ground, showing the final frame of the death animation for good.

```
public enum AnimationStates
{
    Walking = 0,
    Attacking = 1,
    Dying = 2,
    Dead = 3
}
```

The final change required to get this code to work is the addition of another `showDialogue()` method overload with just one button instead of two.

```
private void showDialogue(string title, string message, string button1)
{
    dialogue.Title = title;
    dialogue.Message = message;
    dialogue.NumButtons = 1;
    dialogue.setButtonText(1, button1);
    dialogue.Visible = true;
}
```

LEVEL UP!

After play testing the Combat demo 5 project a few times, I'm extremely pleased with the decision to use a turn-based combat system instead of real time. This slows down the game, gives it more character, and allows the player to become more involved in the gameplay. Combat in a traditional pen-and-paper RPG is not a quick "hack-n-slash" affair that ends in seconds—the players must calculate the results of each attack, roll the dice for their attack roll and damage roll, while the defender often has "succeed or fail" rolls to block the attack, based on their abilities. It is this interaction that makes the game fun. Simply swinging the weapon as fast as the game will let you and mopping up the loot afterward takes away a huge amount of the fun factor. However, there most certainly is a balance to be found: you don't want to bore your player with micro managing his character. One type of combat we did not address in this already lengthy chapter is ranged attacks (of the bow and spell variety). As it turns out, these types of attacks tend to get handled very much like melee attacks but with a little bit more range, so all we need to do is increase the attack radius around each monster to allow for ranged weapons. Perhaps that is an attribute best handled by the weapon's stats? Ironically, that is the very subject we're covering in the next chapter.

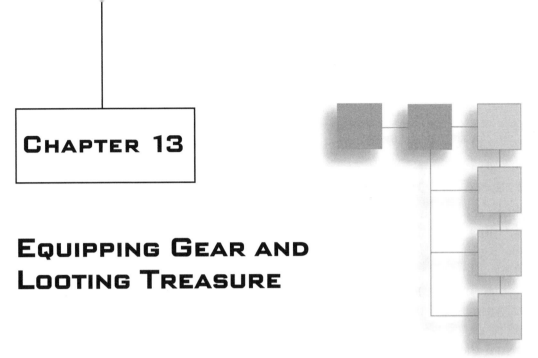

CHAPTER 13

EQUIPPING GEAR AND LOOTING TREASURE

This chapter focuses on the development of an item editor to make creating and managing game items (such as swords, armor pieces, rings, and other gear found in a typical RPG) easier for a designer. We will also build a looting system so that monsters will drop gold and gear items at random when they fall, and a simple inventory screen that allows the player to equip items and move items around in their "bag of loot." If you have ever tried to create an RPG without an editor like this, I'm sure you ran into the same roadblock that I have when it comes to working with items. Just giving the player a sword tends to be a hard-coded, manual process, with less than favorable results. Even just storing items in a text file and reading them in is better than manually creating arrays of items in code, unless your game is on the extremely simple side with just "hack & slash" gameplay without much depth. Since our goal is to send the player on quests before we finish this book, having items that satisfy the quests is essential! For an example of how the item data is used, we'll put that on hold until the next chapter and just focus on editing in this one.

Here's what we'll cover in this chapter:

- Item images
- Looking up items
- The Item class
- Item editor

- Looting treasure
- Managing inventory

ITEM EDITOR DESIGN

Some role-playing games are so focused on inventory micro-management that they lose track of the fun factor and replace real gameplay with an almost never-ending job of sorting and dealing with stuff (also called "loot"). I've seen some RPGs allow the player to carry around *tons* of stuff (I mean literally *thousands* of pounds of items)! This is, of course, completely ridiculous. But some players like micro-management. I guess there's room for those types of games, as long as there are players for them. I've always been a fan of the simpler approach—giving the player simple weapon, armor, and modifier items. Why should the player spend hours of game time swapping armor items when a single suit of armor would be easier to deal with? (Some games allow you to configure chest, leggings, helmet, bracers, and so on, individually.) There's certainly some realism in this, but does it make a game more *fun*?

The item editor is a bit different from the character editor that we developed back in Chapter 10. While characters are stored one per .char file, many items are stored in a .item file. The editor has a File menu, which allows you to start a new item database, load an existing file, or save the current file to a new file. The item editor is shown in Figure 13.1.

The editor was designed to work with groups of items in a file. The example shown here contains some weapons and armor items, but it would be better to organize the items into separate groups (weapons, armor, rings, etc.) so that it's easier to manage and search for specific items. Another approach is to just store everything in a single item database, which is perfectly okay but it's just harder to find and edit items when there are so many in a single file.

This editor does make it possible for players to cheat on your game. By giving the filenames a different extension besides .xml, we can at least hide the data from casual wanna-be hackers, but anyone with bare minimum skills will try opening the .item file in a text editor and immediately see that it is an editable text file containing .xml tables. There are ways to get around this problem, but that subject is beyond the scope of this book. Experience has shown me that for

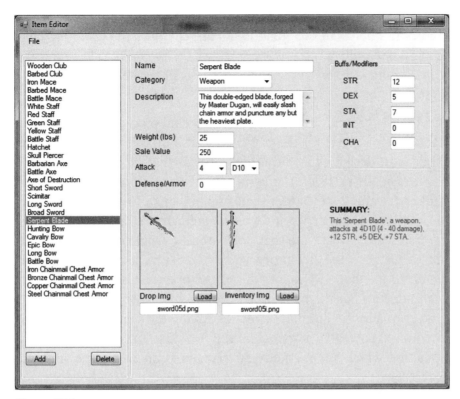

Figure 13.1
The item editor works with an entire list of items at a time.

players who want to hack a game file, whether it's a core database or a saved game, no effort short of hard encryption will prevent them from doing so. If someone wants to hack your game that badly, take it as a compliment.

Item Images

The item editor works with just single-frame bitmaps, with support for two versions for each item: a *drop* image and an *inventory* image. The drop image is usually smaller and oriented with the ground tiles, while the inventory image is often oriented straight-on so it looks better in an inventory screen (the player's equipment). Neither image is suitable for both purposes. If you try to use the inventory image as a drop item, it will look funny on the ground at the wrong angle. However, one alternative is to bring up a "loot window" showing the contents of an item rather than dropping items directly onto the ground. A loot window does eliminate quite a bit of work since we do not need to keep track of two different images *in addition* to the added code to allow the player to pick up items on the ground.

An advantage to the ground image is that you can place individual items anywhere in the dungeon level for the player to find. But, due to the extra work required, I think most designers would rather have their artists working on new gameplay art rather than extra *drop* images. This is why in most games you'll most often find crates and boxes rather than usable items in the dungeon. Since we have both versions of the artwork for every item from Reiner, we can use them with the item editor. Just note that both are not absolutely necessary and it's acceptable to just use the inventory version, as long as you have a loot window come up in the game whenever the player opens a container. I kind of like the realism added when items drop to the ground when an NPC falls in combat (maybe even add the dramatic effect of having the items scatter around the body randomly). Since it's fairly common to "loot the corpse" in most computer RPGs, use whichever method you want in your own game since the artwork is available.

What if we were to add multiple image frame support to the item editor, so that batches of item artwork could be stored on a sprite sheet? That's a distinct possibility. At the very least, we could store both the drop and inventory image together in a two-frame image. The problem is, the artwork is not all uniform in size, with the drop items being somewhat smaller (in Reiner's). Sure, you could enlarge the images to a fixed size all around, but will that save time in the long run versus just adding both image filenames into the item editor fields?

There is the additional problem of having literally hundreds of asset files in the game's folder. The limited set of item images used so far already accounts for a large number of files cluttering the game's main folder. A definite improvement would be to store the images in a sub-folder like .\assets under the main folder, and then prefix all of the image filenames stored in the item editor database with .\assets. So, a filename field such as "drop plate 1.png" would become ".\assets \drop plate 1.png." You can do any such manipulation in the game code while loading these assets.

Looking Up Items

I wanted to use an auto-increment identifier for each item in the item editor database and then use the ID in quests and in the player's inventory. But, though an identifier-based database is required for a professional project, it's not the best choice for an amateur game with multi-purpose tools like what we have for the Dungeon Crawler game. Instead of using an ID, the Item.Name property will be used to look up the data for an item. All that is required to make this work effectively is to ensure that your items each have a unique name. If you want to have three rings called "Magic Ring," be sure to add a qualifier to the name like "Magic Ring +1" or something to uniquely identify each item. Since the name is the lookup field, the first item matching the name will be used in a lookup.

Item Class

As with the previous level editor and character editor, the new item editor includes a class (called Item) that makes the data available to our game. The Item class is meant to handle a single item from the editor database (which is stored in an XML file). In our game code, we will need to load the .item file with additional code and then use the Item class for each item that is loaded. In other words, there is no overall "Items" class that loads an entire .item file, saved by the editor, and makes those items available to the game. Perhaps there should be?

```
public class Item
{
    private string p_name;
    private string p_desc;
    private string p_dropfile;
    private string p_invfile;
    private string p_category;
    private float p_weight;
    private float p_value;
    private int p_attacknumdice;
    private int p_attackdie;
    private int p_defense;
    private int p_buffStr;
    private int p_buffDex;
    private int p_buffSta;
    private int p_buffInt;
```

```csharp
    private int p_buffCha;

    public Item()
    {
        p_name = "new item";
        p_desc = "";
        p_dropfile = "";
        p_invfile = "";
        p_category = "";
        p_weight = 0;
        p_value = 0;
        p_attacknumdice = 0;
        p_attackdie = 0;
        p_defense = 0;
        p_buffStr = 0;
        p_buffDex = 0;
        p_buffSta = 0;
        p_buffInt = 0;
        p_buffCha = 0;
    }

    public string Name
    {
        get { return p_name; }
        set { p_name = value; }
    }

    public string Description
    {
        get { return p_desc; }
        set { p_desc = value; }
    }

    public string DropImageFilename
    {
        get { return p_dropfile; }
        set { p_dropfile = value; }
    }

    public string InvImageFilename
```

```
{
    get { return p_invfile; }
    set { p_invfile = value; }
}

public string Category
{
    get { return p_category; }
    set { p_category = value; }
}

public float Weight
{
    get { return p_weight; }
    set { p_weight = value; }
}

public float Value
{
    get { return p_value; }
    set { p_value = value; }
}

public int AttackNumDice
{
    get { return p_attacknumdice; }
    set { p_attacknumdice = value; }
}

public int AttackDie
{
    get { return p_attackdie; }
    set { p_attackdie = value; }
}

public int Defense
{
    get { return p_defense; }
    set { p_defense = value; }
}
```

```csharp
public int STR
{
    get { return p_buffStr; }
    set { p_buffStr = value; }
}

public int DEX
{
    get { return p_buffDex; }
    set { p_buffDex = value; }
}

public int STA
{
    get { return p_buffSta; }
    set { p_buffSta = value; }
}

public int INT
{
    get { return p_buffInt; }
    set { p_buffInt = value; }
}

public int CHA
{
    get { return p_buffCha; }
    set { p_buffCha = value; }
}

public string Summary
{
    get {
        string text = "This '" + p_name + "', ";

        string weight = "";
        if (p_weight > 50) weight = "a very heavy ";
        else if (p_weight > 25) weight = "a heavy ";
        else if (p_weight > 15) weight = "a ";
        else if (p_weight > 7) weight = "a light ";
```

```
    else if (p_weight > 0) weight = "a very light ";
    text += weight;

    if (p_category == "Weapon") text += "weapon";
    else if (p_category == "Armor") text += "armor item";
    else if (p_category == "Necklace") text += "necklace";
    else if (p_category == "Ring") text += "ring";
    else text += p_category.ToLower() + " item";

    if (p_attacknumdice != 0)
    {
        text += ", attacks at " + p_attacknumdice.ToString()
            + "D" + p_attackdie.ToString()
            + " (" + p_attacknumdice.ToString() + " - "
            + (p_attackdie * p_attacknumdice).ToString()
            + " damage)";
    }

    if (p_defense != 0)
        text += ", adds " + p_defense.ToString() +
            " armor points";

    string fmt = "+#;-#";
    if (p_buffStr != 0)
        text += ", " + p_buffStr.ToString(fmt) + " STR";

    if (p_buffDex != 0)
        text += ", " + p_buffDex.ToString(fmt) + " DEX";

    if (p_buffSta != 0)
        text += ", " + p_buffSta.ToString(fmt) + " STA";

    if (p_buffInt != 0)
        text += ", " + p_buffInt.ToString(fmt) + " INT";

    if (p_buffCha != 0)
        text += ", " + p_buffCha.ToString(fmt) + " CHA";

    return text + ".";
}
```

```
    }

    public override string ToString()
    {
        return p_name;
    }
}
```

Item Editor Project

Like the character editor from a few chapters back, the item editor was created with Visual Basic. (The only editor written in C# is the level editor.) The item editor is completely self-contained and it can create new item files from scratch as well as edit existing files. One nice feature is auto-save: while editing items, if you click on a different item in the list or close the editor, the current item is automatically saved. This takes out some of the tedium from editing a large number of items—just point, click, and edit, without concern for saving at every step.

Obviously, there is a form filled with controls that are not listed here, because the user interface is too complex to build from scratch (as in a tutorial-style walkthrough). The complete source code for the item editor is available in the project in the chapter resources.

LOOTING TREASURE

There are two ways to handle looting: by dropping items directly on the ground, or by opening up a loot window from a dead monster or container (such as a treasure chest). Since we're already heavily invested in code for the inventory manager (coming up later in the chapter), I will forego the loot window and instead just drop items directly on the ground for pickup. We can treat drop items in the game code like monsters as far as range and targeting are concerned—when an item is in range, we can highlight it with a colored circle. Yes, there is a slight conflict when there are many items on top of each other or when a monster is in the way, but we can assume the player will clear out any bad guys from the immediate vicinity before looting. Both attacking and looting will use the Space key so it's just a matter of whether a loot item or a monster is closer in range.

For the Looting demo, I have removed all living monsters and just dropped items randomly near the player's start position to speed up the demo a bit. In the finished game coming up two chapters from now, we will use this code to drop random items directly on the ground when a monster dies. The code *already* does this, but in the interest of speeding up testing of the inventory system, as the monsters are created, they are immediately killed so that the loot can be dropped (which is unfair, I know, but necessary for the sake of this important research!).

Hint

There are quite a few reusable functions in the `Form1` code of the Looting demo in this chapter that can be moved inside the `Game` class once we're confident that they're working correctly. It is sometimes better to keep uncertain code close at hand while working on it for quick editing without searching through your project's classes. Remember, we aren't going over *every line of code*, so consider this chapter an overview, not a tutorial.

Preparing to Loot

We need four variables to get started. As you can see, the item database is handled by a single class, `Items`, which we'll go over shortly. `DrawableItem` is a simple structure that extends `Item` in order to make it drawable. You could easily make the argument that this should be a class that inherits from `Item`, and I might agree with you—this is just one of those times where a structure seemed easier, and it works just as well in the end.

```
public struct DrawableItem
{
    public Item item;
    public Sprite sprite;
}

bool lootFlag = false;
List<DrawableItem> treasure;
int lootTarget = 0;
Items items;
```

The `treasure` object is created as a linked list of `DrawableItem` structures. A linked list is an advanced container that we can go through with the `ForEach` looping statement, and it's more convenient than an array because we can add as many items to it as we want.

```
treasure = new List<DrawableItem>();
```

The items variable is created and initialized in the main program startup code as well.

```
items = new Items();
if (!items.Load("items.item"))
{
    MessageBox.Show("Error loading file items.item");
    Application.Exit();
}
```

The Inventory variable is actually found inside Game and is declared with public scope so it's visible anywhere in the game. We need to access the player's inventory easily so that is why I put it in the Game class.

```
public Inventory Inven;
```

Despite being found in Game, the Inven variable is initialized in our main program, not in the Game constructor. This is also where default items can be added to the player's inventory, such as the items listed here. Perhaps in the final game, when the player creates a new character, some items will be added based on their class? Another common approach is to make the player earn gear from the start, and give him basically just a dagger and rags to wear. I gave the player these four items for testing purposes, but it demonstrates the power of the Items class, because sure enough, these four items show up in the inventory screen.

```
game.Inven = new Inventory(ref game, new Point((800 - 532) / 2, 50));
game.Inven.AddItem(items.getItem("Iron Chainmail"));
game.Inven.AddItem(items.getItem("Long Sword"));
game.Inven.AddItem(items.getItem("Small Shield"));
game.Inven.AddItem(items.getItem("Cape of Stamina"));
```

To add sample piles of loot for testing the inventory system, I just use a real .char file with the loot properties set and then immediately kill the monster that would have been visible in the game world (i.e., the dungeon). There are a pair of functions that make this all possible (and fairly automatic too, thanks to the Items class). The number of loot piles is not that important; I just used 20 and positioned them all within close range of the player's starting location.

```
for (int n=1; n<21; n++)
{
    Character monster = new Character(ref game);
    monster.Load("skeleton sword shield.char");
    monster.Position = new Point(game.Random(100,1200),
        game.Random(100,1200));
    monster.AnimationState = Character.AnimationStates.Dead;
    monster.Alive = false;
    //add some loot
    DropLoot(ref monster);
}
```

Stumbling Upon Loot

The doTreasure() function in the Looting demo project should look very familiar! It's essentially the same as the doMonsters() function from the previous chapter! There are a few differences, of course, because we don't actually *fight* with treasure, we pick it up. So, instead of a variable called fightRadius, we have lootRadius, and instead of monsterCenter, we have itemCenter. The logic is somewhat complex, though. I didn't want to make it overly complex, but it just turned out that way, mainly because of the way in which dialogue works. We usually can't just say, "Show this message to the player" and then forget about it—we have to wait for the player to click a button and then hide the dialogue window. Figure 13.2 shows a bunch of gold on the ground with one highlighted under the player's feet. An interesting side effect of this code is that you can loot many items without having to close the window (with the OK button), and it will just display the name of the next item looted.

Figure 13.3 is the message displayed (via the Dialogue class) when the player picks up gold. Gold is a special case that must be handled differently than regular items because it is not added to inventory, just to the Player.Gold property.

The second condition in doTreasure() occurs when the player is standing over a real item that can be picked up. When that is the case (rather than gold), a message displays information about the item. Do you recall the Item.Summary property from Chapter 12? We use it to display a quick tidbit of information about the item with any buffs it provides the player and any attack or defense values. This handy property works great here as well, telling the player at a

Figure 13.2
Dropped items are highlighted as the player walks over them.

glance what the item can do for him. Figure 13.4 shows the message after picking up an item. Note that this is the item shown in the character editor file as a drop item!

Here is the `doTreasure()` function. Fortunately, there are a lot of code comments so you should be able to make out what each section of code does. Just remember that this function looks at *all* of the items in the treasure container (funny variable names, don't you think?). Another interesting aspect of this code is that it prevents the player from picking up any more items if inventory is full! How cool is that? And we're still at the prototype stage for this inventory thing.

```
private void doTreasure()
{
    PointF relativePos = new PointF(0,0);
    const int lootRadius = 40;
```

Figure 13.3
The amount of gold looted is specified in the character editor.

```
PointF heroCenter = game.Hero.CenterPos;
PointF itemCenter = new PointF(0,0);
double dist;

foreach (DrawableItem it in treasure)
{
    //is item in view?
    if (it.sprite.X > level.ScrollPos.X - 64
        && it.sprite.X < level.ScrollPos.X + 23 * 32 + 64
        && it.sprite.Y > level.ScrollPos.Y - 64
        && it.sprite.Y < level.ScrollPos.Y + 17 * 32 + 64)
    {
        //get relative position of item on screen
        relativePos.X = it.sprite.X - level.ScrollPos.X;
```

Figure 13.4
This dropped item corresponds to the "Small Shield" selected in the character editor.

```
relativePos.Y = it.sprite.Y - level.ScrollPos.Y;

//get center of item
itemCenter = relativePos;
itemCenter.X += it.sprite.Width / 2;
itemCenter.Y += it.sprite.Height / 2;

//get distance to the item
dist = game.Hero.CenterDistance(itemCenter);

//is player trying to pick up this loot?
if (dist < lootRadius)
{
    game.Device.DrawEllipse(new Pen(Color.Magenta, 2),
        itemCenter.X - it.sprite.Width / 2,
        itemCenter.Y - it.sprite.Height / 2,
```

```
                    it.sprite.Width, it.sprite.Height);

            if (lootFlag)
            {
                //collect gold or item
                if (it.item.Name == "gold" && it.item.Value > 0)
                {
                    game.Hero.Gold += (int)it.item.Value;
                    treasure.Remove(it);
                    showDialogue("LOOT", it.item.Value.ToString() +
                        " GOLD", "OK");
                }
                else
                {
                    if (game.Inven.AddItem(it.item))
                    {
                        treasure.Remove(it);
                        showDialogue("LOOT", it.item.Summary, "OK");
                    }
                    else
                        showDialogue("OVERLOADED!", "You are overloaded" +
                            " with too much stuff!", "OK");
                }

                //wait for user
                if (dialogue.Selection == 1)
                {
                    lootFlag = false;
                    dialogue.Selection = 0;
                }
                break;
            }
        }

        //draw the monster sprite
        it.sprite.Draw((int)relativePos.X, (int)relativePos.Y);
    }
  }
}
```

Items Class

The Items class is a helper class to handle the items database. The Items class reads in the entire .item file and is used to drop items when a monster is killed, as well as to show items in the player's inventory. So, this class is very important—it keeps our main code tidy by providing a very useful helper function called getItem(). When creating an object using this class during program initialization, be sure to use Load() to load the .item file needed by the game. This should be the same .item file you used to specify drop items in the character editor.

```
public class Items
{
    //keep public for easy access
    public List<Item> items;

    public Items()
    {
        items = new List<Item>();
    }

    private string getElement(string field, ref XmlElement element)
    {
        string value = "";
        try
        {
            value = element.GetElementsByTagName(field)[0].InnerText;
        }
        catch (Exception){}
        return value;
    }

    public bool Load(string filename)
    {
        try
        {
            //open the xml file
            XmlDocument doc = new XmlDocument();
            doc.Load(filename);
            XmlNodeList list = doc.GetElementsByTagName("item");
            foreach (XmlNode node in list)
```

```
        {
            //get next item in table
            XmlElement element = (XmlElement)node;
            Item item = new Item();

            //store fields in new Item
            item.Name = getElement("name", ref element);
            item.Description = getElement("description", ref element);
            item.DropImageFilename = getElement("dropimagefilename",
                ref element);
            item.InvImageFilename = getElement("invimagefilename",
                ref element);
            item.Category = getElement("category", ref element);
            item.Weight = Convert.ToSingle(getElement("weight",
                ref element));
            item.Value = Convert.ToSingle(getElement("value",
                ref element));
            item.AttackNumDice = Convert.ToInt32(getElement(
                "attacknumdice", ref element));
            item.AttackDie = Convert.ToInt32(getElement("attackdie",
                ref element));
            item.Defense = Convert.ToInt32(getElement("defense",
                ref element));
            item.STR = Convert.ToInt32(getElement("STR", ref element));
            item.DEX = Convert.ToInt32(getElement("DEX", ref element));
            item.STA = Convert.ToInt32(getElement("STA", ref element));
            item.INT = Convert.ToInt32(getElement("INT", ref element));
            item.CHA = Convert.ToInt32(getElement("CHA", ref element));

            //add new item to list
            items.Add(item);
        }
    }
    catch (Exception) { return false; }
    return true;
}

public Item getItem(string name)
{
    foreach (Item it in items)
```

```
        {
            if (it.Name == name) return it;
        }
        return null;
    }
}
```

Character Class

A slightly improved character editor is needed for this chapter. Do you remember the three drop-item fields that have gone unused so far? Now we can finally enable those three drop-down combo list controls and fill them with items from the item database. This is where things start to get *very* interesting! I'll show you the results in a bit. Some changes have been made to the Character class to support the three drop-item fields that are now functional. Check Character.cs to see the complete new class. Because of these changes, .char files saved with the old version of the character editor will generate an error. Please use the new character editor to save any characters you have created into the new format. Figure 13.5 shows the new character editor. Well, it's the same old editor, but with the three item-drop fields now working! Take a look at the item name and quantity: one "Small Shield."

Take note of this, as I'll show you this item in the game shortly. Take note also of the gold fields: minimum (5) to maximum (10). This is the random amount of gold that this monster will drop when killed. You can use any amount you want here, but just be sure that dropped gold is consistent with item prices at vendors that will be selling the player gear (and buying their drop items, most likely, as well). If your most awesome epic sword costs 250 gold, and the typical skeleton warrior drops 10–20 gold, then the player will be earning enough to buy the best weapon in the game within just a few minutes! I think many monsters will need to be set to a gold range of 0 to 1, so that only one gold is dropped 25 percent of the time. (In the item-drop code, a random number makes sure that items only drop at this rate—and that might even be too high! This is one of those factors that may need to be adjusted when gameplay testing reveals that monsters are dropping way too much gear, making the player rich very quickly. You want the player to struggle! If the game becomes too easy too fast, your player will become bored with it.)

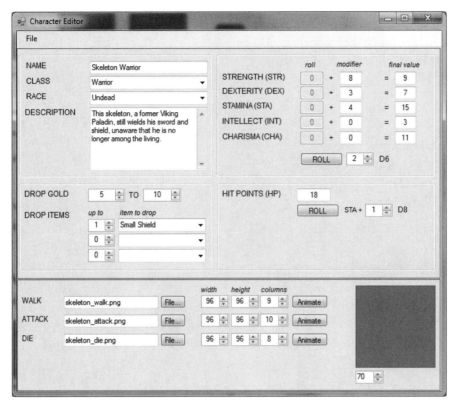

Figure 13.5
Setting the gold and drop items in the character editor.

Here is the new code in the updated Character class (note changes in bold):

```
public class Character
{
    public enum AnimationStates
    {
        Walking = 0,
        Attacking = 1,
        Dying = 2,
        Dead = 3,
        Standing = 4
    }

    private Game p_game;
```

```
        private PointF p_position;
        private int p_direction;
        private AnimationStates p_state;

        //character file properties;
        private string p_name;
        private string p_class;
        private string p_race;
        private string p_desc;
        private int p_str;
        private int p_dex;
        private int p_sta;
        private int p_int;
        private int p_cha;
        private int p_hitpoints;
        private int p_dropGold1;
        private int p_dropGold2;
        private string p_walkFilename;
        private Sprite p_walkSprite;
        private Size p_walkSize;
        private int p_walkColumns;
        private string p_attackFilename;
        private Sprite p_attackSprite;
        private Size p_attackSize;
        private int p_attackColumns;
        private string p_dieFilename;
        private Sprite p_dieSprite;
        private Size p_dieSize;
        private int p_dieColumns;
        private int p_experience;
        private int p_level;
        private bool p_alive;
        private int p_dropnum1;
        private int p_dropnum2;
        private int p_dropnum3;
        private string p_dropitem1;
        private string p_dropitem2;
        private string p_dropitem3;

        public Character(ref Game game)
```

```
{
    p_game = game;
    p_position = new PointF(0, 0);
    p_direction = 1;
    p_state = AnimationStates.Standing;

    //initialize loadable properties
    p_name = "";
    p_class = "";
    p_race = "";
    p_desc = "";
    p_str = 0;
    p_dex = 0;
    p_sta = 0;
    p_int = 0;
    p_cha = 0;
    p_hitpoints = 0;
    p_dropGold1 = 0;
    p_dropGold2 = 0;
    p_walkSprite = null;
    p_walkFilename = "";
    p_walkSize = new Size(0, 0);
    p_walkColumns = 0;
    p_attackSprite = null;
    p_attackFilename = "";
    p_attackSize = new Size(0, 0);
    p_attackColumns = 0;
    p_dieSprite = null;
    p_dieFilename = "";
    p_dieSize = new Size(0, 0);
    p_dieColumns = 0;
    p_experience = 0;
    p_level = 1;
    p_dropnum1 = 0;
    p_dropnum2 = 0;
    p_dropnum3 = 0;
    p_dropitem1 = "";
    p_dropitem2 = "";
    p_dropitem3 = "";
}
```

```
...  //**** note: some code was omitted here ***

public int DropNum1
{
    get { return p_dropnum1; }
    set { p_dropnum1 = value; }
}

public int DropNum2
{
    get { return p_dropnum2; }
    set { p_dropnum2 = value; }
}

public int DropNum3
{
    get { return p_dropnum3; }
    set { p_dropnum3 = value; }
}

public string DropItem1
{
    get { return p_dropitem1; }
    set { p_dropitem1 = value; }
}

public string DropItem2
{
    get { return p_dropitem2; }
    set { p_dropitem2 = value; }
}

public string DropItem3
{
    get { return p_dropitem3; }
    set { p_dropitem3 = value; }
}

...  //**** note: some code was omitted here ***
```

```
public void Draw(int x, int y)
{
    int startFrame, endFrame;
    switch (p_state)
    {
        case AnimationStates.Standing:
            p_walkSprite.Position = p_position;
            if (p_direction > -1)
            {
                startFrame = p_direction * p_walkColumns;
                endFrame = startFrame + p_walkColumns - 1;
                p_walkSprite.CurrentFrame = endFrame;
            }
            p_walkSprite.Draw(x,y);
            break;

        case AnimationStates.Walking:
            p_walkSprite.Position = p_position;
            if (p_direction > -1)
            {
                startFrame = p_direction * p_walkColumns;
                endFrame = startFrame + p_walkColumns - 1;
                p_walkSprite.AnimationRate = 30;
                p_walkSprite.Animate(startFrame, endFrame);
            }
            p_walkSprite.Draw(x,y);
            break;

        case AnimationStates.Attacking:
            p_attackSprite.Position = p_position;
            if (p_direction > -1)
            {
                startFrame = p_direction * p_attackColumns;
                endFrame = startFrame + p_attackColumns - 1;
                p_attackSprite.AnimationRate = 30;
                p_attackSprite.Animate(startFrame, endFrame);
            }
            p_attackSprite.Draw(x,y);
            break;
```

```
        case AnimationStates.Dying:
            p_dieSprite.Position = p_position;
            if (p_direction > -1)
            {
                startFrame = p_direction * p_dieColumns;
                endFrame = startFrame + p_dieColumns - 1;
                p_dieSprite.AnimationRate = 30;
                p_dieSprite.Animate(startFrame, endFrame);
            }
            p_dieSprite.Draw(x,y);
            break;

        case AnimationStates.Dead:
            p_dieSprite.Position = p_position;
            if (p_direction > -1)
            {
                startFrame = p_direction * p_dieColumns;
                endFrame = startFrame + p_dieColumns-1;
                p_dieSprite.CurrentFrame = endFrame;
            }
            p_dieSprite.Draw(x,y);
            break;
    }
}

... //**** note: some code was omitted here ***

public bool Load(string filename)
{
    try
    {
        //open the xml file
        XmlDocument doc = new XmlDocument();
        doc.Load(filename);
        XmlNodeList list = doc.GetElementsByTagName("character");
        XmlElement element = (XmlElement)list[0];

        //read data fields
        string data;
        p_name = getElement("name", ref element);
```

```
p_class = getElement("class", ref element);
p_race = getElement("race", ref element);
p_desc = getElement("desc", ref element);

data = getElement("str", ref element);
p_str = Convert.ToInt32(data);

data = getElement("dex", ref element);
p_dex = Convert.ToInt32(data);

data = getElement("sta", ref element);
p_sta = Convert.ToInt32(data);

data = getElement("int", ref element);
p_int = Convert.ToInt32(data);

data = getElement("cha", ref element);
p_cha = Convert.ToInt32(data);

data = getElement("hitpoints", ref element);
p_hitpoints = Convert.ToInt32(data);

data = getElement("anim_walk_filename", ref element);
p_walkFilename = data;

data = getElement("anim_walk_width", ref element);
p_walkSize.Width = Convert.ToInt32(data);

data = getElement("anim_walk_height", ref element);
p_walkSize.Height = Convert.ToInt32(data);

data = getElement("anim_walk_columns", ref element);
p_walkColumns = Convert.ToInt32(data);

data = getElement("anim_attack_filename", ref element);
p_attackFilename = data;

data = getElement("anim_attack_width", ref element);
p_attackSize.Width = Convert.ToInt32(data);
```

```
                data = getElement("anim_attack_height", ref element);
                p_attackSize.Height = Convert.ToInt32(data);
                data = getElement("anim_attack_columns", ref element);
                p_attackColumns = Convert.ToInt32(data);

                data = getElement("anim_die_filename", ref element);
                p_dieFilename = data;

                data = getElement("anim_die_width", ref element);
                p_dieSize.Width = Convert.ToInt32(data);

                data = getElement("anim_die_height", ref element);
                p_dieSize.Height = Convert.ToInt32(data);

                data = getElement("anim_die_columns", ref element);
                p_dieColumns = Convert.ToInt32(data);

                data = getElement("dropgold1", ref element);
                p_dropGold1 = Convert.ToInt32(data);

                data = getElement("dropgold2", ref element);
                p_dropGold2 = Convert.ToInt32(data);

                data = getElement("drop1_num", ref element);
                p_dropnum1 = Convert.ToInt32(data);

                data = getElement("drop2_num", ref element);
                p_dropnum2 = Convert.ToInt32(data);

                data = getElement("drop3_num", ref element);
                p_dropnum3 = Convert.ToInt32(data);

                p_dropitem1 = getElement("drop1_item", ref element);
                p_dropitem2 = getElement("drop2_item", ref element);
                p_dropitem3 = getElement("drop3_item", ref element);
            }
            catch (Exception ex)
            {
                MessageBox.Show(ex.Message);
                return false;
```

```
        }
        //create character sprites
        try
        {
            if (p_walkFilename != "")
            {
                p_walkSprite = new Sprite(ref p_game);
                p_walkSprite.Image = LoadBitmap(p_walkFilename);
                p_walkSprite.Size = p_walkSize;
                p_walkSprite.Columns = p_walkColumns;
                p_walkSprite.TotalFrames = p_walkColumns * 8;
            }
            if (p_attackFilename != "")
            {
                p_attackSprite = new Sprite(ref p_game);
                p_attackSprite.Image = LoadBitmap(p_attackFilename);
                p_attackSprite.Size = p_attackSize;
                p_attackSprite.Columns = p_attackColumns;
                p_attackSprite.TotalFrames = p_attackColumns * 8;
            }
            if (p_dieFilename != "")
            {
                p_dieSprite = new Sprite(ref p_game);
                p_dieSprite.Image = LoadBitmap(p_dieFilename);
                p_dieSprite.Size = p_dieSize;
                p_dieSprite.Columns = p_dieColumns;
                p_dieSprite.TotalFrames = p_dieColumns * 8;
            }
        }
        catch (Exception ex)
        {
            MessageBox.Show(ex.Message);
            return false;
        }
        return true;
    }

... //**** note: some code was omitted here ***


}
```

Dropping Loot

In the main program code are two functions: `DropLoot()` and `DropTreasureItem()`, which cause the items to appear in the dungeon level (via the treasure container). The code to draw items is similar to the code for drawing trees found way back in Chapter 8, "Adding Objects to the Dungeon," and similar to drawing monsters in the previous few chapters. We just need to figure out whether the item is within the scrolling viewport and then draw it at the relative position. This figure shows the drop count "maxxed out" in the character editor to 300 items! Now, remember, there is still only a 25 percent chance that any one of those will drop, but on average we will see about 25 of each item out of that maximum setting of 100. Figure 13.6 shows the data in the character editor.

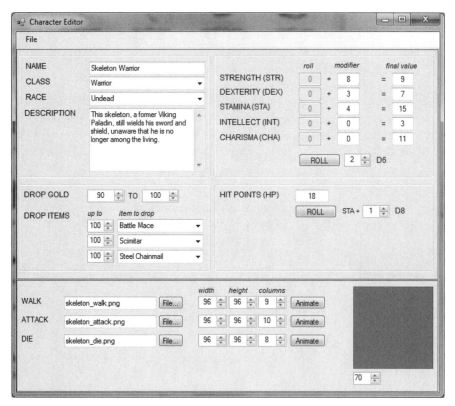

Figure 13.6
This skeleton character has a ridiculous number of drops!

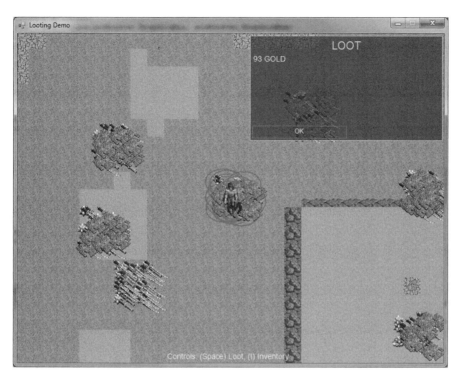

Figure 13.7
The gold is picked up first when there's a huge pile of dropped items.

I have to admit, I was a little surprised that the game was able to handle this large number of item drops so easily. It works like a charm even with scores of items piled on top of each other. The inventory fills up before you can even loot it all. Because of this, the code accounts for gold first, so when you go to a pile of loot the gold is picked up first (as shown in Figure 13.7).

The DropLoot() function is listed next. Gold is handled with custom code that requires the gold.png image, so be sure to include that among the many images now required for inventory. A helper function called DropTreasureItem() keeps the code tidy.

```
public void DropLoot(ref Character srcMonster)
{
    int count = 0;
    int rad = 64;
```

```
//any gold to drop?
Item itm = new Item();
int gold = game.Random(srcMonster.DropGoldMin, srcMonster.DropGoldMax);
itm.Name = "gold";
itm.DropImageFilename = "gold.png";
itm.InvImageFilename = "gold.png";
itm.Value = gold;
Point p = new Point(0, 0);
p.X = (int)srcMonster.X + game.Random(rad) - rad / 2;
p.Y = (int)srcMonster.Y + game.Random(rad) - rad / 2;
DropTreasureItem(ref itm, p.X, p.Y);

//any items to drop?
if (srcMonster.DropNum1 > 0 && srcMonster.DropItem1 != "")
{
    count = game.Random(1, srcMonster.DropNum1);
    for (int n = 1; n < count; n++)
    {
        //25% chance for drop
        if (game.Random(100) < 25)
        {
            itm = items.getItem(srcMonster.DropItem1);
            p.X = (int)srcMonster.X + game.Random(rad) - rad / 2;
            p.Y = (int)srcMonster.Y + game.Random(rad) - rad / 2;
            DropTreasureItem(ref itm, p.X, p.Y);
        }
    }
}
if (srcMonster.DropNum2 > 0 && srcMonster.DropItem2 != "")
{
    count = game.Random(1, srcMonster.DropNum2);
    for (int n = 1; n < count; n++)
    {
        //25% chance for drop
        if (game.Random(100) < 25)
        {
            itm = items.getItem(srcMonster.DropItem2);
            p.X = (int)srcMonster.X + game.Random(rad) - rad / 2;
            p.Y = (int)srcMonster.Y + game.Random(rad) - rad / 2;
            DropTreasureItem(ref itm, p.X, p.Y);
```

```
            }
        }
    }
    if (srcMonster.DropNum3 > 0 && srcMonster.DropItem3 != "")
    {
        count = game.Random(1, srcMonster.DropNum3);
        for (int n = 1; n < count; n++)
        {
            //25% chance for drop
            if (game.Random(100) < 25)
            {
                itm = items.getItem(srcMonster.DropItem3);
                p.X = (int)srcMonster.X + game.Random(rad) - rad / 2;
                p.Y = (int)srcMonster.Y + game.Random(rad) - rad / 2;
                DropTreasureItem(ref itm, p.X, p.Y);
            }
        }
    }
}
```

The helper function, DropTreasureItem(), verifies that the Item.DropImageFilename property contains a valid filename, then adds a new sprite to the treasure container. The game code looks for sprites to draw and interact with in the dungeon level—not Items—so that is why we need the DrawableItem structure. It's a relatively trivial amount of code, wherein the Item and Sprite are each initialized here and added to the list container that handles all drop items in the game.

```
public void DropTreasureItem(ref Item itm, int x, int y)
{
    DrawableItem drit;
    drit.item = itm;
    drit.sprite = new Sprite(ref game);
    drit.sprite.Position = new Point(x, y);
    if (drit.item.DropImageFilename == "")
    {
        MessageBox.Show("Error: Item '" + drit.item.Name +
            "' image file is invalid.");
        Application.Exit();
```

```
    }
    drit.sprite.Image = game.LoadBitmap(drit.item.DropImageFilename);
    drit.sprite.Size = drit.sprite.Image.Size;
    treasure.Add(drit);
}
```

Managing Inventory

Isn't it great that the game engine has been developed up to the point where we can begin discussing higher level topics like inventory? It feels as if all the hard work getting to this point was justified. Now what I'm going to do is explain the approach I've decided to take with Dungeon Crawler when it comes to managing inventory. There are many different approaches or possible directions we could take with an inventory system. One possibility is to give the player a "backpack" in which all inventory items are stored (this is used in a lot of games). Another approach is to display a list of inventory items by name (popular in online MUDs (multi-user dungeons). We could limit the player to a fixed number of inventory items, or base the limit on weight, in which case every item in the game would need to have a weight property.

Another approach is to follow more of an arcade-style inventory system where the player only possesses what he needs. In other words, the player has a weapon, armor, and modifiers like rings and amulets. The player wields a single weapon, based on the character's class (i.e., axe, sword, bow, or staff), wears a complete suit of armor (i.e., leather, studded, scale, or chain), and then has the option of wearing rings or amulets. Those *modifiers* or *buffs* help to boost the player's stats (such as strength or intelligence). The Inventory class keeps track of 30 items total—that's 9 worn items plus 21 items being carried.

Figure 13.8 shows the inventory window after the player has picked up a bunch of sample items from the Looting demo. If you fight the same hostile NPCs, odds are you will end up with several of the same drop items after a while. This Inventory class is *awesome!* You can move stuff around in the "bag," equip items, remove items. The same inventory window also shows the player's basic stats—level, experience, strength, gold, etc. If you want to have a separate screen for that, you are welcome to duplicate the Inventory class and then make the necessary changes. I wanted to keep it simple for this game, to keep the code on the shorter side.

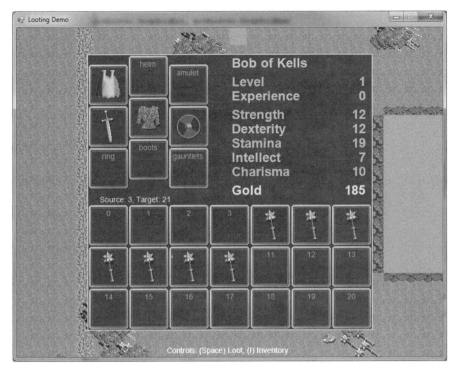

Figure 13.8
Items can be moved around in the inventory system!

Inventory Class

The Inventory class does double duty as a container for the player's inventory *and* it produces the rendered output of the inventory screen that the player uses to manage his stuff. This is by far the largest class we've seen with quite a few lines of code! The inventory system has to keep track of the mouse position, highlighting buttons when the mouse moves over them, drawing the inventory and equipped items, and the player's stats. Whew, this class does a lot! The great thing about it is that all of the inventory buttons are positioned in code as rectangles, so if you want to redo the inventory/character screen, you can move the gear buttons around.

```
public class Inventory
{
    public struct Button
    {
```

```
        public Rectangle rect;
        public string text;
        public Bitmap image;
        public string imagefile;
    }

    private int BTN_HEAD;
    private int BTN_CHEST;
    private int BTN_LEGS;
    private int BTN_RTHAND;
    private int BTN_LTHAND;
    private int BTN_RTFINGER;
    private int BTN_LTFINGER;

    private Game p_game;
    private Font p_font;
    private Font p_font2;
    private PointF p_position;
    private Button[] p_buttons;
    private int p_selection;
    private int p_sourceIndex;
    private int p_targetIndex;
    private Point p_mousePos;
    private MouseButtons p_mouseBtn;
    private int p_lastButton;
    private MouseButtons p_oldMouseBtn;
    private bool p_visible;
    private Bitmap p_bg;
    private Item[] p_inventory;

    public Inventory(ref Game game, Point pos)
    {
        p_game = game;
        p_position = pos;
        p_bg = game.LoadBitmap("char_bg3.png");
        p_font = new Font("Arial", 24, FontStyle.Bold, GraphicsUnit.Pixel);
        p_font2 = new Font("Arial", 14, FontStyle.Regular,
            GraphicsUnit.Pixel);
        p_selection = 0;
        p_mouseBtn = MouseButtons.None;
```

```
        p_oldMouseBtn = p_mouseBtn;
        p_mousePos = new Point(0, 0);
        p_visible = false;
        p_lastButton = -1;
        CreateInventory();
        CreateButtons();
    }

    public void CreateInventory()
    {
        p_inventory = new Item[30];
        for (int n = 0; n < p_inventory.Length - 1; n++)
        {
            p_inventory[n] = new Item();
            p_inventory[n].Name = "";
        }
    }

    public bool AddItem(Item itm)
    {
        for (int n = 0; n < 20; n++)
        {
            if (p_inventory[n].Name == "")
            {
                CopyInventoryItem(ref itm, ref p_inventory[n]);
                return true;
            }
        }
        return false;
    }

    public void CreateButtons()
    {
        int rx=0, ry=0, rw=0, rh=0, index=0;

        //create inventory buttons
        p_buttons = new Button[30];
        for (int y = 0; y < 3; y++)
        {
            for (int x = 0; x < 7; x++)
```

```
        {
            rx = (int)p_position.X + 6 + x * 76;
            ry = (int)p_position.Y + 278 + y * 76;
            rw = 64;
            rh = 64;
            p_buttons[index].rect = new Rectangle(rx, ry, rw, rh);
            p_buttons[index].text = index.ToString();
            index += 1;
        }
    }

    //create left gear buttons
    rx = (int)p_position.X + 6;
    ry = (int)p_position.Y + 22;
    p_buttons[index].rect = new Rectangle(rx, ry, rw, rh);
    p_buttons[index].text = "cape";
    index += 1;

    ry += 76;
    p_buttons[index].rect = new Rectangle(rx, ry, rw, rh);
    p_buttons[index].text = "weapon 1";
    BTN_RTHAND = index;
    index += 1;

    ry += 76;
    p_buttons[index].rect = new Rectangle(rx, ry, rw, rh);
    p_buttons[index].text = "ring";
    index += 1;

    //create center gear buttons
    rx = (int)p_position.X + 82;
    ry = (int)p_position.Y + 6;
    p_buttons[index].rect = new Rectangle(rx, ry, rw, rh);
    p_buttons[index].text = "helm";
    BTN_HEAD = index;
    index += 1;

    ry += 76;
    p_buttons[index].rect = new Rectangle(rx, ry, rw, rh);
    p_buttons[index].text = "chest";
```

```
        BTN_CHEST = index;
        index += 1;

        ry += 76;
        p_buttons[index].rect = new Rectangle(rx, ry, rw, rh);
        p_buttons[index].text = "boots";
        BTN_LEGS = index;
        index += 1;

        //create right gear buttons
        rx = (int)p_position.X + 158;
        ry = (int)p_position.Y + 22;
        p_buttons[index].rect = new Rectangle(rx, ry, rw, rh);
        p_buttons[index].text = "amulet";
        index += 1;

        ry += 76;
        p_buttons[index].rect = new Rectangle(rx, ry, rw, rh);
        p_buttons[index].text = "weapon 2";
        BTN_LTHAND = index;
        index += 1;

        ry += 76;
        p_buttons[index].rect = new Rectangle(rx, ry, rw, rh);
        p_buttons[index].text = "gauntlets";
        index += 1;
    }

    public bool Visible
    {
        get { return p_visible; }
        set { p_visible = value; }
    }

    public int Selection
    {
        get { return p_selection; }
        set { p_selection = value; }
    }
```

```
//get/set position in pixels
public PointF Position
{
    get { return p_position; }
    set { p_position = value; }
}

public int LastButton
{
    get { return p_lastButton; }
    set { p_lastButton = value; }
}

private void Print(int x, int y, string text)
{
    Print(x, y, text, Brushes.White);
}

private void Print(int x, int y, string text, Brush color)
{
    p_game.Device.DrawString(text, p_font, color, x, y);
}

//print text right-justified from top-right x,y
private void PrintRight(int x, int y, string text, Brush color)
{
    SizeF rsize = p_game.Device.MeasureString(text, p_font);
    p_game.Device.DrawString(text, p_font, color, x - rsize.Width, y);
}

public void updateMouse(Point mousePos, MouseButtons mouseBtn)
{
    p_mousePos = mousePos;
    p_oldMouseBtn = p_mouseBtn;
    p_mouseBtn = mouseBtn;
}

public void Draw()
{
    if (!p_visible) return;
```

```
        int tx, ty;

        //draw background
        p_game.DrawBitmap(ref p_bg, p_position.X, p_position.Y);
        p_game.Device.DrawRectangle(new Pen(Color.Gold, 2), p_position.X - 1,
            p_position.Y - 1, p_bg.Width + 2, p_bg.Height + 2);

        //print player stats
        int x = 400;
        int y = (int)p_position.Y;
        int ht = 26;
        Print(x, y, p_game.Hero.Name, Brushes.Gold);
        y += ht + 8;
        PrintRight(660, y, p_game.Hero.Level.ToString(), Brushes.Light-
Green);
        Print(x, y, "Level", Brushes.LightGreen);
        y += ht;
        PrintRight(660, y, p_game.Hero.Experience.ToString(),
            Brushes.LightBlue);
        Print(x, y, "Experience", Brushes.LightBlue);
        y += ht + 8;
        PrintRight(660, y, p_game.Hero.STR.ToString(), Brushes.LightGreen);
        Print(x, y, "Strength", Brushes.LightGreen);
        y += ht;
        PrintRight(660, y, p_game.Hero.DEX.ToString(), Brushes.LightBlue);
        Print(x, y, "Dexterity", Brushes.LightBlue);
        y += ht;
        PrintRight(660, y, p_game.Hero.STA.ToString(), Brushes.LightGreen);
        Print(x, y, "Stamina", Brushes.LightGreen);
        y += ht;
        PrintRight(660, y, p_game.Hero.INT.ToString(), Brushes.LightBlue);
        Print(x, y, "Intellect", Brushes.LightBlue);
        y += ht;
        PrintRight(660, y, p_game.Hero.CHA.ToString(), Brushes.LightGreen);
        Print(x, y, "Charisma", Brushes.LightGreen);
        y += ht + 8;
        PrintRight(660, y, p_game.Hero.Gold.ToString(),
            Brushes.LightGoldenrodYellow);
        Print(x, y, "Gold", Brushes.LightGoldenrodYellow);
        y += ht;
```

```
//draw the buttons
for (int n = 0; n < p_buttons.Length - 1; n++)
{
    Rectangle rect = p_buttons[n].rect;

    //draw button border
    p_game.Device.DrawRectangle(Pens.Gray, rect);

    //print button label
    if (p_buttons[n].image == null)
    {
        SizeF rsize = p_game.Device.MeasureString(p_buttons[n].text,
            p_font2);
        tx = (int)(rect.X + rect.Width / 2 - rsize.Width / 2);
        ty = rect.Y + 2;
        p_game.Device.DrawString(p_buttons[n].text, p_font2,
            Brushes.DarkGray, tx, ty);
    }
}


//check for (button click
for (int n = 0; n < p_buttons.Length - 1; n++)
{
    Rectangle rect = p_buttons[n].rect;
    if (rect.Contains(p_mousePos))
    {
        if (p_mouseBtn == MouseButtons.None && p_oldMouseBtn ==
            MouseButtons.Left)
        {
            p_selection = n;
            if (p_sourceIndex == -1)
                p_sourceIndex = p_selection;
            else if (p_targetIndex == -1)
                p_targetIndex = p_selection;
            else
            {
                p_sourceIndex = p_selection;
                p_targetIndex = -1;
            }
            break;
```

```
            }
            p_game.Device.DrawRectangle(new Pen(Color.Red, 2.0f), rect);
        }
    }

    string text = "Source: " + p_sourceIndex.ToString() + ", Target: " +
        p_targetIndex.ToString();
    if (p_sourceIndex == p_targetIndex)
        text += " : same item";

    if (p_selection != -1 && p_sourceIndex != -1 && p_targetIndex != -1)
    {
        if (p_buttons[p_sourceIndex].image == null)
            text += " : source is empty";
        else if (p_buttons[p_targetIndex].image != null)
            text += " : target is in use";
        else
        {
            text += " : good to move!";
            MoveInventoryItem(p_sourceIndex, p_targetIndex);
            p_selection = -1;
        }
    }
    p_game.Device.DrawString(text, p_font2, Brushes.White,
        p_position.X + 20, p_position.Y + 255);

    //draw equipment
    for (int n = 0; n < p_inventory.Length - 1; n++)
    {
        DrawInventoryItem( n );
    }
}

private void DrawInventoryItem(int index)
{
    string filename = p_inventory[index].InvImageFilename;
    if (filename.Length > 0)
    {
        //try to avoid repeatedly loading image
        if (p_buttons[index].image == null || p_buttons[index].imagefile
```

```
                      != filename)
              {
                  p_buttons[index].imagefile = filename;
                  p_buttons[index].image = p_game.LoadBitmap(filename);
              }
              GraphicsUnit unit = GraphicsUnit.Pixel;
              RectangleF srcRect = p_buttons[index].image.GetBounds( ref unit );
              RectangleF dstRect = p_buttons[index].rect;
              p_game.Device.DrawImage(p_buttons[index].image, dstRect,
                  srcRect, GraphicsUnit.Pixel);
          }
      }


      private void MoveInventoryItem(int source, int dest)
      {
          CopyInventoryItem(ref p_inventory[source], ref p_inventory[dest]);
          p_inventory[source].Name = "";
          p_inventory[source].InvImageFilename = "";
          p_buttons[source].imagefile = "";
          p_buttons[source].image = null;
      }


      public void CopyInventoryItem(int source, int dest)
      {
          CopyInventoryItem(ref p_inventory[source], ref p_inventory[dest]);
      }


      public void CopyInventoryItem(ref Item srcItem, ref Item dstItem)
      {
          dstItem.Name = srcItem.Name;
          dstItem.Description = srcItem.Description;
          dstItem.AttackDie = srcItem.AttackDie;
          dstItem.AttackNumDice = srcItem.AttackNumDice;
          dstItem.Category = srcItem.Category;
          dstItem.Defense = srcItem.Defense;
          dstItem.DropImageFilename = srcItem.DropImageFilename;
          dstItem.InvImageFilename = srcItem.InvImageFilename;
          dstItem.Value = srcItem.Value;
          dstItem.Weight = srcItem.Weight;
          dstItem.STR = srcItem.STR;
```

```
        dstItem.DEX = srcItem.DEX;
        dstItem.CHA = srcItem.CHA;
        dstItem.STA = srcItem.STA;
        dstItem.INT = srcItem.INT;
    }

}
```

Player Class

The Player class is a bit of a pushover at this point, because we're getting a bit ahead of ourselves delving into the player's game state data for just the Looting demo project, but I wanted to at least show you what's in the class at this early stage since it's in the project. The only thing here is the Gold property. In the final chapter, this class will be responsible for keeping track of all the player's information, and for saving and loading the game.

```
public class Player : Character
{
    private int p_gold;

    public Player(ref Game game) : base(ref game)
    {
        p_gold = 0;
    }

    public int Gold
    {
        get { return p_gold; }
        set { p_gold = value; }
    }

    public override string ToString()
    {
        return base.Name;
    }

    public void LoadGame(string filename) { }
    public void SaveGame(string filename) { }
}
```

Level Up!

That successfully finishes off the item editor and inventory system! I'm pleased with how these new features turned out. The editor has been developed with a different goal in mind than the other editors, in that many items are stored in a single xml file rather than one item per file. This makes it quite easy to edit many items quickly by simply clicking each item in the list and making changes to it. Since the editor automatically saves changes made to items, this works quite well. Just be sure to save the file when you're done editing.

When I look at the inventory screen, I think it looks good because there isn't a whole lot of code there and it works so well. But you know what's still missing? You can equip items to *any* gear slot, and they don't actually do anything for the player yet. Granted, but that's some easy logic now that inventory is working. The focus in this chapter was just getting the items created with the editor and getting the inventory system to display the right items, allow the player to pick up loot, and let the player move stuff around. The good news is, the code is already in place to make that happen, and we'll be able to apply inventory item modifiers to the player's stats.

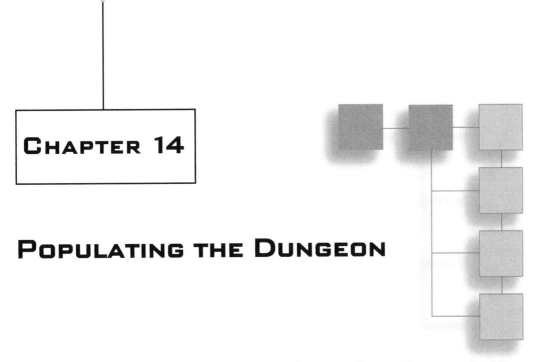

CHAPTER 14

POPULATING THE DUNGEON

This chapter builds on the work developed previously in Chapter 8, "Adding Objects to the Dungeon," with a new emphasis on working within the collidable structure of a dungeon level containing solid walls. The level editor uses tile properties that we have thus far not put to use—Data 1, 2, 3, and 4. These fields will be used to place specific items in the dungeon via the item editor covered in the previous chapter. As you know, every item has an identifier (ID #) as well as a name. We can add an item to the dungeon at any tile location by using either of those fields. Since every tile has these data properties, there's no need to specify an X,Y location for an item because it will automatically be positioned over its parent tile! This same technique for adding treasure and pick-up items to the dungeon will be used to position *monsters* in each level!

One thing you'll notice in the code starting in this chapter is more error-handling code with tests to make sure stuff is loaded correctly before continuing. Taking control over errors as basic as a missing file improve the player's experience and gives your game polish. Allowing hard crash errors to pop up gives the player a bad impression of your game. It's bad enough that an error occurs, but taking control and reporting the error in the game itself shows due diligence on the programmer's part—and most players are willing to accept that, while they may not accept an unhandled error.

Here is a quick outline of what we'll cover:

- Player spawn
- Treasure caches
- Monster spawns

PLAYER SPAWN

The first thing I want to address is the entrance to the dungeon. In most of the examples so far we have been using just a generic overworld scene with grass and dirt tiles without enforcing collision with solid tiles (i.e., walls), despite collision at the player's feet already working. So, where does the player begin? Since a dungeon will be made up of many levels, there must be a door or staircase or other type of portal object that allows the player to move from one level to the next. It seems intuitive that the "downward" staircase on level one should correspond with the player's starting location below on level two, as far as orientation is concerned. But, there is no requirement that every level have the same dimensions! We have the potential for *huge* levels with the dimensions that the level editor supports.

Some game designers (like yourself?) might really enjoy creating a large level using that much space. As a demonstration game, I will not be working very hard to make creative and cunning level designs—I just need to show *you* how they work, so *you* can create creatively ingenious gameplay designs for players to enjoy! So, my example levels will be small and to the point, enough to give you guidance on how things work, without trying to pretend that my example game is production quality, so to speak.

Tip

Remember, you can replace the artwork used for the dungeon level by simply replacing the palette image as long as the tiles are compatible with the level (walls = walls, floors = floors, etc.). The sample art used here is just a sample to show what is possible!

Dungeon Entrance

The player spawn point in a dungeon level should represent a ladder or stairway *up* to the next level, and the goal should be to find the next opening *down* to go to the next level. This means we need to spawn the player at a specific location in

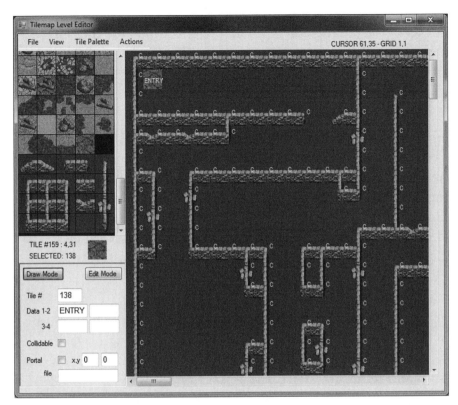

Figure 14.1
Creating a new player spawn flag in the level file.

the dungeon level every time—no more random or fixed locations! We're going to write some code to make this happen and then re-use that code for positioning treasures and monsters in the level as well.

Take a look at Figure 14.1. At the upper-left corner of the level is a highlighted tile. I chose a meaningless tile to place there simply to show the player's spawn point. In a real game you would want to add new tile artwork representing a ladder or stairway. You can use *any* of the four data fields to represent the player spawn flag. I'm just going to use Data 1, the first of the four fields. But what goes here? These fields can contain text or numeric values. What if we use text? In that case, you might actually write "ENTRY" here; and for the exit tile, "EXIT." That does seem more intuitive than numbers or codes, doesn't it? This is really a matter of preference. Some programmers might prefer numbers, while others prefer codes or text. I suspect designers would prefer text because then the level is self-documenting (and I agree with the benefit of that!). The bottom line is, the game engine needs to know what to look for, so whatever you use as an identifier flag, just be consistent. I'm going to use ENTRY for the player's spawn point.

Now, speaking of the exit tile, do we really need one? Not really. There is already a portal system built into the game, and it works well. So, to exit a level, you might still show the player a ladder going down but just set that tile to a portal. Now, regarding the portal X,Y fields, those will not be needed, just the filename. Why? Because the player spawn (ENTRY) will kick in as soon as a level is loaded. It is definitely reasonable to load a level and use those X,Y values to start the player at a specific location if your game would use such a feature.

Positioning the Player

Now let's write some code to position the player. This means the level must be loaded *before* the player is positioned. So, we'll keep the existing player (Hero) creation code in place, but then make sure to set the player's position after loading the level and retrieving the "ENTRY" tile.

What I mean by *player* is actually the *scroll position*, not the location of the hero sprite on the screen. The sprite stays near the center of the screen most of the time, while the level scrolls underneath like a background. It's the *scroll position* that must be set, with the player sprite over the top of that specific tile.

I just thought of something. What if there's no player spawn flag anywhere in the level? What will happen to the player then? There are *walls* all through the dungeon levels so it will not do to just pick a fixed position or random location. What about just looking for a non-collidable tile and positioning the player there? No, I don't like accounting for conditions that should be assumed. We decide that our game will use a certain tile data flag to represent the player's spawn location, and if that is missing then the game needs to quit with an error message, just as if a sprite file is missing. Either way, it's up to you, but I'm going to opt for the error approach. But, it would be helpful to at least explain in the error message what is missing so a designer who is testing their level can easily fix it.

Tip

Want to really throw the player a curve ball? Make the hero a *skeleton* or other monster sprite and all the monsters actually *hero* sprites, and have the monster work his way *up* from the depths of the dungeon to encounter would-be heroes making their way *down*! Then pillage the spawn town at the top to win! Better yet, let the player unlock this feature by beating the game and then play in reverse!

After positioning the scroller to the spawn tile, the level will be drawn with that tile at the upper-left corner of the screen, so we need to adjust it a bit. If possible, it would be preferable to move the scroller so that the spawn is somewhat near the center of the screen, assuming the spawn tile isn't near the edge of the level. One easy way to do that is to just forcibly adjust the scroll position left and up by one-half of the screen (measured in tiles). Perhaps something like 12 tiles over and 9 tiles up? By calling Level.Update() immediately after, the boundary will be enforced and auto-adjusted. This works if the spawn tile is not near the edge of the level, but fails if it is, so that is a start but not a complete solution. We need to figure out exactly where the target tile is on the screen after the scroll position is updated and then move the player sprite there.

Why does it have to be so complicated?

It's time for a game engine assumption! Yes, we could write a complex algorithm to allow the player to spawn anywhere in the level. This is not a problem *at all* for treasure and monsters, because they are rendered relative to the scroll window, but it *is* a problem for the player sprite which is rendered in sync with the scroll window.

Here is the assumption: *The spawn point must be in the upper-left corner of the level within one screen worth of tiles.*

The level will be set to a position of 0,0, and the player sprite will be positioned within that range of tiles without having to deal with any relative positioning. The player sprite is not merely drawn relative to the scroll position, it is at the very core of the scrolling code. So, we can't easily manipulate it to handle any location on the tilemap without writing a lot of conditional code. Figure 14.2 shows the location of a player spawn tile (note the grid coordinates at the top), while Figure 14.3 shows the game running with the player sprite spawned at that location. Here is some sample source code to give you the basic idea:

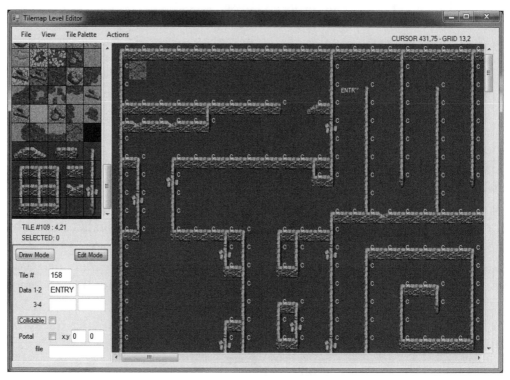

Figure 14.2
Setting a new spawn point in the editor.

```
Point target = new Point(0, 0);
bool found = false;
for (int y = 0; y < 128; y++)
{
    if (found) break;
    for (int x = 0; x < 128; x++)
    {
        target = new Point(x-1, y-1);
        Level.tilemapStruct tile = level.getTile(x,y);
        if (tile.data1.ToUpper() == "ENTRY")
        {
            found = true;
            game.Hero.Position = new Point(
                target.X * 32, target.Y * 32-16);
            break;
```

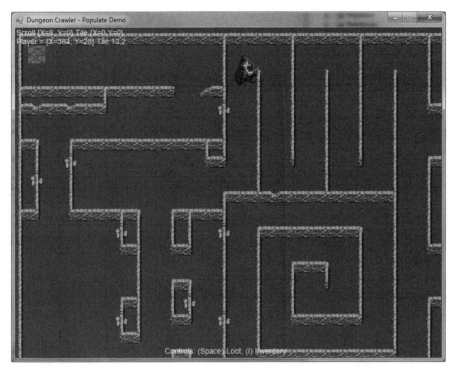

Figure 14.3
Running the game to see the player sprite spawn over the correct tile.

```
        }
    }
}
```

Enforcing Tile Collision

Collision with tiles already works, but we have just been ignoring this property. To enforce collision with walls and other impassable tiles, what's needed is a pair of variables to keep track of the player's previous step. When the player runs into a collidable tile, then the sprite is moved back to the previous step—and the sprite will simply stop moving in that direction even if the player holds down the movement key.

The Level class will be modified to make collision a little easier, and at the same time, the old code in doScrolling() will be moved into Level.Update() now that this code is well established and fully tested, to make movement and the scroller somewhat automatic. In our usual doScroller() function, a call to Level.Update() and Level.Draw() will be made, and that will take care of it. (There will be some additional code in Level to make it all work—refer to the project sources for the complete listing.)

```
private PointF p_oldScrollPos;
private PointF p_oldPlayerPos;
```

The Update() function now incorporates all of the scrolling logic, and now calls on a new helper function, fillScrollBuffer().

```
public void Update()
{
    int steps = 4;

    p_oldScrollPos = p_scrollPos;
    p_oldPlayerPos = p_game.Hero.Position;

    //up key movement
    if (p_game.keyState.up)
    {
        if (p_game.Hero.Y > 300 - 48)
        {
            //p_oldPlayerPos = p_game.Hero.Position;
            p_game.Hero.Y -= steps;
        }
        else
        {
            //p_oldScrollPos = p_scrollPos;
            p_scrollPos.Y -= steps;
            if (p_scrollPos.Y <= 0)
                p_game.Hero.Y -= steps;
        }
    }
```

```
        }
    //down key movement
    else if ( p_game.keyState.down)
    {
        if (p_game.Hero.Y < 300 - 48)
        {
            //p_oldPlayerPos = p_game.Hero.Position;
            p_game.Hero.Y += steps;
        }
        else
        {
            //p_oldScrollPos = p_scrollPos;
            p_scrollPos.Y += steps;
            if (p_scrollPos.Y >= (127 - 19) * 32)
                p_game.Hero.Y += steps;
        }
    }


    //left key movement
    if (p_game.keyState.left)
    {
        if (p_game.Hero.X > 400 - 48)
        {
            //p_oldPlayerPos = p_game.Hero.Position;
            p_game.Hero.X -= steps;
        }
        else
        {
            //p_oldScrollPos = p_scrollPos;
            p_scrollPos.X -= steps;
            if (p_scrollPos.X <= 0)
                p_game.Hero.X -= steps;
        }
    }


    //right key movement
    else if ( p_game.keyState.right)
    {
        if (p_game.Hero.X < 400 - 48)
        {
```

```
            //p_oldPlayerPos = p_game.Hero.Position;
            p_game.Hero.X += steps;
        }
        else
        {
            //p_oldScrollPos = p_scrollPos;
            p_scrollPos.X += steps;
            if (p_scrollPos.X >= (127 - 25) * 32)
                p_game.Hero.X += steps;
        }
    }

    //resolve collidable tile
    Point pos = p_game.Hero.GetCurrentTilePos();
    p_currentTile = getTile(pos.X, pos.Y);
    p_collidableFlag = p_currentTile.collidable;
    if (p_collidableFlag)
    {
        p_game.Hero.Position = p_oldPlayerPos;
        p_scrollPos = p_oldScrollPos;
    }

    //resolve portal tile
    p_portalFlag = p_currentTile.portal;
    if (p_currentTile.portal)
    {
        p_portalTarget = new Point(p_currentTile.portalx -
            pos.X / 32, p_currentTile.portaly - pos.Y / 32);
    }

    //fill the scroll buffer only when moving
    if (p_scrollPos != p_oldScrollPos)
    {
        p_oldScrollPos = p_scrollPos;

        //validate X range
        if (p_scrollPos.X < 0) p_scrollPos.X = 0;
        if (p_scrollPos.X > (127 - p_windowSize.Width) * p_tileSize)
            p_scrollPos.X = (127 - p_windowSize.Width) * p_tileSize;
```

```
        //validate Y range
        if (p_scrollPos.Y < 0) p_scrollPos.Y = 0;
        if (p_scrollPos.Y > (127 - p_windowSize.Height) * p_tileSize)
            p_scrollPos.Y = (127 - p_windowSize.Height) * p_tileSize;

        //calculate sub-tile size
        p_subtile.X = p_scrollPos.X % p_tileSize;
        p_subtile.Y = p_scrollPos.Y % p_tileSize;

        //fill scroll buffer with tiles
        fillScrollBuffer();
    }
}

private void fillScrollBuffer()
{
    for (int tx = 0; tx < p_windowSize.Width + 1; tx++)
    {
        for (int ty = 0; ty < p_windowSize.Height + 1; ty++)
        {
            int sx = (int)p_scrollPos.X / p_tileSize + tx;
            int sy = (int)p_scrollPos.Y / p_tileSize + ty;
            int tilenum = p_tilemap[sy * 128 + sx].tilenum;
            drawTileNumber(tx, ty, tilenum);
        }
    }
}
```

With this new code in the Level class, the player will not be able to walk through collidable tiles any longer! At last, the dungeon crawler is starting to work as intended! To begin organizing the project, I have moved the level variable from Form1 to Game, where it has been renamed to World. So, to work with the tile scroller, you would use game.World as a global variable. The new Form1.doScrolling() function is much simplified:

```
private void doScrolling()
{
    game.World.Update();
    game.World.Draw(0, 0, 800, 600);
}
```

TREASURE CACHES

The *same* code to position the player will be used to add treasure to the level. But, there is one major difference: while there was just *one* player starting location, there will be *many* treasure tiles (which is entirely dependent on the level designer, of course). The character editor has item drop fields that were used in the previous chapter to show how monsters can drop loot when killed. One interesting benefit of this fact is that we could use a character file to drop random loot in the dungeon. Instead of manually adding specific loot items to specific tiles in the dungeon, you could instead simulate a monster dropping loot at that location (as if it has been killed during combat). That would add some randomness to the regular treasure drops in the dungeon because loot items have a percent chance of being dropped—this would add some variability, increasing replay value of a level, and hence, the replay value of the game.

Creating Treasure

The global treasure list has been moved to the Game class in an attempt to further strengthen it as a true RPG engine. Here is the new Treasure variable:

```
public List<DrawableItem> Treasure;
```

Although defined here, we must create the object still in Form1_Load as usual, and in the proper order relative to other objects:

```
game.Treasure = new List<Game.DrawableItem>();
```

First, let's see how to just add an item to the dungeon with a straightforward function called DropTreasureItem. You will pass the item object and X,Y position of the tile where the item will go. Given the two fairly large functions, I believe Treasure might need to be handled in a whole new class. I'm thinking about creating a new Combat class to handle these things. We'll see that in the next and final chapter.

```
public void DropTreasureItem(ref Item itm, int x, int y)
{
    Game.DrawableItem drit;
    drit.item = itm;
    drit.sprite = new Sprite(ref game);
    drit.sprite.Position = new Point(x, y);

    if (drit.item.DropImageFilename == "")
```

```
    {
        MessageBox.Show("Error: Item '" + drit.item.Name +
            "' image file is invalid.");
        Application.Exit();
    }

    drit.sprite.Image = game.LoadBitmap(drit.item.DropImageFilename);
    drit.sprite.Size = drit.sprite.Image.Size;
    game.Treasure.Add(drit);
}
```

This function, of course, is dependent on the item database, so we have to load an item file first before trying to drop any items into the dungeon. (I know, this is fundamental, but I'm just being thorough!). The items database has been moved into Game as well, under the variable name Items.

```
game.Items = new Items();
if (!game.Items.Load("items.item"))
{
    MessageBox.Show("Error loading items");
    Application.Exit();
}
```

Now, open up items.item in the item editor tool and find an item you want to drop for the player, like this Small Shield shown in Figure 14.4. I know it's not as great as, say, a bar of gold. Okay, fine, then go ahead and get some artwork of a gold bar and add it to the items database and give a million of them to your players if you want!

This item is called "Small Shield," so that is how we'll grab it out of the database to add to the global Treasure list. I'm going to be a bit inconsistent with error handling here by just showing the basic code to do it. You'll want to add error handling to make sure the item exists before trying to drop it into the dungeon.

```
Item item = game.Items.getItem("Small Shield");
DropTreasureItem(ref item, 10*32, 1*32);
```

Figure 14.5 shows the shield in the dungeon at exactly the location we expected to find it! (Note the player's tile position.) Picking up the shield (with the Space key) adds it to the inventory, which can be brought up with the I key. None of this code has changed since it was developed in Chapter 13. (See Figure 14.6.) Isn't it amazing how synergistic source code can be at a certain point? When

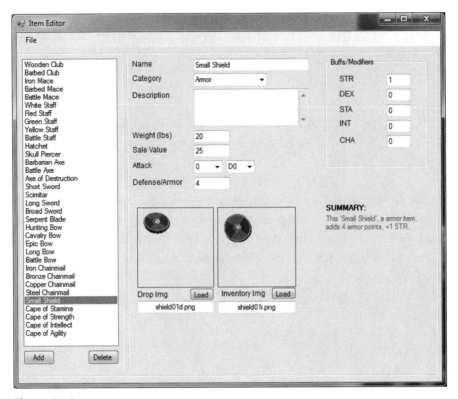

Figure 14.4
Let's find a good item to drop inside the dungeon.

these features start to seriously come together and the game engine starts to take shape, we will spend less time on difficult source code and more time on designing the gameplay.

Dropping Loot-Style Treasure

We have this really great function from Chapter 13 available, called DropLoot(), so let's give it a try without actually adding a monster to the level (we'll give the player sprite a short break). First, a review of the function is in order:

```
public void DropLoot(ref Character srcMonster)
{
    int count = 0;
    int rad = 64;
```

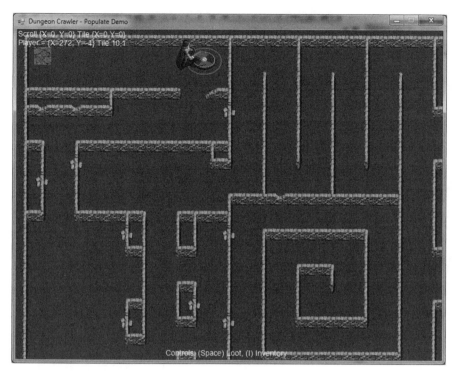

Figure 14.5
The shield magically appears in the dungeon at tile 10,1.

```
//any gold to drop?
Item itm = new Item();
int gold = game.Random(srcMonster.DropGoldMin, srcMonster.DropGoldMax);
itm.Name = "gold";
itm.DropImageFilename = "gold.png";
itm.InvImageFilename = "gold.png";
itm.Value = gold;
Point p = new Point(0, 0);
p.X = (int)srcMonster.X + game.Random(rad) - rad / 2;
p.Y = (int)srcMonster.Y + game.Random(rad) - rad / 2;
DropTreasureItem(ref itm, p.X, p.Y);

//any items to drop?
if (srcMonster.DropNum1 > 0 && srcMonster.DropItem1 != "")
{
```

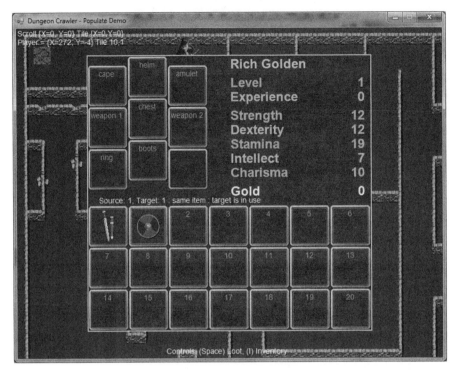

Figure 14.6
The item has been added to the player's inventory.

```
count = game.Random(1, srcMonster.DropNum1);
for (int n = 1; n < count; n++)
{
    //25% chance for drop
    if (game.Random(100) < 25)
    {
        itm = game.Items.getItem(srcMonster.DropItem1);
        p.X = (int)srcMonster.X + game.Random(rad) - rad / 2;
        p.Y = (int)srcMonster.Y + game.Random(rad) - rad / 2;
        DropTreasureItem(ref itm, p.X, p.Y);
    }
}
if (srcMonster.DropNum2 > 0 && srcMonster.DropItem2 != "")
{
    count = game.Random(1, srcMonster.DropNum2);
```

```
        for (int n = 1; n < count; n++)
        {
            //25% chance for drop
            if (game.Random(100) < 25)
            {
                itm = game.Items.getItem(srcMonster.DropItem2);
                p.X = (int)srcMonster.X + game.Random(rad) - rad / 2;
                p.Y = (int)srcMonster.Y + game.Random(rad) - rad / 2;
                DropTreasureItem(ref itm, p.X, p.Y);
            }
        }
    }
    if (srcMonster.DropNum3 > 0 && srcMonster.DropItem3 != "")
    {
        count = game.Random(1, srcMonster.DropNum3);
        for (int n = 1; n < count; n++)
        {
            //25% chance for drop
            if (game.Random(100) < 25)
            {
                itm = game.Items.getItem(srcMonster.DropItem3);
                p.X = (int)srcMonster.X + game.Random(rad) - rad / 2;
                p.Y = (int)srcMonster.Y + game.Random(rad) - rad / 2;
                DropTreasureItem(ref itm, p.X, p.Y);
            }
        }
    }
}
```

Fire up the character editor tool and create a new fake monster to be used just for an item drop. You can create as many custom item drops as you want using this tool. I have created one called "Dummy Drop 1," shown in Figure 14.7. The animations don't matter for our purposes here, but they still must be filled in with valid images because the .char file loader requires it.

```
Character loot = new Character(ref game);
if (!loot.Load("dummydrop1.char"))
{
    MessageBox.Show("Error loading loot file");
    Application.Exit();
}
```

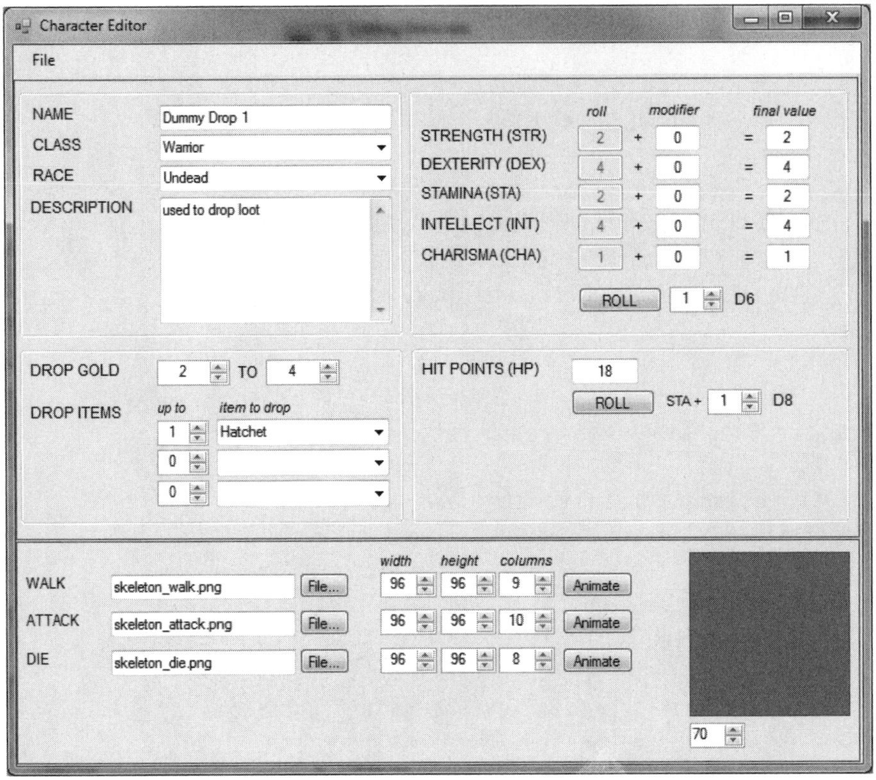

Figure 14.7
A dummy character used to drop loot.

```
loot.Position = new Point(8*32,2*32);
DropLoot(ref loot);
```

Figure 14.8 shows the game running, with the gold drop in the location as expected (tile 8,2). What did *not* show up is the "Hatchet" item, but that is to be expected because the items are only dropped by random chance while gold is *always* dropped.

Designing Treasure Drops

The last way to add treasure items to the dungeon is from right inside the level editor itself—or, more specifically, using the tile property fields. We have already seen how to use the Data1 field to set the player's spawn tile. Similar code can be written to look for an item drop code. In this case, there are some decisions that

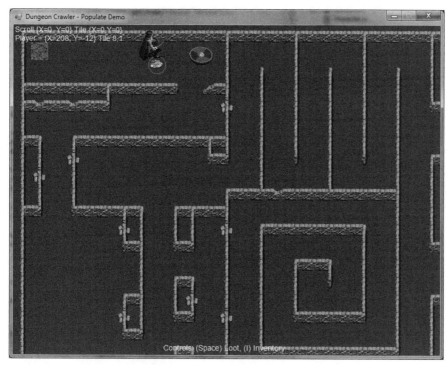

Figure 14.8
The gold has been added to the dungeon like monster loot.

must be made (cooperatively between the designer and programmer, if more than one person is working on the game): How will items be identified in the dungeon levels? Will the item name just be added to Data1, or the item number, or some sort of code?

This is really up to you, but I will give you some pointers on just *one* way to do it. We already know where the item will be located in the level because it will be added right over the top of the tile it belongs to. So, really, all we need is the item name. I'm not even sure if quantity is needed! Do we ever want to add like 50 magic rings or hatchets? No, I don't think so! You can if you want, it's no big deal to just use one of the other data fields for quantity. I'm going to use a code word, "ITEM," to mean that an item should be dropped at that tile location. The Data2 field will contain the item name. See Figure 14.9.

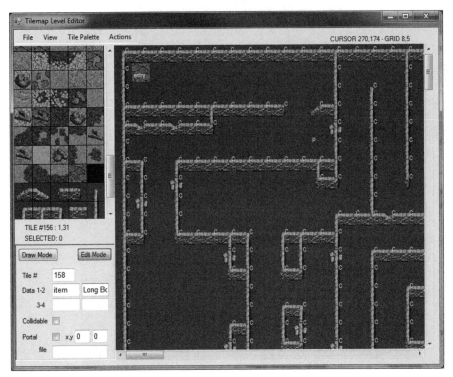

Figure 14.9
A "Long Bow" item has been added to a dungeon tile.

To add items to the dungeon automatically based on tile properties adds a huge element of design power to the game engine! The code to search for the "ITEM" flag and add the associated item to the dungeon will be similar to the code used to position the player. But, instead of breaking when the first item is found, as was done with the player spawn tile, this code needs to keep going and scan the tile records of the entire level. See Figure 14.10.

```
for (int y = 0; y < 128; y++)
{
    for (int x = 0; x < 128; x++)
    {
        Item it = null;
        Level.tilemapStruct tile = game.World.getTile(x, y);
        if (tile.data1.ToUpper() == "ITEM" && tile.data2 != "")
        {
```

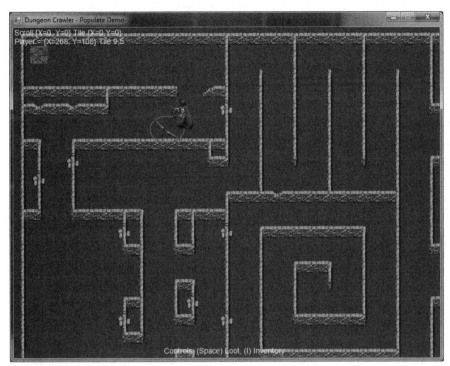

Figure 14.10
Adding items to the dungeon automatically via the level data.

```
        it = game.Items.getItem(tile.data2);
        DropTreasureItem(ref it, x*32, y*32);
    }
  }
}
```

Tip

Some of the item artwork is obviously too large for the dungeon. It's an easy matter to shrink the drop image to a manageable size that better corresponds with the dungeon, but you may not want to change the inventory image because the inventory uses a fixed icon size. Even so, it will still work with smaller images, so that's entirely up to you.

MONSTER SPAWNS

Dungeon Crawler now has all the code we need to position the player at a spawn point, and to add items and gold to the dungeon at any desired tile. All of this code will just make it that much easier to add monsters to the level as well. Like the items, we can add a monster manually one at a time, or use a tile data field. The latter is definitely preferred because then a designer can create the levels without having to dig into any code!

Tip

There's no combat in this chapter's examples, nor do the monsters move. The point is just to demonstrate how to position things inside the level.

Adding Monsters

First, we'll see how to add a single monster manually in code. This example just creates a small array with room for 10 monsters for starters.

```
monsters = new Character[10];
monsters[0] = new Character(ref game);
monsters[0].Load("zombie.char");
monsters[0].Position = new PointF(1 * 32, 4 * 32);
```

Combat is not a priority right now, so combat code has been stripped out of the doMonsters() function. Not to worry, it will be back in the next chapter. Figure 14.11 shows that a zombie has been added to the dungeon at tile location 2,5.

```
private void doMonsters()
{
    PointF relativePos;
    PointF heroCenter;
    PointF monsterCenter;
    heroCenter = game.Hero.CenterPos;
    for (int n = 0; n < monsters.Length; n++)
    {
        if (monsters[n] != null)
        {
            //is monster in view?
            if (monsters[n].X > game.World.ScrollPos.X &&
                monsters[n].X < game.World.ScrollPos.X + 23 * 32 &&
                monsters[n].Y > game.World.ScrollPos.Y &&
                monsters[n].Y < game.World.ScrollPos.Y + 17 * 32)
            {
                //get relative position on screen
                relativePos = new PointF(
```

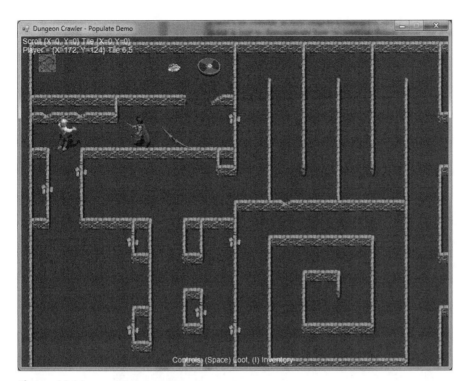

Figure 14.11
A zombie! Uhhhnnnnn! Brains!

```
            Math.Abs(game.World.ScrollPos.X - monsters[n].X),
            Math.Abs(game.World.ScrollPos.Y - monsters[n].Y));

        //get center
        monsterCenter = relativePos;
        monsterCenter.X += monsters[n].GetSprite.Width / 2;
        monsterCenter.Y += monsters[n].GetSprite.Height / 2;

        //draw the monster sprite
        monsters[n].Draw(relativePos);
    }
  }
}
}
```

Monsters by Design

That was a no-brainer. Next, we'll add monsters using tile data. What shall the data field flag be called for monsters? Oh, I don't know, how about "MONSTER"? Now, the second piece of data we need to know in order to add a monster is the .char file. For the example, I'm just using zombie.char, but feel free to use whatever file you want. And, of course, for a polished game the monsters will be selectively added to specific rooms and locations (usually to guard treasure!). Figure 14.12 shows the editor with a bunch of monster tile data entered. This is *not* looking good for our player. Fortunately, the monsters don't know how to move in this disabled example.

This will be a limited example with support for only 10 monsters, so if you edit the level file and make *every tile* a monster spawn, it just won't work. Don't do

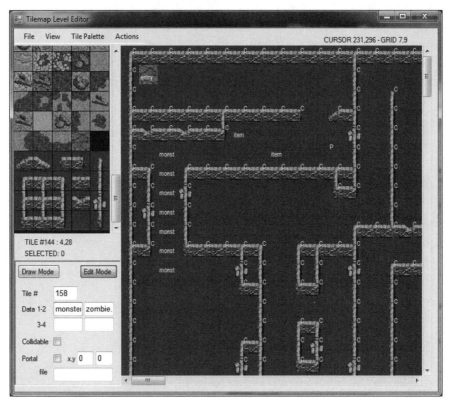

Figure 14.12
Adding a bunch of zombie flags to the level.

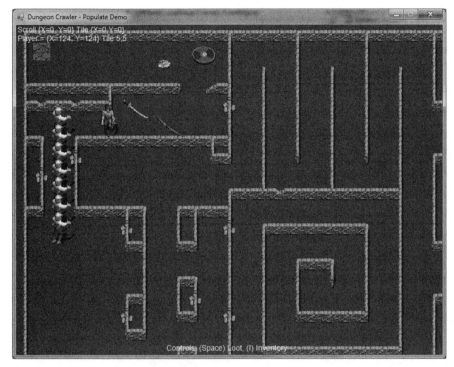

Figure 14.13
Uhh, a little help here? (*If it's not too much trouble!*)

that. You could start a zombie apocalypse. Don't force me to write an apocalypse handler into the code! Figure 14.13 shows our heroic but scared player character facing a horde. He really needs decent gear.

```
int count = 0;
for (int y = 0; y < 128; y++)
{
    for (int x = 0; x < 128; x++)
    {
        Level.tilemapStruct tile = game.World.getTile(x, y);
        if (tile.data1.ToUpper() == "MONSTER" && tile.data2 != "")
        {
            monsters[count] = new Character(ref game);
            monsters[count].Load(tile.data2);
            monsters[count].Position = new PointF((x-1) * 32, (y-1) * 32);
            count++;
```

```
            }
        }
    }
```

LEVEL UP!

We have a custom level editor and an engine that talks to it. What more is there to say? The hard stuff is done. All we have to do now is make improvements and tie some things together and add a story, a title screen, and so forth. The final chapter wraps these things up.

CHAPTER 15

DEEP PLACES OF THE WORLD

"Be on your guard. There are older and fouler things than Orcs in the deep places of the world."

—Gandalf, *The Fellowship of the Ring*, J.R.R. Tolkien

This final chapter covers several important concepts that will give the dungeon crawler engine some much-needed polish. My goal is to make it as easy as possible for you to create your own RPG, by giving just enough information in the example to show how things work, but without going so far into the gameplay that it's difficult to understand how the sample game works. I wouldn't call this a complete game by any means; it is an RPG *engine. The gameplay is up to you!* Among the topics covered are a line-of-sight (LOS) object visibility algorithm; a lantern that lights up the area near the player; character generation; and Lua script support. The final example includes these features and more, including loading and saving the game and rudimentary monster A.I. Along the way, many small but significant improvements have been made to the classes (especially the Game class) to accommodate these new requirements of the engine. All of the editors are in the runtime folder for the game in this chapter's resource files (www.courseptr.com/downloads) for easy access, so if you want to make changes to the game, just fire up the editors and start editing. You have all the tools you need to build your own game, and we will just go over a few new ones in this final chapter.

Here is a quick summary of what we'll cover:

- Line of sight

- Torch light radius

- Scroller optimizations

- Lua script language

- Finishing touches

GOING DEEPER

Everything is starting to really take shape in the dungeon crawler engine. Now we can add treasure and items and monsters in code or via the level editor data. The monsters aren't too bright yet, but they just need some A.I. code to make them move and attack which will be handled in the last chapter. There's one big issue that I want to address because it's a stable of this genre—line of sight.

A really complex game engine would hide everything that isn't directly in the player's line of sight. We could create a node search system to determine whether an object or monster is visible to the player, and then hide them if they are behind a wall or around a corner. But, I was thinking about a simpler way to handle line of sight. Well, simple is a relative term; what I think of as simple, you might have a hard time understanding, and vice versa! How do you tell when something is in view? Well, the only practical way to handle that is to use the `collidable` property, because we have no other way of identifying walls or obstacles. `Collidable` could be used for a small statue or water fountain or something solid that you can see past but not walk through, so there are potential problems with `collidable`, but in general—and for our game— collidable is only really used for wall tiles that are impassible.

Line of Sight (Ray Casting)

Our code already checks to see when an object should be drawn when it is in the current scrolling viewport. But, an item or monster is still drawn even if one or more walls separate them from the player sprite! Wouldn't it be really great if objects only came into view when nothing is obstructing your line of sight? That would make a *big* difference in the gameplay, add to replay value, and quite simply, make the game more *scary*!

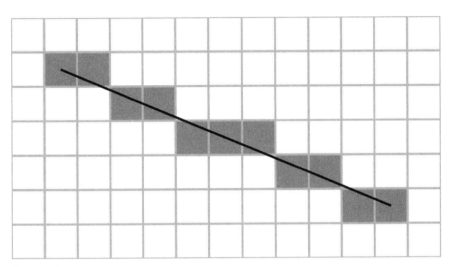

Figure 15.1
Drawing a line using tiles with the Bresenham algorithm.

How do you calculate line of sight? Good question! There's an age-old algorithm invented long ago by a computer scientist named Bresenham, who figured out a very fast way to draw lines on a computer screen. Prior to Bresenham, programmers used trigonometry to draw lines, but Bresenham lines use if statements and counters instead, making it much faster. (See Figure 15.1.) Treat the player's position as the starting point, and the target object's position as the end point, and calculate the points on a line connecting them using *whole tiles* for each pixel. There will only be a few steps in the "line" to calculate. At each step, we check to see whether the tile is *collidable*, and if any tile is, then we know the object is not visible to the player.

This technique is more popularly called *ray casting*.

Another approach is possible. We could simulate firing a bullet from the player to the monster in a straight line, and actually move it along several pixels at a time. As the theoretical bullet is moving along, we figure out which tile it is over at each step, look at the `collidable` property of that tile, and deal with that result in the same way. This avoids the Bresenham algorithm, replacing it with just a simple direction calculation, and by starting at the center of a tile, that step could jump one full tile's worth of pixels (32) at a time. The problem with this second solution, although *simpler*, is that the startup is math heavy—you have to calculate the *angle* from the player to the monster using sine and cosine, which comes out as X and Y velocity values.

Note

For a detailed description of the Bresenham line algorithm, including historical details, take a look at this Wikipedia article: http://en.wikipedia.org/wiki/Bresenham's_line_algorithm.

For a working example, any kind of object will do, so I've stripped out everything but the essentials, leaving in just enough of the game so that treasure items are visible as the player walks around, but they can't be picked up. Here is a function, objectIsVisibleLOS(), that treats the tilemap as pixels while calculating a Bresenham line between the player and any other tile location.

The objectIsVisibleLOS() function is self-contained, calculating the player's tile position automatically, and only requires one parameter—the *relative* location on the screen (in pixel coordinates). Since objects beyond the viewport will be culled anyway, only objects in the viewport need to be tested for line of sight. The Line of Sight demo project demonstrates the technique, as shown in Figure 15.2.

```
private bool objectIsVisibleLOS(PointF target)
{
    //get player's tile position
    Point p0 = new Point((int)game.Hero.FootPos.X-8,
        (int)game.Hero.FootPos.Y);
    Point line0 = p0;

    //get target tile position
    Point p1 = new Point((int)target.X, (int)target.Y);
    Point line1 = p1;

    //begin calculating line
    bool steep = Math.Abs(p1.Y - p0.Y) > Math.Abs(p1.X - p0.X);
    if (steep)
    {
        //swap points due to steep slope
        Point tmpPoint = new Point(p0.X,p0.Y);
        p0 = new Point(tmpPoint.Y, tmpPoint.X);
```

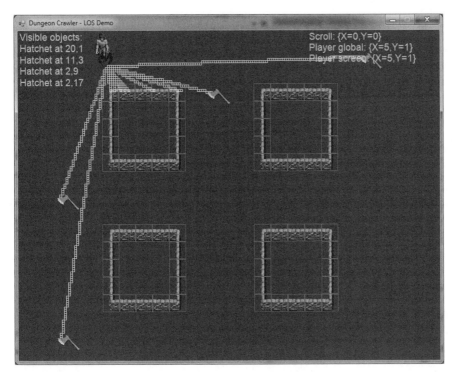

Figure 15.2
Line of sight (LOS) ray casting is used to hide objects that should not be visible to the player.

```
        tmpPoint = p1;
        p1 = new Point(tmpPoint.Y, tmpPoint.X);
}

int deltaX = (int)Math.Abs(p1.X - p0.X);
int deltaY = (int)Math.Abs(p1.Y - p0.Y);
int error = 0;
int deltaError = deltaY;
int yStep = 0, xStep = 0;
int x = p0.X, y = p0.Y;

if (p0.Y < p1.Y) yStep = 4;
else yStep = -4;

if (p0.X < p1.X) xStep = 4;
else xStep = -4;
```

```
int tmpX = 0, tmpY = 0;

while (x != p1.X)
{
    x += xStep;
    error += deltaError;

    //move one along on the Y axis
    if ((2*error) > deltaX)
    {
        y += yStep;
        error -= deltaX;
    }

    //flip the coords if steep
    if (steep)
    {
        tmpX = y;
        tmpY = x;
    }
    else
    {
        tmpX = x;
        tmpY = y;
    }

    //make sure coords are legal
    if (tmpX >= 0 & tmpX < 1280 & tmpY >= 0 & tmpY < 1280 )
    {
        //is this a collidable tile?
        Level.tilemapStruct ts = game.World.getTile(tmpX/32, tmpY/32);
        if (ts.collidable) return false;
        else
        {
            //draw this step of path toward target
            game.Device.DrawRectangle(Pens.Azure, tmpX + 14,
                tmpY + 14, 4, 4);
        }
    }
    else
```

```
        //not legal coords
        return false;
}

    return true;
}
```

Figure 15.3 shows another view of the demo with the player at the center of the four walled-off rooms, making it impossible to see what's inside (there's an item in each room). Note that the line-of-sight rays terminate when they reach a collidable tile, while those without obstruction continue to the target item. This is not a 100 percent foolproof algorithm. There are some cases where an object will be visible when it shouldn't be, because the algorithm is *fast* and sometimes the ray's points fall in between tiles. One improvement would be to use the player's lantern radius *and* the ray casting line-of-sight algorithm to hide objects

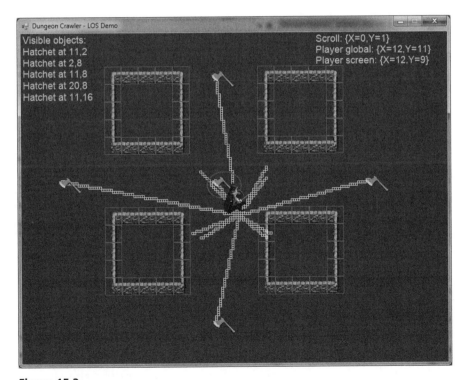

Figure 15.3
The items placed inside the walled rooms are invisible due to LOS.

that are either blocked or outside the player's viewing range. This is the technique I recommend using, with both rather than just line of sight alone.

Torch Light Radius

Having line-of-sight culling is a huge improvement over just drawing everything in the viewport, as far as improving the game's realism. That, combined with another new technique in drawing the level—torch light radius—will make the player truly feel as if he is walking through a dark, dank, cold dungeon. Since line of sight causes only objects within view to be drawn, we can take advantage of that with this additional effect to make the player's experience *perfect* for this genre. It goes without saying that dungeons don't come with halogen lights on the ceiling—a real underground tunnel and room system would be pitch black, and the player would have to be carrying a torch—there's just no way around that. I'm not a big fan of micro-management, so I just give the player a permanent torch, but some game designers are cruel enough to cause the torch to burn out!

The key to making the dungeon level look dark everywhere except near the player is by using a radius value, highlighting all tiles within a certain range around the player. All tiles in that range are drawn normally, while all other tiles are drawn with a level of darkness (perhaps 50 percent white). GDI+ has a feature that we could use to draw some of the tiles darker that are beyond the light radius around the player. By using `ImageAttribute`, it is possible to set the gamma level to increase or decrease the lighting of an image. In testing, however, this proved to be too slow for the game, causing performance to drop significantly (because the actual pixels of the image were being manipulated). Instead, we'll just have to manipulate the *artwork*. If you are intrigued by the `ImageAttribute` approach—don't be. In practice, anything you can do easily with artwork is a far better solution than trying to do it in code. Try to keep your code as straightforward as possible, without all kinds of conditions and options, and put some requirements on the artwork instead for better results.

The Torch Light demo is shown in Figure 15.4. The first and most obvious problem with this is the square-shape of the lit area (where it really *should* be round in shape). The second problem with this demo is that areas beyond a wall appear to be lit even though the lantern should not be penetrating the wall. It

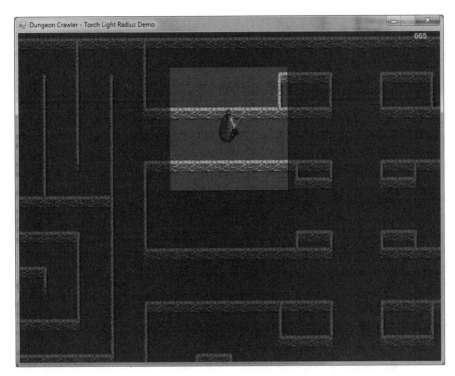

Figure 15.4
Lighting up a small area around the player to simulate a lantern.

would seem we need to combine the lantern code with the ray-casting line-of-sight code for object visibility *as well as* for lighting. The *great* thing about this problem, strange as that may sound, is that we have all the code we need to make any such changes we want to make—to both object visibility and to the lighting around the player.

How do you want to tackle it? Are these issues important for your own game design goals? I can only give you the tools, but you must make the game! These examples are meant to teach concepts, not to create a fun gameplay experience. So, use these concepts and the code I'm sharing with you in creative ways while creating your own dungeon crawler!

The dark tile set is just a copy of the normal palette.bmp image with the brightness turned down and saved as a new file, palette_dark.bmp. Some changes must be made to the Level class to make this work. Another Bitmap variable is needed to handle the dark tiles:

```
private Bitmap p_bmpTilesDark;
```

The loadPalette() function is modified to require both palette filenames:

```
public bool loadPalette(string lightTiles, string darkTiles, int columns)
{
    p_columns = columns;
    try {
        p_bmpTiles = new Bitmap(lightTiles);
        p_bmpTilesDark = new Bitmap(darkTiles);
        fillScrollBuffer();
    }
    catch (Exception) { return false; }
    return true;
}
```

The function fillScrollBuffer() draws the tiles representing the current scroll buffer. This function is called only when the player moves one full tile width or height (32 pixels), at which point the buffer must be re-filled with tiles at the new scroll position. This function, in turn, calls on a helper called drawTile-Number(), to actually do the physical drawing of the tile image. This function has not changed since the Level class was originally created.

```
private void fillScrollBuffer()
{
    Point currentTile = new Point((int)p_scrollPos.X / p_tileSize,
        (int)p_scrollPos.Y / p_tileSize);

    for (int tx = 0; tx < p_windowSize.Width + 1; tx++)
    {
        for (int ty = 0; ty < p_windowSize.Height + 1; ty++)
        {
            int rx = currentTile.X   + tx;
            int ry = currentTile.Y + ty;
            int tilenum = p_tilemap[ry * 128 + rx].tilenum;

            Point playerTile = p_game.Hero.GetCurrentTilePos();
            if ((Math.Abs(rx - (playerTile.X + currentTile.X)) <= 3) &&
                (Math.Abs(ry - (playerTile.Y + currentTile.Y)) <= 3))
```

```
        {
            //draw tile using light tileset
            drawTileNumber(ref p_bmpTiles, tx, ty, tilenum);
        }
        else
        {
            //draw tile using dark tileset
            drawTileNumber(ref p_bmpTilesDark, tx, ty, tilenum);
        }
    }
  }
}
```

Even more sophisticated forms of lighting can be adopted, such as using an adaptation of the line-of-sight code developed recently to cause the light range to stop when it hits a wall. If you are going for an even more realistic look for your own game, you might try this. In simple experiments I found it fairly easy to look for collidable tiles while drawing the lighter tiles. Creative coding could produce interesting special effects like a flashlight-style light or a lamp light that swings back and forth as the player walks.

Scroller Optimizations

The scroller engine now built into the Level class is not optimized. In our efforts to get a scrolling level to move and draw, no concern was given to performance. But, there is a built-in capability to optimize the scroller which will result in at least a 10x frame rate increase. Presently, the fillScrollBuffer() function is called *any time* the player moves—even a pixel. This is highly inefficient. But, again, the important thing is to get a game to *work* first, then worry about performance later. Now is that time! By adding the gamma light modifications to the tile renderer, there is an added strain on the engine to maintain a steady frame rate. By making a few modifications to the scroller, based on the scroll buffer image, the game loop will run so much faster!

The first thing we might do to speed up the game is to take a look again at the doUpdate() and doScrolling() functions. Level.Update() contains user input code, so we need the scroller to continue as it has for consistent player movement. But, the problem is Level.Update() *also* contains engine-level scroll buffer code. We could detach the scroll buffer code from the player movement code so it can be run in a faster part of the engine (outside of the time-limited user input cycle). We must be careful with changes like this, though, because the game's parts are now highly interconnected; detaching any one piece or changing its behavior might affect other systems.

Another optimization that might be made is to the scroll buffer code. As you may recall, the scroll buffer is one full tile (32 pixels) larger around the edges than the screen. The scroll buffer is then shifted in whatever direction the player is moving until it has moved 32 pixels, at which point the scroll buffer must be re-filled. *In theory!* As a matter of fact, that isn't happening at all—the scroll buffer is being refilled *every step* the player makes! Instant 10–20x performance boost here.

Open up the `Level.Update()` function, and down near the bottom there is a block of code beginning with this:

```
//fill the scroll buffer only when moving
if (p_scrollPos != p_oldScrollPos || p_game.Hero.Position != p_oldPlayerPos)
```

At the bottom of that code block is a call to `fillScrollBuffer()`. This is where the optimization will be made! Can you figure it out? In fairness, the game *works* as is; this is an important but not *essential* modification. If you need help with it, come by my forum to chat about it with others—maybe you will be the first person to figure it out? (www.jharbour.com/forum).

Tip

As a reward, I will give away a free book to the first person who posts a solution to this optimization!

Lua Script Language

Scripting is a subject that might seem to belong back in Part II, "Building the Dungeon," since it is a core engine-level feature. But, until all of the classes were built for the dungeon crawler engine, there really was nothing we could do with a script language—which must necessarily be based on existing features within a game's source code. A script language *can* be used to create almost an entire game, if the engine behind it supports gameplay functions, but until now we have not had enough of a working example to make use of scripting. The script language of choice here is Lua, which will be briefly introduced along with code to tie Lua scripts into the game engine.

When you combine the versatility that a data-driven game engine like this one affords, along with a custom level editor, you already have a great combination for making a great game. But when you add script support to the mix, things get even *more* interesting! We have progressed to the point in both the game and the editors where, sure, we could get by with the excellent tools and code already in hand, but I want to raise the cool factor even higher with the addition of scripting support.

Now, let me disclaim something first: Yes, scripting is cool and adds incredible power to a game project, but it requires a lot of extra effort to make it work effectively.

The cool factor is that we can call C# functions from within a Lua script file! Likewise, we can call Lua functions from our C# code—interpreted Lua functions! But what about all of the global variables in a Lua source code file? The variables are automatically handled by the Lua engine when a script file is loaded. I'm not going to delve into a full-blown tutorial on the Lua language, because I just don't have time or space. Instead, we're just going to use it and you'll see how useful a scripting language is by watching it put to use.

Hint

There is one really big drawback to Lua: once you have "seen the light," you may never go back to writing a game purely with a compiled language like Basic or C# again! Lua is so compelling that you'll wonder how in the world you ever got anything done before you discovered it!

Installing Lua

The key to adding Lua support to our C# code is an open-source project called LuaInterface, hosted at the LuaForge website: http://luaforge.net/projects/luainterface/. The sources for LuaInterface are housed in a Google Code Subversion (SVN) repository at http://code.google.com/p/luainterface, with support for Visual C# 2008. I have included a project with this chapter that has the pre-compiled version of LuaInterface ready to use.

Definition

Lua is the Portuguese word for "Moon." The official spelling is LUA, with all caps, but I prefer to spell it without all caps because that leads the reader to assume it's an acronym rather than a word.

Installing LuaInterface

After compiling the LuaInterface project, you'll get a file called LuaInterface.dll which contains the .NET assembly for the project. You will also need the Lua runtime library file, lua51.dll. Copy LuaInterface.dll and lua51.dll to any project that needs Lua support and you'll be all set. (Note also that these files must always be distributed with your game.) Whether you compiled it yourself or just copied it from the chapter resource files, create a new C# project. Then, open the Project menu and select Add Reference. Locate the LuaInterface.dll file and select it, as shown in Figure 15.5.

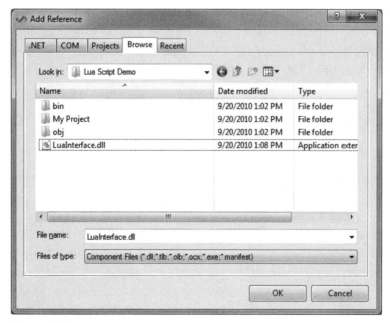

Figure 15.5
Adding the LuaInterface.dll file to the project.

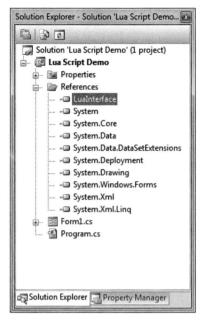

Figure 15.6
List of referenced components in this project.

Nothing will seem to change in the project. To verify that the component has been added, open Project, Properties, and bring up the References tab, where you should see the component among the others available to your project. See Figure 15.6.

Testing LuaInterface

Here is our first short example program that loads a Lua script file. The form for this program has a `TextBox` control, which is used as a simple console for printing out text from both the Lua script and our Basic code. Figure 15.7 shows the result of the program.

```
public partial class Form1 : Form
{
    private TextBox textBox1;
    public Lua lua;

    public Form1()
    {
```

Figure 15.7
We now have Lua script language support for our game.

```csharp
    InitializeComponent();
}

private void Form1_Load(object sender, EventArgs e)
{
    this.Text = "Lua Script Demo";
    textBox1 = new TextBox();
    textBox1.Dock = DockStyle.Fill;
    textBox1.Multiline = true;
    textBox1.Font = new Font("System", 14, FontStyle.Regular);
    this.Controls.Add(textBox1);

    //create lua object
    lua = new Lua();

    //link a C# function to Lua
    lua.RegisterFunction("DoPrint", this, this.GetType().
        GetMethod("DoPrint"));

    //load lua script file
    lua.DoFile("script.lua");

    //get globals from lua
    string name = lua.GetString("name");
    double age = lua.GetNumber("age");
```

```
        DoPrint("name = " + name);
        DoPrint("age = " + age.ToString());


    }

    //this function is visible to Lua script
    public void DoPrint(string text)
    {
        textBox1.Text += text + "\r\n";
    }
}
```

Hint

The LuaInterface.dll requires the .NET Framework 2.0, not the later versions such as 3.5. If you are using Visual C# 2010, it will default to the later version of the .NET Framework. To get LuaInterface to work with your Visual C# 2010 project, you may need to switch to .NET Framework 2.0 (which is done via Project Properties). You may also need to manually set the target from "Any CPU" to "x86" to get the Lua library to work with Visual C# 2010.

First, the TextBox control is created and added to the form with the Multiline property set to true so the control acts like a console rather than an entry field.

Next, the LuaInterface.Lua object is created. That object, called lua, is then used to register a C# function called DoPrint() (note that it must be declared with *public* scope in order for Lua to see it!). Next, lua.DoFile() is called to load the script code in the script.lua file. This file must be located in the .\bin\Debug folder where the executable file is created at compile time. So, we can think of a script file like any game asset file, equivalent to a bitmap file or an audio file.

When DoFile() is called, that not only opens the script file, it also executes the code. This is one of the two ways to open a script file. The second way is to use LoadFile() instead, which simply loads the script into memory, registers the functions and globals, but does not start executing statements yet.

After the script has been loaded and run, then we can tap into the lua object to retrieve globals from the lua object, as well as call functions in the script code. In this example, we just grab two globals (name and age) and print out their values. This demonstrates that Lua can see our Basic function and call it, and that we can tap into the globals, which is the *most important* thing!

Here is the script.lua file for this project:

```
-This is my first Lua Script!
-create some globals
name = "Rich Golden"
age = 24
-call a function in the program
DoPrint( "Welcome to " .. _VERSION )
```

The last line in the script.lua file calls DoPrint(), which is not a Lua function; it's a function in our C# program! As soon as a function is registered with Lua using RegisterFunction(), it becomes visible to the script code.

Hint

Do you see that odd-looking pair of dots in the last line of the script file? The double dot is how you combine strings in Lua (also called *concatenation*).

Sharing Tile Data with Lua

Now that we have a Lua linkage in our project, we should give Lua access to the game engine. I want to be able to scroll the game world to any location with a function call, as well as read the data for any tile on the tilemap, including the tile under the player's current position, for obvious reasons. Once those things are done, then it will be possible to add Lua functions to the tilemap via the level editor. At that point, the game engine becomes less of a factor for gameplay code. Any variable in the engine can be sent to the Lua code as a global, and vice versa! This level of cooperation along with the runtime interpretation of Lua script makes it an extremely valuable addition to the game.

Hint

If you get the unusual runtime error shown below, that usually means the program could not find the lua51.dll file which is a dependent of LuaInterface.dll. Be sure both dll files are located in the .\bin\Debug folder of your project.

An unhandled exception of type 'System.InvalidOperationException' occurred in Lua Script Demo.exe. Additional information: An error occurred creating the form. See Exception.InnerException for details. The error is: Could not load file or assembly 'lua51, Version=0.0.0.0, Culture=neutral, PublicKeyToken =1e1fb15b02227b8a' or one of its dependencies. The system cannot find the file specified.

Incorporating Script Into the Engine

The great thing about the source code for the dungeon crawler is that all of the "big pieces" are in classes that are initialized in Form1_Load(). Furthermore, all of the real work is being done in the doUpdate() function, which calls doScrolling (), doMonsters(), doHero(), etc. This is a very clean way to build a game, because it is easy to add new things to it, and we can see easily what's happening in this game at a glance without wading through hundreds of lines of code muddying up these main functions. The way this code is structured *also* makes it possible to *script* much of it with Lua!

In order to give the script something to *work on*, we have to call a function in the script file. When a script is opened, if there is no function, then it is simply parsed and no more processing takes place. You can continue to use the script global variables but no work takes place in the script unless you tell it to do something from the C# game code. In our Form1_Load() source code, we have a function called doUpdate() that does timing, calls all of the update functions, displays info on the screen, etc.—in other words, this is our workhorse function, the core loop of the game. We're going to plug the Lua update into the game loop along with the other "do" functions.

Hint

The script.lua file *must* be in the \bin\Debug folder just like bitmap files and other assets.

All of the components of the game can be selectively loaded with script functions, and almost total control is given to the script to override what happens in the default C# code (in Form1_Load() and doUpdate()). Let's briefly review the properties available. Note that most are all read-only properties. Making changes to them does not affect the game, as they are just intended to supply information to the script. The exception is ScrollX and ScrollY, which are both sent to the script and *back* to C#, so you can change the player's current location in the world with these properties. Open the final project to see these script functions in action.

- WindowTitle
- ScrollX

- ScrollY
- PortalFlag
- CollidableFlag
- Health
- HP
- QuestNumber
- QuestSummary
- QuestCompleteFlag
- MessageResult

Here are the functions available to our Lua script, which are tied in to the C# code.

- LoadLevel()
- LoadItems()
- LoadQuests()
- LoadHero()
- DropGold()
- AddCharacter()
- Write()
- Message()

FINISHING TOUCHES

Unfortunately, we are out of room and time to go into any more detail on the finished game! You will have to open the completed Dungeon Crawler game in the chapter resources to see the final version of the game! Here are features currently in the game that we did not have time to cover (because this is not a 500-page book):

1. Monster A.I.

2. Loading and saving the game

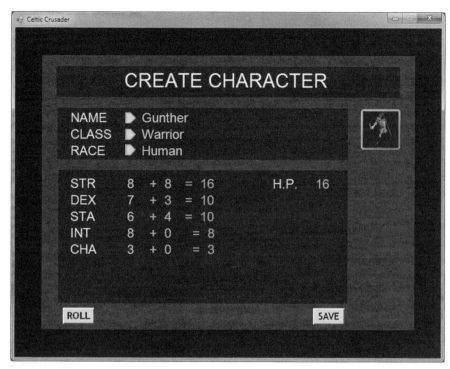

Figure 15.8
Rolling the stats for a new character.

3. Loading level files using portals.

4. Creating player characters (Figure 15.8).

5. Combining line of sight and light radius for both monsters and items.

6. Shifting most of the startup code to Lua.

At any rate, you now have enough tools to create your own RPG! Of course, no game is ever truly *finished*, it's just "good enough" to play, so maybe you will do something fun with this RPG engine?

Level Up!

You are now a level 15 game programmer who is ready to take your skills and abilities to build your own dungeon crawler RPG! In the words of Yoda, "No more training do you require. Already know you that which you need." But one task remains before your training is complete—you must build your own game. I hope you have enjoyed the journey of learning how to build a custom role-playing game. It has been a blast to work on this game! Happy exploring!

INDEX